It's another great book from CGP...

GCSE Core Science is all about **understanding how science works**.
And not only that — understanding it well enough to be able to **question**
what you hear on TV and read in the papers.

But don't panic. This book includes all the **science facts** you need to learn,
and shows you how they work in the real world. It even includes
a **free** Online Edition you can read on your computer or tablet.

How to get your free Online Edition

Just go to **cgpbooks.co.uk/extras** and enter this code...

1447 0712 1356 1050

By the way, this code only works for one person. If somebody else has used
this book before you, they might have already claimed the Online Edition.

CGP — still the best! ☺

Our sole aim here at CGP is to produce the highest
quality books — carefully written, immaculately presented
and dangerously close to being funny.

Then we work our socks off to get them
out to you — at the cheapest possible prices.

Contents

Published by CGP

From original material by Richard Parsons.

Editors:
Joe Brazier, Emma Elder, Ben Fletcher, Murray Hamilton, Helen Ronan, Lyn Setchell,
Julie Wakeling, Dawn Wright.

Contributors:
Mike Bossart, Paddy Gannon, Gemma Hallam, Andy Rankin, Adrian Schmit, Andy Williams.

ISBN: 978 1 84146 726 9

With thanks to Hayley Thompson and Jane Towle for the proofreading.
With thanks to Jan Greenway, Laura Jakubowski and Laura Stoney for the copyright research.

Graph to show trend in atmospheric CO_2 concentration and global temperature on page 127
based on data by EPICA Community Members 2004 and Siegenthaler et al. 2005.

With thanks to Science Photo Library for permission to use the image on page 133.

Every effort has been made to locate copyright holders and obtain permission to reproduce
sources. For those sources where it has been difficult to trace the originator of the work,
we would be grateful for information. If any copyright holder would like us to make an
amendment to the acknowledgements, please notify us and we will gladly update the book
at the next reprint. Thank you.

Groovy website: www.cgpbooks.co.uk

Printed by Elanders Ltd, Newcastle upon Tyne.
Jolly bits of clipart from CorelDRAW®

The Scientific Process

Before you get started with the really fun stuff, it's a good idea to understand exactly <u>how</u> the world of science <u>works</u>. Investigate these next few pages and you'll be laughing all day long on results day.

Scientists Come Up with Hypotheses — Then Test Them

Hundreds of years ago, we thought demons caused illness.

1) Scientists try to <u>explain</u> things. Everything.

2) They start by <u>observing</u> or <u>thinking about</u> something they don't understand — it could be anything, e.g. planets in the sky, a person suffering from an illness, what matter is made of... anything.

3) Then, using what they already know (plus a bit of insight), they come up with a <u>hypothesis</u> — a possible <u>explanation</u> for what they've observed.

4) The next step is to <u>test</u> whether the hypothesis might be <u>right or not</u> — this involves <u>gathering evidence</u> (i.e. <u>data</u> from <u>investigations</u>).

5) To gather evidence the scientist uses the hypothesis to make a <u>prediction</u> — a statement based on the hypothesis that can be <u>tested</u> by carrying out <u>experiments</u>.

6) If the results from the experiments match the prediction, then the scientist can be <u>more confident</u> that the hypothesis is <u>correct</u>. This <u>doesn't</u> mean the hypothesis is <u>true</u> though — other predictions based on the hypothesis might turn out to be <u>wrong</u>.

Scientists Work Together to Test Hypotheses

1) Different scientists can look at the <u>same evidence</u> and interpret it in <u>different ways</u>. That's why scientists usually work in <u>teams</u> — they can share their <u>different ideas</u> on how to interpret the data they find.

2) Once a team has come up with (and tested) a hypothesis they all agree with, they'll present their work to the scientific community through <u>journals</u> and <u>scientific conferences</u> so it can be judged — this is called the <u>peer review</u> process.

3) Other scientists then <u>check</u> the team's results (by trying to <u>replicate</u> them) and carry out their own experiments to <u>collect more evidence</u>.

4) If all the experiments in the world back up the hypothesis, scientists start to have a lot of <u>confidence</u> in it. (A hypothesis that is <u>accepted</u> by pretty much every scientist is referred to as a <u>theory</u>.)

5) However, if another scientist does an experiment and the results <u>don't</u> fit with the hypothesis (and other scientists can <u>replicate</u> these results), then the hypothesis is in trouble. When this happens, scientists have to come up with a new hypothesis (maybe a <u>modification</u> of the old explanation, or maybe a completely <u>new</u> one).

Then we thought it was caused by 'bad blood' (and treated it with leeches).

Scientific Ideas Change as New Evidence is Found

Now we know most illnesses are due to microorganisms.

1) Scientific explanations are <u>provisional</u> because they only explain the evidence that's <u>currently available</u> — new evidence may come up that can't be explained.

2) This means that scientific explanations <u>never</u> become hard and fast, totally indisputable <u>fact</u>. As <u>new evidence</u> is found (or new ways of <u>interpreting</u> existing evidence are found), hypotheses can <u>change</u> or be <u>replaced</u>.

3) Sometimes, an <u>unexpected observation</u> or <u>result</u> will suddenly throw a hypothesis into doubt and further experiments will need to be carried out. This can lead to new developments that <u>increase</u> our <u>understanding</u> of science.

You expect me to believe that — then show me the evidence...

If scientists think something is true, they need to produce evidence to convince others — it's all part of <u>testing a hypothesis</u>. One hypothesis might survive these tests, while others won't — it's how things progress. And along the way some hypotheses will be disproved — i.e. shown not to be true.

Quality of Data

Evidence is the key to science — but not all evidence is equally good.
The way evidence is gathered can have a big effect on how trustworthy it is...

The Bigger the Sample Size the Better

1) Data based on small samples isn't as good as data based on large samples.
   A sample should be representative of the whole population (i.e. it should share as many of
   the various characteristics in the population as possible) — a small sample can't do that as well.

2) The bigger the sample size the better, but scientists have to be realistic when choosing how big.
   For example, if you were studying how lifestyle affects people's weight it'd be great to study everyone in
   the UK (a huge sample), but it'd take ages and cost a bomb. Studying a thousand people is more realistic.

Evidence Needs to be Reliable (Repeatable and Reproducible)

Evidence is only reliable if it can be repeated (during an experiment) AND other scientists can reproduce it too
(in other experiments). If it's not reliable, you can't believe it.

> RELIABLE means that the data can be repeated, and reproduced by others.

> EXAMPLE: In 1989, two scientists claimed that they'd produced 'cold fusion' (the energy source of
> the Sun — but without the big temperatures). It was huge news — if true, it would have meant free
> energy for the world... forever. However, other scientists just couldn't reproduce the results —
> so the results weren't reliable. And until they are, 'cold fusion' isn't going to be accepted as fact.

Evidence Also Needs to Be Valid

> VALID means that the data is reliable AND answers the original question.

> EXAMPLE: DO POWER LINES CAUSE CANCER?
> Some studies have found that children who live near overhead power lines are more likely to develop
> cancer. What they'd actually found was a correlation (relationship) between the variables "presence of
> power lines" and "incidence of cancer" — they found that as one changed, so did the other.
> But this evidence is not enough to say that the power lines cause cancer, as other explanations might
> be possible. For example, power lines are often near busy roads, so the areas tested could
> contain different levels of pollution from traffic. So these studies don't show a definite link
> and so don't answer the original question.

Don't Always Believe What You're Being Told Straight Away

1) People who want to make a point might present data in a biased way, e.g. by overemphasising
   a relationship in the data. (Sometimes without knowing they're doing it.)

2) And there are all sorts of reasons why people might want to do this — for example, companies might
   want to 'big up' their products. Or make impressive safety claims.

3) If an investigation is done by a team of highly-regarded scientists it's sometimes taken more seriously
   than evidence from less well known scientists.

4) But having experience, authority or a fancy qualification doesn't necessarily mean the evidence is good
   — the only way to tell is to look at the evidence scientifically (e.g. is it reliable, valid, etc.).

RRRR — Remember, Reliable means Repeatable and Reproducible...

By now you should have realised how important trustworthy evidence is (even more important than a good supply
of spot cream). Without it (the evidence, not the spot cream), you just can't believe what you're being told.

Limits of Science and the Issues it Creates

Science can give us amazing things — cures for diseases, space travel, heated toilet seats...
But science has its limitations — there are questions that it just can't answer.

Some Questions Are Unanswered, Others are Unanswerable

1) Some questions are unanswered — we don't know everything and we never will. We'll find out more as new hypotheses are suggested and more experiments are done, but there'll always be stuff we don't know.

2) For example, we don't know what the exact impacts of global warming are going to be. At the moment scientists don't all agree on the answers because there isn't enough reliable and valid evidence.

3) Then there's the other type... questions that all the experiments in the world won't help us answer — the "Should we be doing this at all?" type questions. There are always two sides...

4) Take embryo screening (which allows you to choose an embryo with particular characteristics). It's possible to do it — but does that mean we should?

5) Different people have different opinions.

For example...
- Some people say it's good... couples whose existing child needs a bone marrow transplant, but who can't find a donor, will be able to have another child selected for its matching bone marrow. This would save the life of their first child — and if they want another child anyway... where's the harm?

- Other people say it's bad... they say it could have serious effects on the new child. In the above example, the new child might feel unwanted — thinking they were only brought into the world to help someone else. And would they have the right to refuse to donate their bone marrow (as anyone else would)?

THE GAZETTE
BONE MARROW BABY'S BROTHER SAVED

THE POST
BONE MARROW BABY BORN: WHAT RIGHTS DOES HE HAVE?

6) The question of whether something is morally or ethically right or wrong can't be answered by more experiments — there is no "right" or "wrong" answer.

7) The best we can do is get a consensus from society — a judgement that most people are more or less happy to live by. Science can provide more information to help people make this judgement, and the judgement might change over time. But in the end it's up to people and their conscience.

Scientific Developments are Great, but they can Raise Issues

Scientific knowledge is increased by doing experiments. And this knowledge leads to scientific developments, e.g. new technologies or new advice. These developments can create issues though. For example:

Economic issues: Society can't always afford to do things scientists recommend (e.g. investing heavily in alternative energy sources) without cutting back elsewhere.

Social issues: Decisions based on scientific evidence affect people — e.g. should fossil fuels be taxed more highly (to invest in alternative energy)? Should alcohol be banned (to prevent health problems)? Would the effect on people's lifestyles be acceptable...

Environmental issues: Genetically modified crops may help us produce more food — but some people think they could cause environmental problems.

Ethical issues: There are a lot of things that scientific developments have made possible, but should we do them? E.g. clone humans, develop better nuclear weapons.

Chips or rice? — totally unanswerable by science...

Science can't tell you whether you should or shouldn't do something. That is up to you and society to decide.

Planning Investigations

The next few pages show how <u>investigations</u> should be carried out — by both <u>professional scientists</u> and <u>you</u>.

To Make an Investigation a Fair Test You Have to Control the Variables

1) In a lab experiment you usually <u>change one variable</u> and <u>measure</u> how it affects the <u>other variable</u>.

> EXAMPLE: you might change only the temperature of an enzyme-controlled reaction and measure how it affects the rate of reaction.

2) To make it a fair test <u>everything else</u> that could affect the results should <u>stay the same</u> (otherwise you can't tell if the thing that's being changed is affecting the results or not — the data won't be reliable or valid).

> EXAMPLE continued: you need to keep the pH the same, otherwise you won't know if any change in the rate of reaction is caused by the change in temperature, or the change in pH.

3) The variable that you <u>change</u> is called the <u>independent</u> variable.

4) The variable that's <u>measured</u> is called the <u>dependent</u> variable.

5) The variables that you <u>keep the same</u> are called <u>control</u> variables.

> EXAMPLE continued:
> Independent = temperature
> Dependent = rate of reaction
> Control = pH

6) Because you can't always control all the variables, you often need to use a <u>control experiment</u> — an experiment that's kept under the <u>same conditions</u> as the rest of the investigation, but doesn't have anything done to it. This is so that you can see what happens when you don't change anything at all.

> Accurate data is data that's close to the true value — see the next page.

The Equipment Used has to be Right for the Job

1) The measuring equipment you use has to be <u>sensitive enough</u> to accurately measure the chemicals you're using, e.g. if you need to measure out 11 ml of a liquid, you'll need to use a measuring cylinder that can measure to 1 ml, not 5 or 10 ml.

2) The <u>smallest change</u> a measuring instrument can <u>detect</u> is called its RESOLUTION. E.g. some mass balances have a resolution of 1 g and some have a resolution of 0.1 g.

3) Also, equipment needs to be <u>calibrated</u> so that your data is <u>more accurate</u>. E.g. mass balances need to be set to zero before you start weighing things.

Experiments Must be Safe

1) Part of planning an investigation is making sure that it's <u>safe</u>.

2) A <u>hazard</u> is something that can <u>potentially cause harm</u>.

3) There are lots of <u>hazards</u> you could be faced with during an investigation, e.g. <u>radiation</u>, <u>electricity</u>, <u>gas</u>, <u>chemicals</u> and <u>fire</u>.

4) You should always make sure that you <u>identify</u> all the hazards that you might encounter.

5) You should also come up with ways of <u>reducing the risks</u> from the hazards you've identified.

6) One way of doing this is to carry out a <u>risk assessment</u>:

> For an experiment involving a <u>Bunsen burner</u>, the risk assessment might be something like this:

> Hazard: Bunsen burner is a fire risk.
> Precautions:
> • Keep flammable chemicals away from the Bunsen.
> • Never leave the Bunsen unattended when lit.
> • Always turn on the yellow safety flame when not in use.

Hazard: revision boredom. Precaution: use CGP books

Labs are dangerous places — you need to know the <u>hazards</u> of what you're doing <u>before you start</u>.

Collecting Data

There are a few things that can be done to make sure that you get the best results you possibly can.

Data Should be as Reliable, Accurate and Precise as Possible

1) When carrying out an investigation, you can improve the reliability of your results (see p. 2) by repeating the readings and calculating the mean (average, see next page). You should repeat readings at least twice (so that you have at least three readings to calculate an average result).

2) To make sure your results are reliable you can cross check them by taking a second set of readings with another instrument (or a different observer).

3) Checking your results match with secondary sources, e.g. studies that other people have done, also increases the reliability of your data.

4) You should always make sure that your results are accurate. Really accurate results are those that are really close to the true answer.

5) You can get accurate results by doing things like making sure the equipment you're using is sensitive enough (see previous page), and by recording your data to a suitable level of accuracy. For example, if you're taking digital readings of something, the results will be more accurate if you include at least a couple of decimal places instead of rounding to whole numbers.

6) You should also always make sure your results are precise. Precise results are ones where the data is all really close to the mean (i.e. not spread out).

Trial Runs Help Figure out the Range and Interval of Variable Values

1) Before you carry out an experiment, it's a good idea to do a trial run first — a quick version of your experiment.

2) Trial runs help you work out whether your plan is right or not — you might decide to make some changes after trying out your method.

3) Trial runs are used to figure out the range of variable values used (the upper and lower limit).

4) And they're used to figure out the interval (gaps) between the values too.

5) Trial runs can also help you figure out how many times the experiment has to be repeated to get reliable results. E.g. if you repeat it two times and the results are all similar, then two repeats is enough.

> Enzyme-controlled reaction example from previous page continued:
>
> • You might do trial runs at 10, 20, 30, 40 and 50 °C. If there was no reaction at 10 or 50 °C, you might narrow the range to 20-40 °C.
>
> • If using 10 °C intervals gives you a big change in rate of reaction you might decide to use 5 °C intervals, e.g. 20, 25, 30, 35...

You Can Check For Mistakes Made When Collecting Data

1) When you've collected all the results for an experiment, you should have a look to see if there are any results that don't seem to fit in with the rest.

2) Most results vary a bit, but any that are totally different are called anomalous results.

3) They're caused by human errors, e.g. by a whoopsie when measuring.

4) The only way to stop them happening is by taking all your measurements as carefully as possible.

5) If you ever get any anomalous results, you should investigate them to try to work out what happened. If you can work out what happened (e.g. you measured something wrong) you can ignore them when processing your results.

Reliable data — it won't ever forget your birthday...

All this stuff is really important — without good quality data an investigation will be totally meaningless. So give this page a read through a couple of times and your data will be the envy of the whole scientific community.

Processing, Presenting and Interpreting Data

The fun doesn't stop once the data's been collected — it then needs to be **processed** and **presented**...

Data Needs to be Organised

Test tube	Result (ml)	Repeat 1 (ml)	Repeat 2 (ml)
A	28	37	32
B	47	51	60
C	68	72	70

1) Data that's been collected needs to be <u>organised</u> so it can be processed later on.

2) <u>Tables</u> are dead useful for <u>organising data</u>.

3) When drawing tables you should always make sure that <u>each column</u> has a <u>heading</u> and that you've included the <u>units</u>.

4) Annoyingly, tables are about as useful as a chocolate teapot for showing <u>patterns</u> or <u>relationships</u> in data. You need to use some kind of graph or mathematical technique for that...

Data Can be Processed Using a Bit of Maths

1) <u>Raw data</u> generally just ain't that useful. You usually have to <u>process</u> it in some way.

2) A couple of the most simple calculations you can perform are the <u>mean</u> (average) and the <u>range</u> (how spread out the data is):

- To calculate the <u>mean</u> <u>**ADD TOGETHER**</u> all the data values and <u>**DIVIDE**</u> by the total number of values. You usually do this to get a single value from several <u>repeats</u> of your experiment.

- To calculate the <u>range</u> find the <u>**LARGEST**</u> number and <u>**SUBTRACT**</u> the <u>**SMALLEST**</u> number. You usually do this to <u>check</u> the accuracy and reliability of the results — the <u>greater</u> the <u>spread</u> of the data, the <u>lower</u> the accuracy and reliability.

Test tube	Result (ml)	Repeat 1 (ml)	Repeat 2 (ml)	Mean (ml)	Range
A	28	37	32	$(28 + 37 + 32) \div 3 = 32.3$	$37 - 28 = 9$
B	47	51	60	$(47 + 51 + 60) \div 3 = 52.7$	$60 - 47 = 13$
C	68	72	70	$(68 + 72 + 70) \div 3 = 70.0$	$72 - 68 = 4$

Different Types of Data Should be Presented in Different Ways

1) Once you've carried out an investigation, you'll need to <u>present</u> your data so that it's easier to see <u>patterns</u> and <u>relationships</u> in the data.

2) Different types of investigations give you <u>different types</u> of data, so you'll always have to <u>choose</u> what the best way to present your data is.

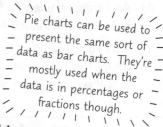

Pie charts can be used to present the same sort of data as bar charts. They're mostly used when the data is in percentages or fractions though.

Bar Charts

If the independent variable is <u>categoric</u> (comes in distinct categories, e.g. blood types, metals) you should use a <u>bar chart</u> to display the data. You also use them if the independent variable is <u>discrete</u> (the data can be counted in chunks, where there's no in-between value, e.g. number of people is discrete because you can't have half a person).

There are some <u>golden rules</u> you need to follow for <u>drawing</u> bar charts:

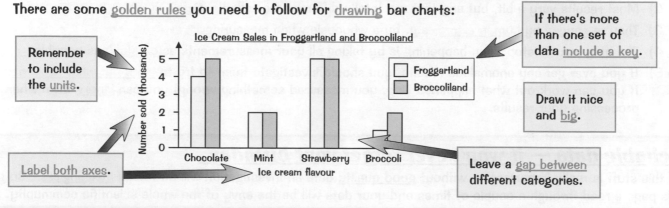

Remember to include the <u>units</u>.

Ice Cream Sales in Froggartland and Broccoliland

If there's more than one set of data <u>include a key</u>.

Draw it nice and <u>big</u>.

Label both axes.

Leave a <u>gap between</u> different categories.

Processing, Presenting and Interpreting Data

Line Graphs

If the independent variable is <u>continuous</u> (numerical data that can have any value within a range, e.g. length, volume, temperature) you should use a <u>line graph</u> to display the data.

Remember to include the <u>units</u>.

The <u>dependent</u> variable (the thing you measure) goes on the <u>y-axis</u> (the <u>vertical</u> one).

The <u>independent</u> variable (the thing you change) goes on the <u>x-axis</u> (the <u>horizontal</u> one).

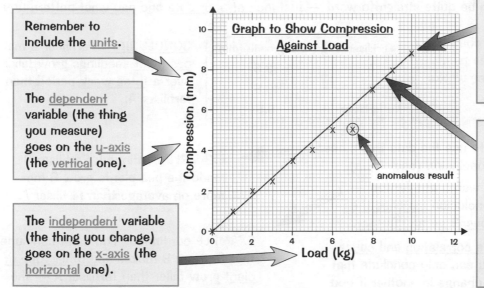

When plotting points, use a <u>sharp pencil</u> and make a <u>neat little cross</u> (don't do blobs).

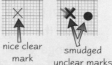

nice clear mark

smudged unclear marks

<u>Don't join the dots up.</u> You should draw a <u>line of best fit</u> (or a <u>curve of best fit</u> if your points make a curve).

When drawing a line (or curve), try to draw the line <u>through</u> or as <u>near</u> to <u>as many points as possible</u>, ignoring anomalous results.

anomalous result

Line Graphs Can Show Relationships in Data

1) Line graphs are great for showing relationships <u>between two variables</u> (just like other graphs).

2) Here are some of the different types of <u>correlation</u> (relationship) shown on line graphs:

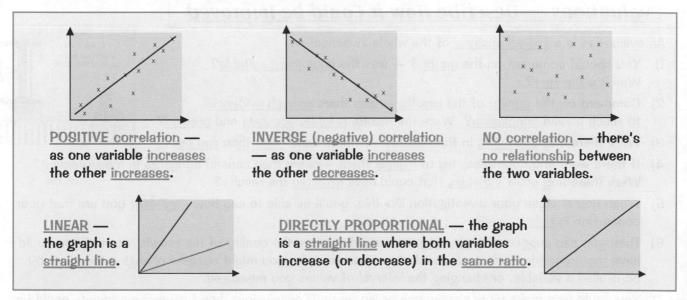

<u>POSITIVE</u> correlation — as one variable <u>increases</u> the other <u>increases</u>.

<u>INVERSE</u> (negative) correlation — as one variable <u>increases</u> the other <u>decreases</u>.

<u>NO</u> correlation — there's <u>no relationship</u> between the two variables.

<u>LINEAR</u> — the graph is a <u>straight line</u>.

<u>DIRECTLY PROPORTIONAL</u> — the graph is a <u>straight line</u> where both variables increase (or decrease) in the <u>same ratio</u>.

3) You've got to be careful not to <u>confuse correlation</u> with <u>cause</u> though. A <u>correlation</u> just means that there's a <u>relationship</u> between two variables. It <u>doesn't always mean</u> that the change in one variable is <u>causing</u> the change in the other.

4) There are <u>three possible reasons</u> for a correlation. It could be down to <u>chance</u>, it could be that there's a <u>third variable</u> linking the two things, or it might actually be that one variable is <u>causing</u> the other to change.

There's a positive correlation between age of man and length of nose hair...

<u>Process</u>, <u>present</u>, <u>interpret</u>... data's like a difficult child — it needs a lot of attention. Go on, make it happy.

Concluding and Evaluating

At the end of an investigation, the <u>conclusion</u> and <u>evaluation</u> are waiting. Don't worry, they won't bite.

A Conclusion is a Summary of What You've Learnt

1) Once all the data's been collected, presented and analysed, an investigation will always involve coming to a <u>conclusion</u>.

2) Drawing a conclusion can be quite straightforward — just <u>look at your data</u> and <u>say what pattern you see</u>.

EXAMPLE: The table on the right shows the heights of pea plant seedlings grown for three weeks with different fertilisers.

Fertiliser	Mean growth (mm)
A	13.5
B	19.5
No fertiliser	5.5

<u>CONCLUSION:</u> Fertiliser <u>B</u> makes <u>pea plant</u> seedlings grow taller over a <u>three week</u> period than fertiliser A.

3) However, you also need to use the data that's been <u>collected</u> to <u>justify</u> the conclusion (back it up).

EXAMPLE continued: Fertiliser B made the pea plants grow 6 mm more on average than fertiliser A.

4) There are some things to watch out for too — it's important that the conclusion <u>matches the data</u> it's based on and <u>doesn't go any further</u>.

5) Remember not to <u>confuse correlation</u> and <u>cause</u> (see previous page). You can only conclude that one variable is <u>causing</u> a change in another if you have controlled all the <u>other variables</u> (made it a <u>fair test</u>).

EXAMPLE continued: You can't conclude that fertiliser B makes <u>any other type of plant</u> grow taller than fertiliser A — the results could be totally different. Also, you can't make any conclusions <u>beyond</u> the three weeks — the plants could <u>drop dead</u>.

Evaluations — Describe How it Could be Improved

An evaluation is a <u>critical analysis</u> of the whole investigation.

I'd value this E somewhere in the region of 250-300k

1) You should comment on the <u>method</u> — was the <u>equipment suitable</u>? Was it a <u>fair test</u>?

2) Comment on the <u>quality</u> of the <u>results</u> — was there <u>enough evidence</u> to reach a valid <u>conclusion</u>? Were the results <u>reliable</u>, <u>accurate</u> and <u>precise</u>?

3) Were there any <u>anomalies</u> in the results — if there were <u>none</u> then <u>say so</u>.

4) If there were any anomalies, try to <u>explain</u> them — were they caused by <u>errors</u> in measurement? Were there any other <u>variables</u> that could have <u>affected</u> the results?

5) When you analyse your investigation like this, you'll be able to say how <u>confident</u> you are that your conclusion is <u>right</u>.

6) Then you can suggest any <u>changes</u> that would <u>improve</u> the quality of the results, so that you could have <u>more confidence</u> in your conclusion. For example, you might suggest changing the way you controlled a variable, or changing the interval of values you measured.

7) You could also make more <u>predictions</u> based on your conclusion, then <u>further experiments</u> could be carried out to test them.

8) When suggesting improvements to the investigation, always make sure that you say <u>why</u> you think this would make the results <u>better</u>.

Evaluation — in my next study I will make sure I don't burn the lab down...

I know it doesn't seem very nice, but writing about where you went <u>wrong</u> is an important skill — it shows you've got a really good understanding of what the investigation was <u>about</u>. It's difficult for me — I'm always right.

The Nervous System

The nervous system allows you to react to what goes on around you — you'd find life tough without it.

Sense Organs Detect Stimuli

A stimulus is a change in your environment which you may need to react to (e.g. a grizzly bear looking hungrily at you). You need to be constantly monitoring what's going on so you can respond if you need to.

1) You have five different sense organs — eyes, ears, nose, tongue and skin.

2) They all contain different receptors. Receptors are groups of cells which are sensitive to a stimulus. They change stimulus energy (e.g. light energy) into electrical impulses.

3) A stimulus can be light, sound, touch, pressure, pain, chemical, or a change in position or temperature.

Sense organs and Receptors
Don't get them mixed up:

The eye is a sense organ — it contains light receptors.

The ear is a sense organ — it contains sound receptors.

The Five Sense Organs and the receptors that each contains:

1) Eyes — Light receptors — sensitive to light. These cells have a nucleus, cytoplasm and cell membrane (just like most animal cells).

2) Ears — Sound receptors — sensitive to sound. Also, "balance" receptors — sensitive to changes in position.

3) Nose — Smell receptors — sensitive to chemical stimuli.

4) Tongue — Taste receptors — sensitive to bitter, salt, sweet and sour, plus the taste of savoury things like monosodium glutamate (MSG) — chemical stimuli.

5) Skin — Sensitive to touch, pressure, pain and temperature change.

Sensory Neurones
The nerve cells that carry signals as electrical impulses from the receptors in the sense organs to the central nervous system.

Relay Neurones
The nerve cells that carry signals from sensory neurones to motor neurones.

Motor Neurones
The nerve cells that carry signals from the central nervous system to the effector muscles or glands.

The Central Nervous System Coordinates a Response

1) The central nervous system (CNS) is where all the information from the sense organs is sent, and where reflexes and actions are coordinated. The central nervous system consists of the brain and spinal cord only.

2) Neurones (nerve cells) transmit the information (as electrical impulses) very quickly to and from the CNS.

3) "Instructions" from the CNS are sent to the effectors (muscles and glands), which respond accordingly.

Effectors
Muscles and glands are known as effectors — they respond in different ways. Muscles contract in response to a nervous impulse, whereas glands secrete hormones.

Your tongue's evolved for Chinese meals — sweet, sour, MSG...

Listen up... the thing with GCSE Science is that it's not just a test of what you know — it's also a test of how well you can apply what you know. For instance, you might have to take what you know about a human and apply it to a horse (easy... sound receptors in its ears, light receptors in its eyes, etc.), or to a snake (so if you're told that certain types of snakes have heat receptors in nostril-like pits on their head, you should be able to work out what type of stimulus those pits are sensitive to). Thinking in an exam... gosh.

Synapses and Reflexes

Neurones transmit information <u>very quickly</u> to and from the brain, and your brain <u>quickly decides</u> how to respond to a stimulus. But <u>reflexes</u> are even quicker...

Synapses Connect Neurones

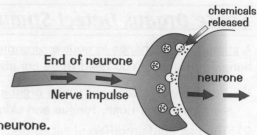

1) The <u>connection</u> between <u>two neurones</u> is called a <u>synapse</u>.

2) The nerve signal is transferred by <u>chemicals</u> which <u>diffuse</u> (move) across the gap.

3) These chemicals then set off a <u>new electrical signal</u> in the <u>next</u> neurone.

Reflexes Help Prevent Injury

1) <u>Reflexes</u> are <u>automatic</u> responses to certain stimuli — they can reduce the chances of being injured.

2) For example, if someone shines a <u>bright light</u> in your eyes, your <u>pupils</u> automatically get smaller so that less light gets into the eye — this stops it getting <u>damaged</u>.

3) Or if you get a shock, your body releases the <u>hormone</u> adrenaline automatically — it doesn't wait for you to <u>decide</u> that you're shocked.

4) The passage of information in a reflex (from receptor to effector) is called a <u>reflex arc</u>.

The Reflex Arc Goes Through the Central Nervous System

5. Impulses travel along a motor neurone, via a synapse.

4. Impulses are passed along a relay neurone, via a synapse.

6. When impulses reach muscle, it contracts.

3. Impulses travel along the sensory neurone.

2. Stimulation of the pain receptor.

1. Cheeky bee stings finger.

1) The neurones in reflex arcs go through the <u>spinal cord</u> or through an <u>unconscious part of the brain</u>.

2) When a <u>stimulus</u> (e.g. a painful bee sting) is detected by receptors, <u>impulses</u> are sent along a <u>sensory neurone</u> to the CNS.

3) When the impulses reach a <u>synapse</u> between the sensory neurone and a relay neurone, they trigger chemicals to be released (see above). These chemicals cause impulses to be sent along the <u>relay neurone</u>.

4) When the impulses reach a <u>synapse</u> between the relay neurone and a motor neurone, the same thing happens. Chemicals are released and cause impulses to be sent along the <u>motor neurone</u>.

5) The impulses then travel along the motor neurone to the <u>effector</u> (in this example it's a muscle).

6) The <u>muscle</u> then <u>contracts</u> and moves your hand away from the bee.

7) Because you don't have to think about the response (which takes time) it's <u>quicker</u> than normal responses.

Here's a <u>block diagram</u> of a <u>reflex arc</u> — it shows what happens, from stimulus to response.

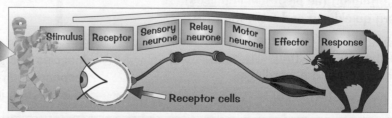

| Stimulus | Receptor | Sensory neurone | Relay neurone | Motor neurone | Effector | Response |

Receptor cells

Don't get all twitchy — just learn it...

Reflexes bypass your conscious brain completely when a quick response is essential — your body just gets on with things. Reflex actions can be used to assess the condition of <u>unconscious</u> casualties or those with <u>spinal injuries</u>. So... if you're asked <u>which bodily system</u> doctors are examining when they tap your knee with a hammer and check that you kick, just work it out. (They're checking parts of your nervous system.)

Hormones

The other way to send information around the body (apart from along nerves) is by using <u>hormones</u>.

Hormones Are Chemical Messengers Sent in the Blood

1) <u>Hormones</u> are <u>chemicals</u> released directly into the <u>blood</u>. They are carried in the <u>blood plasma</u> to other parts of the body, but only affect particular cells (called <u>target cells</u>) in particular places. Hormones control things in organs and cells that need <u>constant adjustment</u>.

2) Hormones are produced in (and secreted by) various <u>glands</u>, as shown on the diagram. They travel through your body at "<u>the speed of blood</u>".

3) Hormones tend to have relatively <u>long-lasting</u> effects.

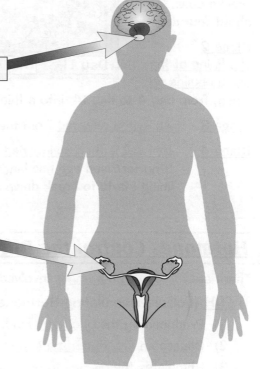

<u>Learn this definition:</u>
<u>HORMONES</u>...
are <u>chemical messengers</u>
which <u>travel in the blood</u>
to <u>activate target cells</u>.

<u>THE PITUITARY GLAND</u>
This produces many
important hormones
including <u>FSH</u> and <u>LH</u>,
which are involved in
the <u>menstrual cycle</u>
(see page 12).

<u>OVARIES</u> — females only
Produce <u>oestrogen</u>, which is
involved in the <u>menstrual cycle</u>
(see page 12).

These are just examples — there are
loads more, each doing its own thing.

Hormones and Nerves Do Similar Jobs, but There Are Differences

<u>NERVES:</u>
1) Very <u>FAST</u> action.
2) Act for a very <u>SHORT TIME</u>.
3) Act on a very <u>PRECISE AREA</u>.

<u>HORMONES:</u>
1) <u>SLOWER</u> action.
2) Act for a <u>LONG TIME</u>.
3) Act in a more <u>GENERAL</u> way.

So if you're not sure whether a response is nervous or hormonal, have a think...

1) If the response is <u>really quick</u>, it's <u>probably nervous</u>. Some information needs to be passed to effectors really quickly (e.g. pain signals, or information from your eyes telling you about the lion heading your way), so it's no good using hormones to carry the message — they're too slow.

2) But if a response <u>lasts for a long time</u>, it's <u>probably hormonal</u>. For example, when you get a shock, a hormone called adrenaline is released into the body (causing the fight-or-flight response, where your body is hyped up ready for action). You can tell it's a hormonal response (even though it kicks in pretty quickly) because you feel a bit wobbly for a while afterwards.

Nerves, hormones — no wonder revision makes me tense...

Hormones control various <u>organs</u> and <u>cells</u> in the body, though they tend to control things that aren't <u>immediately</u> life-threatening. For example, they take care of all things to do with sexual development, pregnancy, birth, breast-feeding, blood sugar level, water content... and so on. Pretty amazing really.

The Menstrual Cycle

The <u>monthly</u> release of an <u>egg</u> from a woman's <u>ovaries</u>, and the build-up and breakdown of the protective lining in the <u>uterus</u> (womb), is called the <u>menstrual cycle</u>.

The Menstrual Cycle Has Four Stages

<u>Stage 1</u>
<u>Day 1 is when the</u>
<u>bleeding starts</u>.
The uterus lining
breaks down for
about four days.

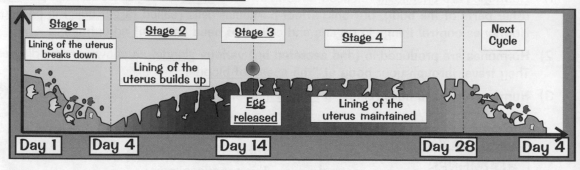

Stage 1 — Lining of the uterus breaks down
Stage 2 — Lining of the uterus builds up
Stage 3 — Egg released
Stage 4 — Lining of the uterus maintained
Next Cycle

Day 1 — Day 4 — Day 14 — Day 28 — Day 4

<u>Stage 2</u>
<u>The lining of the</u>
<u>uterus builds up</u>
<u>again</u>, from day 4 to day 14, into a thick spongy layer full of blood vessels, ready to receive a fertilised egg.

<u>Stage 3</u>   <u>An egg is released</u> from the ovary at day 14.

<u>Stage 4</u>   <u>The wall is then maintained</u> for about 14 days, until day 28.
If no fertilised egg has landed on the uterus wall by day 28, the spongy lining starts to break down again and the whole cycle starts again.

Hormones Control the Different Stages

There are <u>three main hormones</u> involved:

1) <u>FSH</u> (Follicle-Stimulating Hormone):

   1) Produced by the <u>pituitary gland</u>.

   2) Causes an <u>egg to mature in one of the ovaries</u>.

   3) Stimulates the <u>ovaries to produce oestrogen</u>.

2) <u>Oestrogen</u>:

   1) Produced in the <u>ovaries</u>.

   2) Causes <u>pituitary</u> to produce <u>LH</u>.

   3) <u>Inhibits</u> the further release of <u>FSH</u>.

3) <u>LH</u> (Luteinising Hormone):

   1) Produced by the <u>pituitary gland</u>.

   2) Stimulates the <u>release of an egg</u> at around the middle of the menstrual cycle.

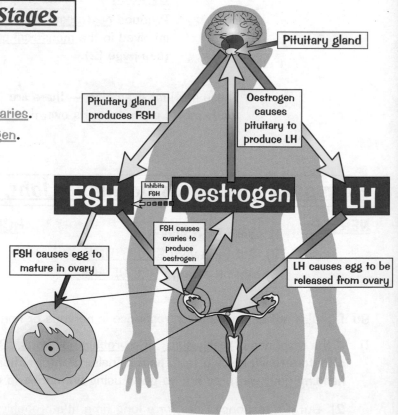

Pituitary gland
Pituitary gland produces FSH
Oestrogen causes pituitary to produce LH
Inhibits FSH
FSH — Oestrogen — LH
FSH causes egg to mature in ovary
FSH causes ovaries to produce oestrogen
LH causes egg to be released from ovary

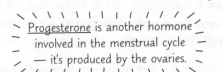
<u>Progesterone</u> is another hormone involved in the menstrual cycle — it's produced by the ovaries.

What do you call a fish with no eye — FSH...

In the exam you could be given a <u>completely new</u> situation and have to answer questions about it.
For example, say you're told that certain women with epilepsy suffer <u>more seizures</u> at certain points of the <u>menstrual cycle</u> and you have to suggest a reason why. Sounds scary, but the key is not to panic.
You know that during the menstrual cycle, <u>hormone</u> levels change — so maybe it's these hormone changes that are <u>triggering</u> the seizures. There are no guarantees, but that'd be a pretty good answer.

Controlling Fertility

The hormones FSH, LH, oestrogen and progesterone can be used to artificially change how fertile a woman is.

Hormones Can Be Used to Reduce Fertility...

1) Oestrogen can be used to prevent the release of an egg — so it can be used as a method of contraception.

2) This may seem kind of strange (since naturally oestrogen helps stimulate the release of eggs). But if oestrogen is taken every day to keep the level of it permanently high, it inhibits the production of FSH, and after a while egg development and production stop and stay stopped.

3) Progesterone (see page 12) also reduces fertility e.g. by stimulating the production of thick cervical mucus which prevents any sperm getting through and reaching an egg.

4) The pill is an oral contraceptive. The first version was made in the 1950s and contained high levels of oestrogen and progesterone (known as the combined oral contraceptive pill).

5) But there were concerns about a link between oestrogen in the pill and side effects like blood clots. The pill now contains lower doses of oestrogen so has fewer side effects.

PROS
1) The pill's over 99% effective at preventing pregnancy.
2) It reduces the risk of getting some types of cancer.

CONS
1) It isn't 100% effective — there's still a very slight chance of getting pregnant.
2) It can cause side effects like headaches, nausea, irregular menstrual bleeding, and fluid retention.
3) It doesn't protect against STDs (sexually transmitted diseases).

6) There's also a progesterone-only pill — it has fewer side effects than the pill (but it's not as effective).

...or Increase It

1) Some women have levels of FSH (Follicle-Stimulating Hormone) that are too low to cause their eggs to mature. This means that no eggs are released and the women can't get pregnant.

2) The hormones FSH and LH can be injected by these women to stimulate egg release in their ovaries.

PROS
It helps a lot of women to get pregnant when previously they couldn't... pretty obvious.

CONS
1) It doesn't always work — some women may have to do it many times, which can be expensive.
2) Too many eggs could be stimulated, resulting in unexpected multiple pregnancies (twins, triplets etc.).

IVF Can Also Help Couples to Have Children

1) IVF ("in vitro fertilisation") involves collecting eggs from the woman's ovaries and fertilising them in a lab using the man's sperm. These are then grown into embryos.

2) Once the embryos are tiny balls of cells, one or two of them are transferred to the woman's uterus (womb) to improve the chance of pregnancy.

3) FSH and LH are given before egg collection to stimulate egg production (so more than one egg can be collected).

PRO Fertility treatment can give an infertile couple a child — a pretty obvious benefit.

CONS
1) Some women have a strong reaction to the hormones — e.g. abdominal pain, vomiting, dehydration.
2) There have been some reports of an increased risk of cancer due to the hormonal treatment (though others have reported no such risk — the position isn't really clear at the moment).
3) Multiple births can happen if more than one embryo grows into a baby — these are risky for the mother and babies (there's a higher risk of miscarriage, stillbirth...).

Different hormones — VERY different effects...

IVF is a relatively young technology — the first test tube baby was born in the late 1970s. But loads of people have been born since then because of it. But IVF, like other ways of controlling fertility, has its pros and cons.

Plant Hormones

Plants <u>don't</u> just grow randomly. Plant hormones make sure they grow in the <u>right direction</u>.

Auxins are Plant Growth Hormones

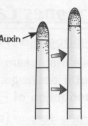

1) <u>Auxins</u> are <u>plant hormones</u> which control <u>growth</u> at the <u>tips</u> of <u>shoots</u> and <u>roots</u>. They move through the plant in <u>solution</u> (dissolved in water).
2) Auxin is produced in the <u>tips</u> and <u>diffuses backwards</u> to stimulate the <u>cell elongation process</u> which occurs in the cells <u>just behind</u> the tips.
3) Auxin <u>promotes</u> growth in the <u>shoot</u>, but actually <u>inhibits</u> growth in the <u>root</u>.
4) Auxins are involved in the growth responses of plants to <u>light</u> (phototropism) and <u>gravity</u> (geotropism).

Auxins Change the Direction of Root and Shoot Growth

SHOOTS ARE POSITIVELY PHOTOTROPIC (grow towards light)

1) When a <u>shoot tip</u> is exposed to <u>light</u>, it accumulates <u>more auxin</u> on the side that's in the <u>shade</u> than the side that's in the light.
2) This makes the cells grow (elongate) <u>faster</u> on the <u>shaded side</u>, so the shoot bends <u>towards</u> the light.

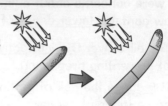

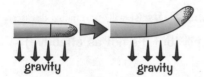

SHOOTS ARE NEGATIVELY GEOTROPIC (grow away from gravity)

1) When a <u>shoot</u> is growing sideways, <u>gravity</u> produces an unequal distribution of auxin in the tip, with <u>more auxin</u> on the <u>lower side</u>.
2) This causes the lower side to grow <u>faster</u>, bending the shoot <u>upwards</u>.

ROOTS ARE POSITIVELY GEOTROPIC (grow towards gravity)

1) A <u>root</u> growing sideways will also have more auxin on its <u>lower side</u>.
2) But in a root the <u>extra</u> auxin <u>inhibits</u> growth. This means the cells on <u>top</u> elongate faster, and the root bends <u>downwards</u>.

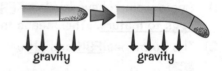

ROOTS ARE NEGATIVELY PHOTOTROPIC (grow away from light)

1) If a <u>root</u> starts being exposed to some <u>light</u>, <u>more auxin</u> accumulates on the more <u>shaded</u> side.
2) The auxin <u>inhibits</u> cell elongation on the shaded side, so the root bends <u>downwards</u>, back into the ground.

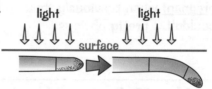

Experiments Have Shown How Auxins Work

Experiment 1 — shows auxins are produced in the tip of the plant.

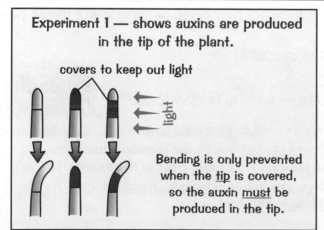

covers to keep out light

Bending is only prevented when the <u>tip</u> is covered, so the auxin <u>must</u> be produced in the tip.

Experiment 2 — shows auxins cause bending by building up on the shaded side of the root

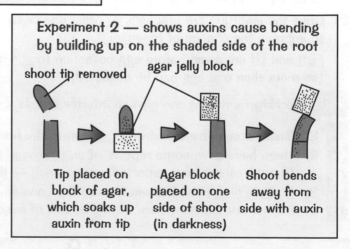

shoot tip removed

agar jelly block

Tip placed on block of agar, which soaks up auxin from tip

Agar block placed on one side of shoot (in darkness)

Shoot bends away from side with auxin

A plant auxin to a bar — 'ouch'...

Shoots grow towards light and roots grow towards gravity — that's not <u>too hard</u> to remember, now, is it.

Commercial Use of Plant Hormones

Plant hormones can be <u>extracted</u>, or <u>artificial copies</u> can be made. They can then be used to do all kinds of useful things, including <u>killing weeds</u>, <u>growing cuttings</u> and <u>ripening fruit</u>.

1) As Selective Weedkillers

1) Most <u>weeds</u> growing in fields of crops or in a lawn are <u>broad-leaved</u>, in contrast to <u>grasses</u> and <u>cereals</u> which have very <u>narrow leaves</u>.

2) <u>Selective weedkillers</u> have been developed from <u>plant growth hormones</u> which only affect the <u>broad-leaved plants</u>.

3) They totally <u>disrupt</u> their normal growth patterns, which soon <u>kills</u> them, whilst leaving the grass and crops <u>untouched</u>.

Unhappy weeds

2) Growing from Cuttings with Rooting Powder

1) A <u>cutting</u> is part of a plant that has been <u>cut off it</u>, like the end of a branch with a few leaves on it.

2) Normally, if you stick cuttings in the soil they <u>won't grow</u>, but if you add <u>rooting powder</u>, which contains a plant <u>growth hormone</u>, they will <u>produce roots</u> rapidly and start growing as <u>new plants</u>.

3) This enables growers to produce lots of <u>clones</u> (exact copies) of a really good plant <u>very quickly</u>.

boring old soil

rooting compound

3) Controlling the Ripening of Fruit

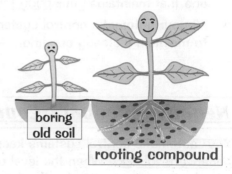

1) Plant hormones can be used to <u>delay the ripening</u> of fruits — either while they are still on the plant, or during <u>transport</u> to the shops.

2) This allows the fruit to be picked while it's still <u>unripe</u> (and therefore firmer and <u>less easily damaged</u>).

3) <u>Ripening hormone</u> is then added and the fruit will ripen on the way to the supermarket and be <u>perfect</u> just as it reaches the shelves.

4) Controlling Dormancy

1) Lots of seeds <u>won't germinate</u> (start growing) until they've been through <u>certain conditions</u> (e.g. a period of <u>cold</u> or of <u>dryness</u>). This is called <u>dormancy</u>.

2) A hormone called <u>gibberellin</u> breaks this dormancy and allows the seeds to <u>germinate</u>.

3) Commercial growers can <u>treat seeds</u> with gibberellin to make them germinate at <u>times of year</u> when they <u>wouldn't</u> normally. It also helps to make sure <u>all</u> the seeds in a batch germinate at the <u>same time</u>.

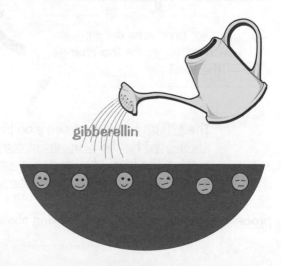

gibberellin

You will ripen when I SAY you can ripen — and NOT BEFORE...

If you want some fruit to ripen, put it into a paper bag with a banana. The banana releases a ripening hormone called <u>ethene</u> which causes the fruit to ripen. Bad apples also release lots of ethene. Unfortunately this means if you've got one bad apple in a barrel, you'll soon have lots of bad apples.

Homeostasis

Homeostasis — a word that strikes fear into the heart of many a GCSE student. But it's really <u>not</u> that bad at all. You might even find it kinda fun. So to kick things off here's a nice, gentle introduction to the topic.

Homeostasis — Maintaining a Constant Internal Environment

1) Homeostasis is all about balancing <u>inputs</u> (stuff going into your body) with <u>outputs</u> (stuff leaving) to <u>maintain a constant internal environment</u>.

I'm not really a doctor — this clipboard isn't holding anything. But take it from me, homeostasis is one important topic.

2) The conditions inside your body need to be kept <u>steady</u>, even when the <u>external environment changes</u>. This is really important because your <u>cells</u> need the <u>right conditions</u> in order to <u>function properly</u>.

3) You have loads of <u>automatic control systems</u> in your body that regulate your internal environment — these include both <u>nervous</u> and <u>hormonal</u> communication systems. For example, there's a control system that maintains your <u>water content</u> (see page 18) and one that maintains your <u>body temperature</u>.

4) All your automatic control systems are made up of <u>three main components</u> which work together to maintain a steady condition — <u>receptors</u>, <u>processing centres</u> and <u>effectors</u>.

Negative Feedback Counteracts Changes

Your automatic control systems keep your internal environment stable using a mechanism called <u>negative feedback</u>. When the level of something (e.g. water or temperature) gets <u>too high</u> or <u>too low</u>, your body uses negative feedback to bring it back to <u>normal</u>.

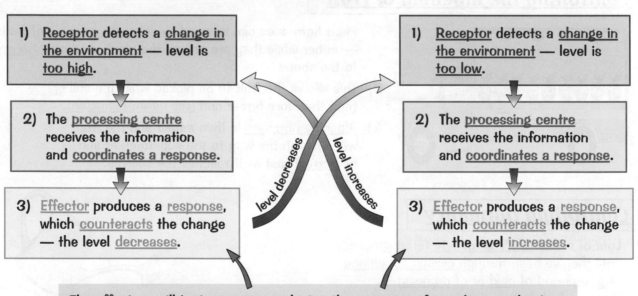

1) <u>Receptor</u> detects a <u>change in the environment</u> — level is <u>too high</u>.

2) The <u>processing centre</u> receives the information and <u>coordinates a response</u>.

3) <u>Effector</u> produces a <u>response</u>, which <u>counteracts</u> the change — the level <u>decreases</u>.

level decreases

level increases

1) <u>Receptor</u> detects a <u>change in the environment</u> — level is <u>too low</u>.

2) The <u>processing centre</u> receives the information and <u>coordinates a response</u>.

3) <u>Effector</u> produces a <u>response</u>, which <u>counteracts</u> the change — the level <u>increases</u>.

The <u>effectors</u> will just carry on producing the responses for as long as they're <u>stimulated</u> by the <u>processing centre</u>. This might cause the <u>opposite problem</u> — making the level change <u>too much</u> (away from the ideal). Luckily the <u>receptor</u> detects if the level becomes <u>too different</u> and negative feedback <u>starts again</u>.

This process happens without you thinking about it — it's all <u>automatic</u>.

Homeostasis — I always thought that was Latin for static caravan...

See, it wasn't so bad, was it? OK, the bit about <u>negative feedback</u> might have confused you at first, but the more you <u>go over it</u>, the more it <u>makes sense</u>. Make sure you've got your head around this <u>homeostasis</u> malarkey because the next two pages are all about <u>how your body uses it</u> to control the levels of different things.

Controlling Ions, Temperature and Blood Sugar

Your body is a fussy old thing — loads of stuff inside it has to be <u>balanced</u> just right. It's such diva...

Your Body Needs Some Things to Be Kept Constant

To keep all your cells working properly, certain things must be <u>kept at the right level</u> — not too high, and not too low.

<u>Bodily levels</u> that need to be controlled include:

1) <u>Ion</u> content
2) <u>Temperature</u>
3) <u>Sugar</u> content
4) <u>Water</u> content (see page 18)

Remember, maintaining a constant internal environment is what homeostasis is all about.

Ion Content Is Regulated by the Kidneys

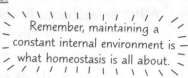
Kidneys

1) <u>Ions</u> (e.g. sodium, Na^+) are taken into the body in <u>food</u>, then absorbed into the blood.

2) If the food contains <u>too much</u> of any kind of ion then the excess ions need to be <u>removed</u>. E.g. a salty meal will contain far too much Na^+.

3) Some ions are lost in <u>sweat</u> (which tastes salty, you'll have noticed).

4) The kidneys will <u>remove the excess</u> from the blood — this is then got rid of in <u>urine</u> (see page 18).

Body Temperature is Controlled by the Brain

All <u>enzymes</u> have an <u>optimum temperature</u> they work best at. For enzymes in the human body it's about <u>37 °C</u>.

1) There's a <u>thermoregulatory centre</u> in the <u>brain</u> which acts as your own <u>personal thermostat</u>.

2) It contains <u>receptors</u> that are sensitive to the <u>blood temperature</u> in the brain. It also receives impulses from the <u>skin</u> that provide information about <u>skin temperature</u>. The brain can <u>respond</u> to this information and bring about changes in the body's temperature. For example:

When You're TOO HOT:

1) <u>Hairs</u> lie flat.

2) <u>Lots of sweat</u> is produced — when sweat <u>evaporates</u> it uses heat from the skin. This transfers heat from your skin to the environment, which <u>cools you down</u>.

3) <u>Blood vessels</u> close to the surface of the skin <u>widen</u>. This allows more blood to flow near the surface, so it can radiate more heat into the surroundings. This is called <u>vasodilation</u>.

If you're exposed to <u>high temperatures</u> you can get <u>dehydrated</u> and you could get <u>heat stroke</u>. This can <u>kill</u> you.

When You're TOO COLD:

1) <u>Hairs</u> stand on end to trap an insulating layer of air which helps keep you warm.

2) <u>Very little sweat</u> is produced.

3) Blood vessels near the surface <u>constrict</u> (<u>vasoconstriction</u>) so that less heat can be transferred from the blood to the surroundings.

4) You <u>shiver</u>, and the movement generates heat in the muscles.

Your body temperature can drop to dangerous levels if you're exposed to <u>very low temperatures</u> for a long time — this is called <u>hypothermia</u>. If you don't get help quickly you can <u>die</u>.

Blood Sugar Level Needs to Be Controlled Too

1) Eating foods containing <u>carbohydrate</u> puts <u>glucose</u> into the blood from the <u>gut</u>.

2) The normal metabolism of cells <u>removes</u> glucose from the blood. But if you do a lot of vigorous <u>exercise</u>, then much more glucose is removed.

3) A hormone called <u>insulin</u> helps to maintain the <u>right level</u> of glucose in your blood, so your cells get a <u>constant supply</u> of <u>energy</u>.

Sweaty and red — I'm so attractive in the heat...

Admittedly this isn't the most <u>thrilling</u> page in the world, but it could be worse. You could be doing <u>maths</u>.

Controlling Water Content

Controlling water content is pretty important — so here's a page all about it. Just for you.

Water Is Lost from the Body in Various Ways

There's a need for the body to constantly balance the water coming in against the water going out. Water is taken into the body as food and drink and is lost from the body in these ways:

1) through the SKIN as SWEAT...
2) via the LUNGS in BREATH...
3) via the kidneys as URINE.

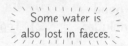
Some water is also lost in faeces.

The balance between sweat and urine can depend on what you're doing, or what the weather's like...

On a COLD DAY, or when you're NOT EXERCISING, you don't sweat much, so you'll produce more urine, which will be pale (since the waste carried in the urine is more diluted).

On a HOT DAY, or when you're EXERCISING, you sweat a lot, and so you will produce less urine, but this will be more concentrated (and hence a deeper colour). You will also lose more water through your breath when you exercise because you breathe faster.

Kidneys Help Balance Substances in the Body

The kidneys balance levels of water, waste and other chemicals in the body by doing the following things...

1) They filter small molecules from the blood, including water, sugar, ions and waste.
2) They reabsorb various things...
   - All the sugar.
   - As much water and ions as the body requires. Water absorption is controlled by ADH (see below).
3) Whatever isn't reabsorbed forms urine, which is excreted by the kidneys and stored in the bladder.

The Concentration of Urine is Controlled by a Hormone

1) The concentration of urine is controlled by a hormone called anti-diuretic hormone (ADH). This is released into the bloodstream by the pituitary gland.

2) The brain monitors the water content of the blood and instructs the pituitary gland to release ADH into the blood according to how much is needed.

3) The whole process of water content regulation is controlled by negative feedback (see page 16). This means that if the water content gets too high or too low a mechanism will be triggered that brings it back to normal.

1) A receptor in the brain detects that the water content is too high.

2) The processing centre in the brain receives the information and coordinates a response.

3) The pituitary gland releases less ADH, so the kidneys reabsorb less water.

water content decreases

water content increases

1) A receptor in the brain detects that the water content is too low.

2) The processing centre in the brain receives the information and coordinates a response.

3) The pituitary gland releases more ADH, so the kidneys reabsorb more water.

So, using negative feedback the amount of water in your body can be closely regulated. Don't forget that the more water your kidneys reabsorb, the less water will pass out as urine.

Bet you didn't realise wee is so exciting...

And as if that wasn't excitement enough, you've got one awesome revision summary coming right up. Lucky you.

Revision Summary for Section 1

Congratulations, you've made it to the end of the first section. I reckon that section wasn't too bad, there's some pretty interesting stuff there — nerves, reflexes, hormones, wee... what more could you want? Actually, I know what more you could want, some questions to make sure you know it all.

1) Describe the structure of the central nervous system and explain what it does.
2) Where would you find the following receptors in a dog: a) smell b) taste c) light d) pressure e) sound?
3) What is a synapse?
4) What is the purpose of a reflex action?
5) Describe the pathway of a reflex arc from stimulus to response.
6) Define "hormone".
7)* Here's a table of data about response times.

Response	Reaction time (s)	Response duration (s)
A	0.005	0.05
B	2	10

    a) Which response (A or B) is carried by nerves?
    b) Which is carried by hormones?

8) Draw a timeline of the 28 day menstrual cycle.
    Label the four stages of the cycle and label when the egg is released.
9) Describe two effects of FSH on the body.
10) State two advantages and two disadvantages of using the contraceptive pill.
11) Briefly describe how IVF is carried out.
12) What are auxins?
13) Shoots are negatively geotropic. How are auxins responsible for this?
14) Give three ways that plant growth hormones are used commercially.
15) What is homeostasis?
16) Name the three main components of the body's automatic control systems.
17) Name four levels that the body keeps constant by homeostasis.
18) Describe how body temperature is reduced when you're too hot.
19) Give two ways that water is gained by the body.
20) Water content is kept steady by homeostasis. Describe how the amount and concentration of urine you produce varies depending on how much exercise you do and how hot it is.
21) Which gland releases ADH?
22) If there is an increase in water content in the blood, will more or less ADH be released?

* Answers on page 140.

Diet and Metabolic Rate

The first thing on the Section 2 menu is... well... <u>food</u>. Obviously. It's where you get your <u>energy</u> from, to do all sorts of things like talking, partying and maybe a bit of <u>revision</u>.

A Balanced Diet Does a Lot to Keep You Healthy

1) For good health, your diet must provide the <u>energy</u> you need (but <u>not more</u>) — see the next page.

2) But that's not all. Because the different <u>food groups</u> have different uses in the body, you need to have the right <u>balance</u> of foods as well.
So you need:

   ...enough <u>carbohydrates</u> to release <u>energy</u>,

   ...enough <u>fats</u> to <u>keep warm</u> and release <u>energy</u>,

   ...enough <u>protein</u> for <u>growth</u>, <u>cell repair</u> and <u>cell replacement</u>,

   ...enough <u>fibre</u> to keep everything moving <u>smoothly</u> through your digestive system,

   ...and tiny amounts of various <u>vitamins</u> and <u>mineral ions</u> to keep your skin, bones, blood and everything else generally healthy.

People's Energy Needs Vary Because of Who They Are...

1) You need <u>energy</u> to fuel the chemical reactions in the body that keep you alive. These reactions are called your <u>metabolism</u>, and the speed at which they occur is your <u>metabolic rate</u>.

2) There are slight variations in the <u>resting metabolic rate</u> of different people. For example, <u>muscle</u> needs more energy than <u>fatty tissue</u>, which means (all other things being equal) people with a higher proportion of muscle to fat in their bodies will have a <u>higher</u> metabolic rate.

3) However, physically <u>bigger</u> people are likely to have a <u>higher</u> metabolic rate than smaller people — the <u>bigger</u> you are, the <u>more energy</u> your body needs to be supplied with (because you have more cells).

4) <u>Men</u> tend to have a slightly <u>higher</u> rate than <u>women</u> — they're slightly <u>bigger</u> and have a larger proportion of <u>muscle</u>. Other <u>genetic factors</u> may also have some effect.

5) And regular <u>exercise</u> can boost your resting metabolic rate because it <u>builds muscle</u>.

...and Because of What They Do

Activity	kJ/min
Sleeping	4.5
Watching TV	7
Cycling (5 mph)	21
Jogging (5 mph)	40
Climbing stairs	77
Swimming	35
Rowing	58
Slow walking	14

1) When you <u>exercise</u>, you obviously need more <u>energy</u> — so your <u>metabolic rate</u> goes up during exercise and stays high for <u>some time</u> after you finish (particularly if the exercise is strenuous).

2) So people who have more <u>active</u> jobs need more <u>energy</u> on a daily basis — builders require more energy per day than office workers, for instance. The table shows the average kilojoules burned per minute when doing different activities.

3) This means your activity level affects the amount of <u>energy</u> your <u>diet should contain</u>. If you do <u>little exercise</u>, you're going to need <u>less energy</u>, so <u>less fat</u> and <u>carbohydrate</u> in your diet, than if you're constantly on the go.

Diet tip — the harder you revise the more calories you burn...

So basically, eating healthily involves eating the <u>right amount</u> of food and the <u>right type</u> of food. You've also got to eat <u>enough food</u> to match your <u>energy needs</u>... or do enough exercise to match your eating habits. Well, what are you waiting for — time to burn off those calories by <u>revising</u> all of this page.

Factors Affecting Health

Being healthy doesn't just mean you look great in your swimwear — it means being free of any diseases too.

Your Health is Affected by Having an Unbalanced Diet...

1) People whose diet is badly out of balance are said to be malnourished.
2) Malnourished people can be fat or thin, or unhealthy in other ways:

Malnourishment is different from starvation, which is not getting enough food of any sort.

Eating too much can lead to obesity...

1) Excess carbohydrate or fat in the diet can lead to obesity.
2) Obesity is a common disorder in developed countries — it's defined as being 20% (or more) over maximum recommended body mass.
3) Hormonal problems can lead to obesity, though the usual cause is a bad diet, overeating and a lack of exercise.
4) Health problems that can arise as a result of obesity include: arthritis (inflammation of the joints), type 2 diabetes (inability to control blood sugar level), high blood pressure and heart disease. It's also a risk factor for some kinds of cancer.

...and other health problems

1) Too much saturated fat in your diet can increase your blood cholesterol level (see below).
2) Eating too much salt can cause high blood pressure and heart problems (see pages 24-25).

Eating too little can also cause problems

1) Some people suffer from lack of food, particularly in developing countries.
2) The effects of malnutrition vary depending on what foods are missing from the diet. But problems commonly include slow growth (in children), fatigue, poor resistance to infection, and irregular periods in women.
3) Deficiency diseases are caused by a lack of vitamins or minerals. For example, a lack of vitamin C can cause scurvy, a deficiency disease that causes problems with the skin, joints and gums.

...Not Getting Enough Exercise...

1) Exercise is important as well as diet — people who exercise regularly are usually healthier than those who don't.
2) Exercise increases the amount of energy used by the body and decreases the amount stored as fat. It also builds muscle so it helps to boost your metabolic rate (see page 20). So people who exercise are less likely to suffer from health problems such as obesity.
3) However, sometimes people can be fit but not healthy — e.g. you can be physically fit and slim, but malnourished at the same time because your diet isn't balanced.

...and Inherited Factors

1) It's not just about what you eat and how much exercise you do — your health can depend on inherited factors too.
2) Some people may inherit factors that affect their metabolic rate, e.g. some inherited factors cause an underactive thyroid gland, which can lower the metabolic rate and cause obesity.
3) Other people may inherit factors that affect their blood cholesterol level. Cholesterol is a fatty substance that's essential for good health — it's found in every cell in the body. Some inherited factors increase blood cholesterol level, which increases the risk of heart disease.

Obesity is an increasingly weighty issue nowadays...

Your health can really suffer if you regularly eat too much, too little, or miss out on a vital nutrient. Exercise is important as well as diet — regular exercise helps to keep you fit. But remember, being fit isn't the same as being healthy — if your diet isn't balanced then you can still be malnourished, even if you do tons of exercise.

Evaluating Food, Lifestyle and Diet

Sometimes you've got to be a bit <u>savvy</u> when working out which is the healthiest food product to eat, or if a <u>claim</u> about a particular slimming diet is actually <u>true</u>.

You Might Have to Evaluate Information on Food and Lifestyle

1) In the exam, you may get asked to <u>evaluate information</u> about how <u>food</u> affects health — panic ye not, just take a look at the food label example below:

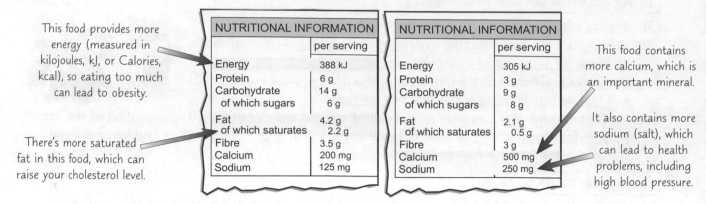

This food provides more energy (measured in kilojoules, kJ, or Calories, kcal), so eating too much can lead to obesity.

There's more saturated fat in this food, which can raise your cholesterol level.

NUTRITIONAL INFORMATION	
	per serving
Energy	388 kJ
Protein	6 g
Carbohydrate	14 g
of which sugars	6 g
Fat	4.2 g
of which saturates	2.2 g
Fibre	3.5 g
Calcium	200 mg
Sodium	125 mg

NUTRITIONAL INFORMATION	
	per serving
Energy	305 kJ
Protein	3 g
Carbohydrate	9 g
of which sugars	8 g
Fat	2.1 g
of which saturates	0.5 g
Fibre	3 g
Calcium	500 mg
Sodium	250 mg

This food contains more calcium, which is an important mineral.

It also contains more sodium (salt), which can lead to health problems, including high blood pressure.

2) You might also get asked to evaluate information about how <u>lifestyle</u> affects health. Your lifestyle includes <u>what you eat</u> and <u>what you do</u>. E.g. a person who eats too much fat or carbohydrate and doesn't do much exercise will increase their risk of <u>obesity</u>. Remember, you may need to use your <u>knowledge</u> of how diet and exercise affect health to answer exam questions — the facts on the previous two pages will help you out.

Watch Out for Slimming Claims that Aren't Scientifically Proven

1) There are loads of <u>slimming products</u> (e.g. diet pills, slimming milkshakes) and <u>slimming programmes</u> (e.g. the Atkins Diet™) around — and they all claim they'll help you <u>lose weight</u>. But how do you know they work...

2) It's a good idea to <u>look out</u> for <u>these things</u>:

- Is the report a scientific study, published in a reputable journal?
- Was it written by a qualified person (not connected with the people selling it)?
- Was the sample of people asked/tested large enough to give reliable results?
- Have there been other studies which found similar results?

A "yes" to one or more of these is a good sign.

E.g. a common way to promote a new <u>diet</u> is to say, "Celebrity A has lost x pounds using it". But effectiveness in <u>one person</u> doesn't mean much. Only a <u>large survey</u> can tell if a diet is more or less effective than just <u>eating less</u> and <u>exercising more</u> — and these aren't done often.

3) Really, all you need to do to lose weight is to <u>take in less energy</u> than you <u>use</u>. So diets and slimming products will only work if you...

- eat <u>less fat or carbohydrate</u> (so that you take in less energy), or
- do <u>more exercise</u> (so that you use more energy).

4) Some claims may be <u>true</u> but a little <u>misleading</u>. E.g. <u>low-fat bars</u> might be low in fat, but eating them without changing the rest of your diet doesn't necessarily mean you'll lose weight — you could still be taking in <u>too much energy</u>.

"Brad Pitt says it's great" is NOT scientific proof...

Learn what to look out for before you put too much faith in what you read. Then buy my book — 100% of the people I surveyed (i.e. both of them) said it had no negative affect <u>whatsoever</u> on their overall wellbeing!

The Circulatory System

Blood is vital. It moves oxygen from your lungs to your cells, carbon dioxide from your cells to your lungs, nutrients from your gut to your cells, hormones from your glands to your cells... oh, I'm exhausted.

The Heart and Blood Vessels Supply Blood to the Body

1) Blood is circulated around the body in tubes called blood vessels. Oxygen and nutrients are carried in the blood to the body cells, and waste substances such as carbon dioxide are carried away from the cells.

2) The heart is a pumping organ that keeps the blood flowing through the vessels. It's actually a double pump — the right side pumps deoxygenated blood to the lungs to collect oxygen and remove carbon dioxide. The left side pumps the oxygenated blood around the body.

3) The heart's made up of muscle cells that keep it beating continually. These cells need their own blood supply to deliver the nutrients and oxygen needed to keep the heart beating continually.

4) Blood is supplied to the heart by two coronary arteries, which branch from the base of the aorta (the biggest artery in the body).

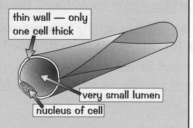

The diagram shows the right and left side of the person in the diagram, not your right and left as you look at them.

There are Three Major Types of Blood Vessel

1) Arteries carry blood away from the heart to the body cells (including the heart muscle).

2) It comes out of the heart at high pressure, so the artery walls have to be strong and elastic. They're much thicker than the walls of veins...

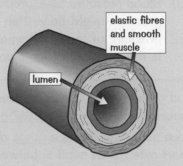

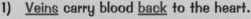

1) Veins carry blood back to the heart.

2) The blood is at a lower pressure in the veins so the walls don't need to be as thick.

3) They have a bigger lumen than arteries, to help the blood flow more easily.

4) They also have valves to help keep the blood flowing in the right direction.

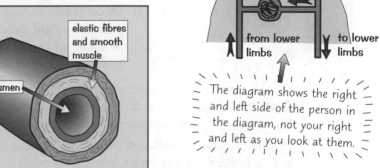

1) Capillaries are branches of arteries that are really tiny — you need a microscope to see them.

2) They carry the blood really close to every cell in the body to exchange substances with them.

3) They have permeable walls, so substances can diffuse in and out.

4) They supply nutrients and oxygen, and take away wastes like CO_2.

5) Their walls are only one cell thick. This increases the rate of diffusion by decreasing the distance over which it happens.

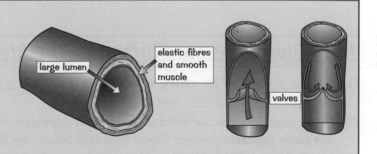

Unbreak my heart — say it's pumping again...

Don't forget that the heart is a double pump that has two jobs — pumping blood to the body, and to the lungs. From two jobs, to three blood vessels — their structures help them with their functions.

Heart Rate and Blood Pressure

Your blood has got to travel a <u>long way</u> around your body and the only way it can do this is if it's <u>under pressure</u>. Your heart <u>beats</u> continuously to keep the blood moving and keep up this pressure.

Your Pulse Rate Can be Used to Measure Your Heart Rate

1) Your <u>heart rate</u> is the number of times your <u>heart beats</u> in <u>one minute</u> — it's measured in <u>BPM</u> (beats per minute).

2) Your <u>pulse rate</u> is the number of times an <u>artery pulsates</u> in <u>one minute</u>.

3) The pulsation of an artery is <u>caused</u> by blood being <u>pumped</u> through it by a <u>heart beat</u>, so you can measure your pulse rate to work out your <u>heart rate</u>.

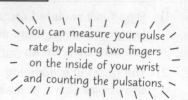
You can measure your pulse rate by placing two fingers on the inside of your wrist and counting the pulsations.

Blood is Pumped Around Your Body Under Pressure

Well, your blood pressure is a little high...

1) When your heart muscle <u>contracts</u>, blood is forced out of the heart — this <u>increases</u> the <u>pressure</u> of your blood. When your heart muscle <u>relaxes</u>, the heart fills with blood and your <u>blood pressure decreases</u>.

2) You can <u>measure</u> your blood pressure by taking a reading of the <u>pressure</u> of the blood <u>against the walls</u> of an <u>artery</u>.

3) Blood pressure measurements have <u>two values</u>, e.g. a person's blood pressure might be written as "135 over 85". The <u>higher</u> value is the pressure of the blood when the heart <u>contracts</u>, and the <u>lower</u> value is the pressure of the blood when the heart <u>relaxes</u>.

> A person's <u>heart rate</u> and <u>blood pressure</u> can be used to check how <u>healthy</u> they are by <u>comparing</u> their measurements against <u>"normal" measurements</u>.
>
> Normal measurements are usually given as a <u>range</u> of values because <u>individuals vary</u>, e.g. a normal resting heart rate for an adult is between 60 and 100 beats a minute.

High Blood Pressure Increases the Risk of Heart Disease

1) The <u>inner lining</u> of an artery is usually <u>smooth</u> and <u>unbroken</u>, but <u>high blood pressure</u> can <u>damage</u> it.

2) <u>Fatty deposits</u> can sometimes <u>build up</u> in damaged areas of arteries — these deposits <u>restrict</u> blood flow and cause the <u>blood pressure</u> in arteries to <u>increase</u>.

Heart disease is just any disease that affects the heart — including heart attacks.

3) If a fatty deposit <u>breaks through</u> the inner lining of an artery, a <u>blood clot</u> may form around it.

4) The <u>blood clot</u> could <u>block</u> the artery completely, or it could <u>break away</u> and block a <u>different artery</u>.

5) If a <u>coronary artery</u> (see previous page) becomes <u>completely blocked</u> an area of the heart muscle will be totally <u>cut off</u> from its blood supply, receiving <u>no oxygen</u>. This causes a <u>heart attack</u>.

6) A heart attack can cause <u>serious damage</u> to the heart or may even cause the <u>death</u> of the heart muscle — which can be <u>fatal</u>.

Don't let exam stress send your blood pressure through the roof...

This page started off nice enough — measuring your <u>pulse rate</u> is something you can do at home, and having your <u>blood pressure</u> taken is always fun. But then it got serious... and it doesn't get much more serious than <u>heart disease</u>. At least now you should understand why having <u>high blood pressure</u> is <u>not</u> a good thing.

Factors Affecting Heart Disease

Your <u>heart</u> is pretty darn important, but certain <u>lifestyle factors</u> can <u>increase</u> your <u>chance</u> of getting <u>heart disease</u>. These risk factors can be identified by <u>epidemiological studies</u>...

Lifestyle Factors Can Increase the Risk of Heart Disease

1) Heart disease can often be linked to <u>lifestyle factors</u>, such as what someone <u>eats</u> and how much <u>exercise</u> they do. Some people might be more at risk because of their <u>genes</u> too. In most people it's a condition caused by one or both of these things.

2) The lifestyle factors that <u>increase</u> the risk of heart disease include:

Smoking

1) Both <u>carbon monoxide</u> and <u>nicotine</u>, found in cigarette smoke, <u>increase</u> the risk of heart disease.

2) Carbon monoxide <u>reduces</u> the amount of <u>oxygen</u> the blood can transport. If <u>heart muscle</u> doesn't receive enough oxygen it can lead to a <u>heart attack</u> (see previous page).

3) Nicotine increases <u>heart rate</u>. The heart contracts more often increasing <u>blood pressure</u>, which increases the risk of <u>heart disease</u>.

Excessive alcohol drinking

Drinking too much alcohol <u>increases</u> the risk of heart disease because it also <u>increases blood pressure</u>.

Misuse of illegal drugs

Drugs like <u>ecstasy</u> and <u>cannabis</u> can also <u>increase</u> the risk of heart disease by causing an <u>increase</u> in <u>heart rate</u>, which increases <u>blood pressure</u>.

Stress

1) People feel stress when they are <u>under pressure</u>, e.g. if they have a lot of work to do in a short amount of time.

2) If a person is stressed for a long period of time it can <u>increase</u> their <u>blood pressure</u> and so <u>increase</u> the risk of heart disease.

Poor diet

A diet high in <u>saturated fat</u> can <u>increase</u> your <u>cholesterol level</u> (see page 21). This increases the risk of <u>heart disease</u>.

3) Heart disease is more common in <u>industrialised countries</u>, such as the UK and USA, than in non-industrialised countries. This is mainly because people in these countries can <u>afford</u> a lot of high-fat food and often <u>don't need</u> to be very physically active.

Epidemiological Studies Can Identify Possible Risk Factors

Epidemiology is the study of <u>patterns</u> of diseases and the <u>factors</u> that affect them. You need to know about how epidemiological studies are used to identify the factors that increase the risk of <u>heart disease</u>.

1) Epidemiological studies can help to identify the <u>lifestyle risk factors</u>. For example, you could study a group of people who all died from heart disease to look for <u>similarities</u> in their lifestyle that may be <u>linked</u> to heart disease, e.g. they were all smokers or they all had a poor diet.

2) They can also involve large scale <u>genetics studies</u> to identify the <u>genetic risk factors</u>. For example, you could map the genetic makeup of a large group of people, then see if there are any <u>genetic similarities</u> between the people who are affected by heart disease.

Contrary to popular belief, lard sandwiches won't keep your heart healthy...

Time for a little bit of <u>common sense</u> — if you know the things that <u>increase</u> the risk of heart disease, <u>cut down on them</u> by changing your lifestyle. It's <u>not</u> rocket science, but it's important that you're aware of it.

Drugs

Drugs alter what goes on in your body. Your body's essentially a seething mass of chemical reactions — drugs can interfere with these reactions, sometimes for the better, sometimes not.

Drugs Change Your Body Chemistry

Some of the chemical changes caused by drugs can lead to the body becoming addicted to the drug. If the drug isn't taken, an addict can suffer physical withdrawal symptoms — and these are sometimes very unpleasant. E.g. heroin, cocaine, nicotine and caffeine are all very addictive.

Drugs can be Medicinal, Recreational or Performance-Enhancing

1) Medicinal drugs are medically useful, like antibiotics. For some of these drugs you don't need a prescription (e.g. paracetamol), but for others you do (e.g. morphine) because they can be dangerous if misused.

2) Recreational drugs are used for fun. These can be legal or illegal (see page 28).

3) Performance-enhancing drugs can improve a person's performance in sport (see below).

Performance-Enhancing Drugs have Health and Ethical Impacts

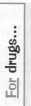

1) Some athletes take performance-enhancing drugs to make them better at sport.

2) There are several different types, including anabolic steroids (that increase muscle size) and stimulants (that increase heart rate).

3) But these drugs can have negative health effects, e.g. steroids can cause high blood pressure.

4) Some of these drugs are banned by law, some are prescription-only, but all are banned by sporting bodies.

5) There are also ethical problems with taking performance-enhancing drugs:

Against drugs...
1) It's unfair if people gain an advantage by taking drugs, not just through training.
2) Athletes may not be fully informed of the serious health risks of the drugs they take.

For drugs...
1) Athletes have the right to make their own decision about whether taking drugs is worth the risk or not.
2) Drug-free sport isn't really fair anyway — different athletes have access to different training facilities, coaches, equipment, etc.

Claims About Drugs need to be Carefully Looked At

Claims about the effects of drugs (both prescribed and non-prescribed) need to be looked at critically. E.g:

STATINS
1) Statins are prescribed drugs used to lower the risk of heart and circulatory disease.
2) There's evidence that statins lower blood cholesterol and significantly lower the risk of heart disease in diabetic patients.
3) The original research was done by government scientists with no connection to the manufacturers. And the sample was big — 6000 patients.
4) It compared two groups of patients — those who had taken statins and those who hadn't. Other studies have since backed up these findings.

So control groups were used. And the results were reproducible.

But research findings are not always so clear cut...

CANNABIS
1) Cannabis is an illegal drug. Scientists have investigated whether the chemicals in cannabis smoke cause mental health problems. The results vary, and are sometimes open to different interpretations.
2) Basically, until more definite scientific evidence is found, no one's sure.

Drugs can kill you or cure you (or anything in between)...

Many people take drugs of some kind, e.g. caffeine in coffee, headache tablets, alcohol, hayfever medicine or an inhaler for asthma. Most of these are okay if you're careful with them and don't go mad. It's misuse that can get you into trouble (e.g. a paracetamol overdose can kill you). Read the packet.

Testing Medicinal Drugs

New drugs are constantly being developed. But before they can be given to the general public, they have to go through a thorough testing procedure. This is what usually happens...

There are Three Main Stages in Drug Testing

 1) Drugs are tested on human cells and tissues in the lab.

2) However, you can't use human cells and tissues to test drugs that affect whole or multiple body systems, e.g. testing a drug for blood pressure must be done on a whole animal because it has an intact circulatory system.

2 1) The next step is to test the drug on live animals. This is to see whether the drug works (produces the effect you're looking for), to find out about its toxicity (how harmful it is) and the best dosage (the dose at which it's most effective).

2) The law in Britain states that any new drug must be tested on two different live mammals. Some people think it's cruel to test on animals, but others believe this is the safest way to make sure a drug isn't dangerous before it's given to humans.

But some people think that animals are so different from humans that testing on animals is pointless.

3 1) If the drug passes the tests on animals then it's tested on human volunteers in a clinical trial.

2) First, the drug is tested on healthy volunteers. This is to make sure that it doesn't have any harmful side effects when the body is working normally. At the start of the trial, a very low dose of the drug is given and this is gradually increased.

3) If the results of the tests on healthy volunteers are good, the drugs can be tested on people suffering from the illness. The optimum dose is found — this is the dose of drug that is the most effective and has few side effects.

4) To test how well the drug works, patients are put into two groups. One is given the new drug, the other is given a placebo (a substance that's like the real drug but doesn't do anything). This is so the doctor can see the actual difference the drug makes — it allows for the placebo effect (when the patient expects the treatment to work and so feels better, even though the treatment isn't doing anything).

5) Clinical trials are blind — the patient in the study doesn't know whether they're getting the drug or the placebo. In fact, they're often double-blind — neither the patient nor the doctor knows until all the results have been gathered. This is so the doctors monitoring the patients and analysing the results aren't subconsciously influenced by their knowledge.

Things Have Gone Wrong in the Past

An example of what can happen when drugs are not thoroughly tested is the case of thalidomide — a drug developed in the 1950s.

1) Thalidomide was intended as a sleeping pill, and was tested for that use. But later it was also found to be effective in relieving morning sickness in pregnant women.

2) Unfortunately, thalidomide hadn't been tested as a drug for morning sickness, and so it wasn't known that it could pass through the placenta and affect the fetus, causing abnormal limb development. In some cases, babies were born with no arms or legs at all.

3) About 10 000 babies were affected by thalidomide, and only about half of them survived.

4) The drug was banned, and more rigorous testing procedures were introduced.

5) More recently thalidomide has been used in the treatment of leprosy and other diseases, e.g. some cancers.

A little learning is a dangerous thing...

The thalidomide story is an example of an attempt to improve people's lives which then caused some pretty tragic knock-on effects. Could the same thing happen today? Well, maybe not the exact same thing, but there's no such thing as perfect knowledge — we're learning all the time, and you can never eliminate risk completely.

Recreational Drugs

Not all drugs are used by people with illnesses — some are just used for <u>fun</u>. But fun comes with <u>risk</u>. Everyone knows that. Just like the time I thought it'd be fun to roller skate around the office. Not advisable.

Recreational Drugs Can Be Illegal or Legal

1) <u>Illegal</u> drugs are often divided into two main classes — <u>soft</u> and <u>hard</u>. Hard drugs are usually thought of as being seriously <u>addictive</u> and generally more <u>harmful</u>.

2) But the terms "soft" and "hard" are a bit <u>vague</u> — they're <u>not</u> scientific descriptions, and you can certainly have problems with <u>soft</u> drug use. E.g. <u>heroin</u> and <u>ecstasy</u> (hard drugs) and <u>cannabis</u> (a soft drug) can all cause <u>heart</u> and <u>circulatory system</u> problems.

There Are Various Reasons Why People Use Recreational Drugs

So if all these recreational drugs are so dangerous, why do so many people use them...

1) When asked why they use cannabis, most <u>users</u> quote either simple <u>enjoyment</u>, <u>relaxation</u> or <u>stress relief</u>. Some say they do it to <u>get stoned</u> or for <u>inspiration</u>.

2) But very often this turns out to be <u>not</u> the <u>whole</u> story. There may be other factors in the user's <u>background</u> or <u>personal life</u> which influence them in choosing to use drugs. It's a <u>personal</u> thing, and often pretty <u>complicated</u>.

And some multiple sclerosis sufferers say cannabis can relieve pain.

Some Studies Link Cannabis and Hard Drug Use — Others Don't

Almost all users of <u>hard drugs</u> have tried <u>cannabis</u> first (though <u>most</u> users of cannabis do <u>not</u> go on to use hard drugs). The <u>link</u> between cannabis and hard drugs isn't clear, but <u>three</u> opinions are common...

<u>Cannabis is a "stepping stone":</u> The effects of cannabis create a desire to try harder drugs.	<u>Cannabis is a "gateway drug":</u> Cannabis use brings people into contact with drug dealers.	<u>It's all down to genetics:</u> Certain people are more likely to take drugs generally, so cannabis users will also try other drugs.

Some Legal Drugs have More of an Impact than Illegal Drugs

1) <u>Tobacco</u> and <u>alcohol</u> are both <u>legal</u> recreational drugs but have a massive impact on people and society:

SMOKING
1) Smoking causes <u>disease</u> of the <u>heart</u>, <u>blood vessels</u> and <u>lungs</u>.
2) Tobacco smoke also causes <u>cancer</u>.
3) <u>Nicotine</u> is the drug found in <u>cigarettes</u> — it's <u>addictive</u> so it's hard to stop smoking.

ALCOHOL
1) Alcohol affects the <u>nervous system</u> and slows down the body's reactions.
2) Too much alcohol leads to <u>impaired judgement</u>, <u>poor coordination</u> and <u>unconsciousness</u>.
3) And excessive drinking can cause <u>liver disease</u> and <u>brain damage</u>.
4) Alcohol is also <u>addictive</u>.

2) <u>Tobacco</u> and <u>alcohol</u> have a bigger impact in the UK than illegal drugs, as <u>so many</u> people take them.

3) The National Health Service spends loads on treating people with <u>lung diseases</u> caused by <u>smoking</u>. Add to this the cost to businesses of people missing days from work, and the figures get pretty scary.

4) The same goes for <u>alcohol</u>. The costs to the NHS are huge, but are pretty small compared to the costs related to <u>crime</u> (police time, damage to people/property) and the <u>economy</u> (lost working days etc.).

5) And in addition to the financial costs, alcohol and tobacco cause <u>sorrow</u> and <u>anguish</u> to people affected by them, either directly or indirectly.

Drinking and smoking — it's so big and clever...

So it's <u>legal</u> drugs that have the most impact on the country as a <u>whole</u>, when you take everything into consideration. Some legal drugs are <u>prescribed</u> by doctors — but these can also have a <u>massive impact</u> on health if people <u>misuse</u> them, e.g. people can become addicted to prescribed <u>painkillers</u> if they're overused.

Fighting Disease

Microorganisms that enter the body and cause disease are called pathogens.
A disease caused by pathogens is known as an infectious disease.

There Are Two Main Types of Pathogen: Bacteria and Viruses

1) Bacteria are very small living cells.
2) They make you feel ill by doing two things:
   a) damaging your cells, b) producing toxins (poisons).
3) Viruses aren't cells — they're much smaller.
4) They replicate inside your cells and damage them — this what makes you feel ill.

> Diseases can also be caused by fungi and protozoa (single-celled organisms).

Your Body Has a Pretty Sophisticated Defence System

1) Your skin, plus hairs and mucus in your respiratory tract (breathing pipework), stop a lot of nasties getting inside your body.

2) And to try and prevent microorganisms getting into the body through cuts, small fragments of cells (called platelets) help blood clot quickly to seal wounds. If the blood contains low numbers of platelets then it will clot more slowly.

3) But if something does make it through, your immune system kicks in. The most important part is the white blood cells. They travel around in your blood and crawl into every part of you, constantly patrolling for microbes. When they come across an invading microbe they have three lines of attack.

1. Consuming Them

White blood cells can engulf foreign cells and digest them.

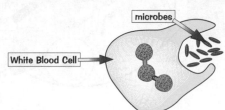

2. Producing Antibodies

1) Every invading cell has unique molecules (called antigens) on its surface.

2) When your white blood cells come across a foreign antigen (i.e. one they don't recognise), they will start to produce proteins called antibodies to lock onto and kill the invading cells. The antibodies produced are specific to that type of antigen — they won't lock on to any others.

3) Antibodies are then produced rapidly and carried around the body to kill all similar bacteria or viruses.

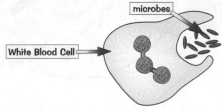

4) Some white blood cells stay around in the blood after the original infection has been fought off — these are called memory cells.

5) Memory cells can reproduce very quickly if the same antigen enters the body for a second time.

6) The memory cells then produce loads of antibodies and kill off the microorganisms before you become ill — this is known as immunity.

3. Producing Antitoxins

These counteract toxins produced by the invading bacteria.

Fight disease — blow your nose with boxing gloves...

If you have a low level of white blood cells, you'll be more susceptible to infections. E.g. HIV/AIDS attacks a person's white blood cells and weakens their immune system, making it easier for other pathogens to invade.

Fighting Disease — Vaccination

Vaccinations have changed the way we fight disease. We don't always have to deal with the problem once it's happened — we can prevent it happening in the first place.

Vaccination — Protects from Future Infections

1) When you're infected with a new microorganism, it takes your white blood cells a few days to learn how to deal with it. But by that time, you can be pretty ill.

2) Vaccinations involve injecting small amounts of dead or inactive microorganisms. These carry antigens, which cause your body to produce antibodies to attack them — even though the microorganism is harmless (since it's dead or inactive). For example, the MMR vaccine contains weakened versions of the viruses that cause measles, mumps and rubella (German measles) all in one vaccine.

3) The body also produces memory cells (see previous page) that recognise the antigens of the microorganisms and stay in the blood.

4) If live microorganisms of the same type appear after that, the memory cells can rapidly mass-produce antibodies to kill off the pathogen. Cool.

5) Some vaccinations "wear off" over time. So booster injections may need to be given to increase levels of antibodies again.

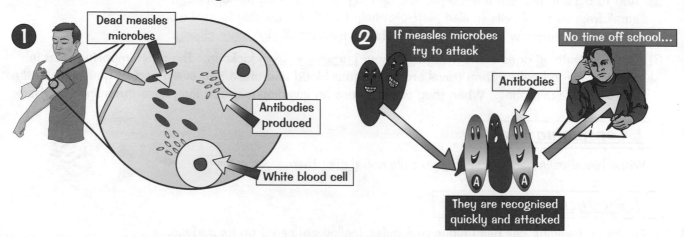

There are Pros and Cons of Vaccination

PROS

1) Vaccines have helped control lots of infectious diseases that were once common in the UK (e.g. polio, measles, whooping cough, rubella, mumps, tetanus...). Smallpox no longer occurs at all, and polio infections have fallen by 99%.

2) Big outbreaks of disease — called epidemics — can be prevented if a large percentage of the population is vaccinated. That way, even the people who aren't vaccinated are unlikely to catch the disease because there are fewer people able to pass it on. But if a significant number of people aren't vaccinated, the disease can spread quickly through them and lots of people will be ill at the same time.

CONS

1) Vaccines don't always work — sometimes they don't give you immunity.

2) You can sometimes have a bad reaction to a vaccine (e.g. swelling, or maybe something more serious like a fever or seizures). But bad reactions are very rare.

Prevention is better than cure...

Deciding whether to have a vaccination means balancing risks — the risk of catching the disease if you don't have a vaccine, against the risk of having a bad reaction if you do. As always, you need to look at the evidence. For example, if you get measles (the disease), there's about a 1 in 15 chance that you'll get complications (e.g. pneumonia) — and about 1 in 500 people who get measles actually die. However, the number of people who have a problem with the vaccine is more like 1 in 1 000 000.

Fighting Disease — Drugs

...a biscuit, nurse? Thanks very much. Sorry, couldn't face that last page — I'm squeamish about needles.*

Some Drugs Just Relieve Symptoms — Others Cure the Problem

1) <u>Painkillers</u> (e.g. aspirin) are drugs that relieve pain (no, really). However, they don't actually tackle the <u>cause</u> of the disease, they just help to reduce the <u>symptoms</u>.

2) Other drugs do a similar kind of thing — reduce the <u>symptoms</u> without tackling the underlying <u>cause</u>. For example, lots of "cold remedies" don't actually <u>cure</u> colds.

3) <u>Antibiotics</u> (e.g. penicillin) work differently — they actually <u>kill</u> (or prevent the growth of) the bacteria causing the problem without killing your own body cells. <u>Different antibiotics</u> kill <u>different types</u> of bacteria, so it's important to be treated with the <u>right one</u>.

4) But antibiotics <u>don't destroy viruses</u> (e.g. <u>flu</u> or <u>cold</u> viruses). Viruses reproduce <u>using your own body cells</u>, which makes it very difficult to develop drugs that destroy just the virus without killing the body's cells.

Bacteria Can Become Resistant to Antibiotics

1) Bacteria can <u>mutate</u> — sometimes the mutations cause them to be <u>resistant</u> to (not killed by) an <u>antibiotic</u>.

2) If you have an <u>infection</u>, some of the bacteria might be <u>resistant</u> to antibiotics.

3) This means that when you <u>treat</u> the infection, only the <u>non-resistant</u> strains of bacteria will be <u>killed</u>.

4) The individual <u>resistant</u> bacteria will <u>survive</u> and <u>reproduce</u>, and the population of the resistant strain will <u>increase</u>. This is an example of natural selection (see page 43).

5) This resistant strain could cause a <u>serious infection</u> that <u>can't</u> be treated by antibiotics. E.g. <u>MRSA</u> (methicillin-resistant *Staphylococcus aureus*) causes serious wound infectious and is resistant to the powerful antibiotic <u>methicillin</u>.

6) To <u>slow down</u> the <u>rate</u> of development of <u>resistant strains</u>, it's important for doctors to <u>avoid</u> <u>over-prescribing</u> antibiotics. So you <u>won't</u> get them for a <u>sore throat</u>, only for something more serious.

You can Investigate Antibiotics by Growing Microorganisms in the Lab

You can test the action of <u>antibiotics</u> or <u>disinfectants</u> by growing cultures of microorganisms:

1) Microorganisms are grown (cultured) in a "<u>culture medium</u>". This is usually <u>agar jelly</u> containing the <u>carbohydrates</u>, <u>minerals</u>, <u>proteins</u> and <u>vitamins</u> they need to grow.

2) <u>Hot</u> agar jelly is poured into shallow round plastic dishes called <u>Petri dishes</u>.

3) When the jelly's cooled and set, <u>inoculating loops</u> (wire loops) are used to transfer microorganisms to the culture medium. The microorganisms then <u>multiply</u>.

4) Paper discs are soaked in different types of <u>antibiotics</u> and placed on the jelly. Antibiotic-resistant bacteria will continue to <u>grow</u> around them but non-resistant strains will <u>die</u>.

colonies of microorganisms

agar jelly

5) The Petri dishes, culture medium and inoculating loops must be <u>sterilised</u> before use, e.g. the inoculating loops are <u>passed through a flame</u>. If equipment isn't sterilised, unwanted microorganisms in the culture medium will <u>grow</u> and <u>affect the result</u>.

inoculating loop

6) The Petri dish must also have a <u>lid</u> to stop any <u>microorganisms in the air</u> contaminating the culture. The lid should be <u>taped on</u>.

7) In the <u>lab at school</u>, cultures of microorganisms are kept at about <u>25 °C</u> because <u>harmful pathogens</u> aren't likely to grow at this temperature.

8) In <u>industrial conditions</u>, cultures are incubated at <u>higher temperatures</u> so that they can grow a lot faster.

Agar — my favourite jelly flavour after raspberry...

Microorganisms might be the perfect <u>pets</u>. You don't have to walk them, they won't get lonely and they hardly cost anything to feed. But whatever you do, do <u>not</u> feed them after midnight.

*That's my excuse, you'll have to think of your own.

Fighting Disease — Past and Future

The treatment of disease has changed somewhat over the last 200 years or so.

Semmelweis Cut Deaths by Using Antiseptics

1) While Ignaz Semmelweis was working in Vienna General Hospital in the 1840s, he saw that women were dying in huge numbers after childbirth from a disease called puerperal fever.

2) He believed that doctors were spreading the disease on their unwashed hands. By telling doctors entering his ward to wash their hands in an antiseptic solution, he cut the death rate from 12% to 2%.

3) The antiseptic solution killed bacteria on doctors' hands, though Semmelweis didn't know this (the existence of bacteria and their part in causing disease wasn't discovered for another 20 years). So Semmelweis couldn't prove why his idea worked, and his methods were dropped when he left the hospital (allowing death rates to rise once again — d'oh).

4) Nowadays we know that basic hygiene is essential in controlling disease (though recent reports have found that a lack of it in some modern hospitals has helped the disease MRSA spread).

Remember, antibiotics kill bacteria (see page 31).

Antibiotic Resistance is Becoming More Common

1) For the last few decades, we've been able to deal with bacterial infections pretty easily using antibiotics. The death rate from infectious bacterial diseases (e.g. pneumonia) has fallen dramatically.

2) But bacteria evolve antibiotic resistance, e.g MRSA bacteria are already resistant to certain antibiotics. And overuse of antibiotics has made this problem worse — by increasing the likelihood of people being infected by antibiotic-resistant strains (see page 31).

3) People who become infected with these bacteria can't easily get rid of them (because antibiotics don't work) and may pass on the infection to others.

4) So antibiotic resistance is a big problem and it's encouraged drug companies to work on developing new antibiotics that are effective against these resistant strains.

5) Meanwhile, bacteria that are resistant to most known antibiotics ('superbugs') are becoming more common.

We Face New and Scary Dangers All the Time

BACTERIA

1) As you know, bacteria can mutate to produce new strains (see page 31).
2) A new strain could be antibiotic-resistant, so current treatments would no longer clear an infection.
3) Or a new strain could be one that we've not encountered before, so no-one would be immune to it.
4) This means a new strain of bacteria could spread rapidly in a population of people and could even cause an epidemic — a big outbreak of disease.

VIRUSES

1) Viruses also tend to mutate often. This makes it hard to develop vaccines against them because the changes to their DNA can lead to them having different antigens.
2) There'd be a real problem if a virus evolved so that it was both deadly and very infectious. (Flu viruses, for example, evolve quickly so this is quite possible.)
3) If this happened, precautions could be taken to stop the virus spreading in the first place (though this is hard nowadays — millions of people travel by plane every day). And vaccines and antiviral drugs could be developed (though these take time to mass produce).
4) But in the worst-case scenario, a flu pandemic could kill billions of people all over the world.

A pandemic is when a disease spreads all over the world.

Aaargh, a giant earwig! Run from the attack of the superbug...

The reality of superbugs is possibly even scarier than giant earwigs. Actually, nothing's more scary than giant earwigs, but microorganisms that are resistant to all our drugs are a worrying thought. It'll be like going back in time to before antibiotics were invented. So far new drugs have kept us one step ahead, but some people think it's only a matter of time until the options run out.

Revision Summary for Section 2

Phew, that's another chunk of biology under your belt. But before you do the most satisfying stretch in the world, I've got a little gift for you... a whole bunch of questions to test just how much of this section you've got to grips with. Don't be sad if you get any wrong — just go back and have another read of the topic and be glad that you're finding out what you do and don't know before the exam. Once you've got them all right, feel free to bend your limbs into weird shapes and let out yelps of joy.

1) Name all the food groups you should eat to have a balanced diet.
2)* Put these jobs in order of how much energy they would need from their food (from highest to lowest):
a) mechanic, b) professional runner, c) secretary.
3) Name five health problems that are associated with obesity.
4) In terms of energy, what does a person have to do to lose weight?
5) The heart is a double pump. Explain what this means.
6) How is the structure of an artery adapted to its function?
7) How is the structure of a vein adapted to its function?
8) Explain why a person's heart rate can be measured by taking their pulse rate.
9) When a blood pressure measurement is taken, what is actually being measured?
10) Describe one way that high blood pressure can cause heart disease.
11)* Have a look at the table below:

Name	Occupation	Cigarettes per day	Exercise per week	Favourite meal
Tricia	Florist	0	5 hours	Houmous and pitta bread
Dave	Stock broker	40	20 minutes	Cheeseburger and chips

a) Who is more at risk from heart disease, Tricia or Dave? Give two reasons for your answer.
b) Give two ways of reducing the risk of heart disease.
12) Explain how epidemiological studies can be used to identify the risk factors for heart disease.
13) Why might an athlete use performance-enhancing drugs like steroids? Why might they not use them?
14) Explain what a placebo is.
15) Briefly describe how a double blind drug trial works.
16) Name a drug that was not tested thoroughly enough and describe the consequences of its use.
17) Describe three opinions about the link between cannabis and hard drug use.
18) Which has the bigger impact on society in the UK, legal or illegal drugs? Explain your answer.
19) Describe three ways in which your immune system defends the body against disease.
20) Describe how the MMR vaccine prevents you getting measles, mumps or rubella.
21) Why shouldn't your doctor give you antibiotics for the flu?
22) Name one type of bacteria that has developed resistance to antibiotics.
23) What practice did Semmelweis introduce in the 1840s?
Explain why this reduced death rates on his ward.

* Answers on page 140.

Genes, Chromosomes and DNA

If you're looking for <u>intrigue</u>, <u>excitement</u> and <u>hilarity</u> — genetics has got it all. Really. You're in for a <u>treat</u>.

1) Most cells in your body have a <u>nucleus</u> — and it's the nucleus that contains your <u>genetic material</u>.

2) The genetic material in the nucleus is arranged into <u>chromosomes</u>. The human cell nucleus contains <u>23 pairs</u> of chromosomes.

nucleus

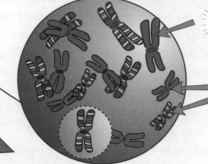

A single <u>chromosome</u>.

3) Each chromosome is <u>one</u> very long <u>molecule of DNA</u> that's <u>coiled up</u> (the coiling is what gives chromosomes their shape).

A <u>pair</u> of <u>chromosomes</u>. (They're always in pairs, one from each <u>parent</u>.)

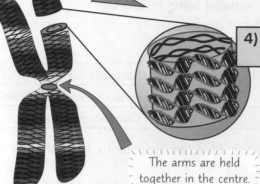

4) A <u>gene</u> is a <u>short length</u> of a chromosome.

DNA molecule

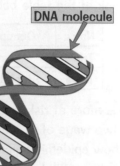

The arms are held together in the centre.

6) Genes can exist in <u>different versions</u>. Each version gives a different form of a <u>characteristic</u>, like blue or brown eyes. The <u>different versions</u> of the <u>same</u> gene are called <u>alleles</u> — see page 36 for more information.

5) Genes <u>control</u> the development of different <u>characteristics</u>, e.g. hair colour, and how an organism <u>functions</u>.

Genes are Instructions for Cells

Each gene is a <u>code</u> for making a certain <u>protein</u>. Proteins are the building blocks of cells. Having different <u>versions</u> of proteins means that we end up with different <u>characteristics</u>.

1) Some proteins are <u>structural</u> proteins. They're part of things like <u>skin</u>, <u>hair</u>, <u>blood</u>, and the <u>cytoplasm</u> in our cells. E.g. <u>collagen</u> is a structural protein that is found in <u>tendons</u>, <u>bones</u> and <u>cartilage</u>.

2) Other proteins are <u>functional</u> proteins. For example, enzymes are proteins that help with <u>digestion</u> by breaking down food molecules — <u>amylase</u> is a digestive enzyme that breaks down <u>starch</u> to maltose.

An Organism's Genotype Describes the Genes It's Got

1) An organism's <u>genotype</u> is all of the genes it has.
2) The <u>characteristics</u> that an organism displays are called its <u>phenotype</u>.

It's hard being a DNA molecule, there's so much to remember...

You need to understand <u>everything</u> on this page — it'll help everything else to make sense later on. To see how much of it you can remember, <u>cover</u> the page, <u>scribble</u> down the main points and then learn the bits you missed.

Reproduction

Ooo err, reproduction... Surely you knew it'd come up at some point. It can happen in two different ways...

Sexual Reproduction Produces Genetically Different Cells

1) Sexual reproduction is where genetic information from two organisms (a father and a mother) is combined to produce offspring which are genetically different to either parent.

2) In sexual reproduction the mother and father produce gametes — e.g. egg and sperm cells in animals.

3) In humans, each gamete contains 23 chromosomes — half the number of chromosomes in a normal cell. (Instead of having two of each chromosome, a gamete has just one of each.)

4) The egg (from the mother) and the sperm cell (from the father) then fuse together (fertilisation) to form a cell with the full number of chromosomes (half from the father, half from the mother).

> SEXUAL REPRODUCTION involves the fusion of male and female gametes.
> Because there are TWO parents, the offspring contain a mixture of their parents' genes.

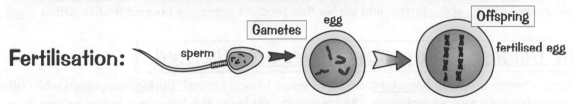

Fertilisation: sperm **Gametes** egg **Offspring** fertilised egg

5) This is why the offspring inherits features from both parents — it's received a mixture of chromosomes from its mum and its dad (and it's the chromosomes that decide how you turn out).

6) This mixture of genetic material produces variation in the offspring. Pretty cool, eh.

Asexual Reproduction Produces Genetically Identical Cells

1) An ordinary cell can make a new cell by simply dividing in two. The new cell has exactly the same genetic information (i.e. genes) as the parent cell — this is known as asexual reproduction.

> In ASEXUAL REPRODUCTION there's only ONE parent. There's no fusion of gametes,
> no mixing of chromosomes and no genetic variation between parent and offspring.
> The offspring are genetically identical to the parent — they're clones.

2) Here's how it works...

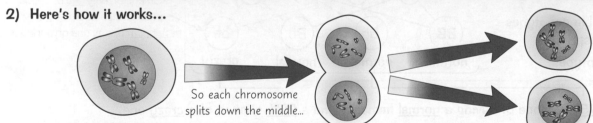

X-shaped chromosomes have two identical halves.

So each chromosome splits down the middle...

...to form two identical sets of 'half-chromosomes' (i.e. two sets of DNA strands). A membrane forms around each set...

...and the DNA replicates itself to form two identical cells with complete sets of X-shaped chromosomes.

3) This is how all plants and animals grow and produce replacement cells.

4) Some organisms also produce offspring using asexual reproduction, e.g. bacteria and certain plants.

 • Some plants produce runners (horizontal stems) that form clones at their tips, e.g. strawberry plants.

 • Other plants produce underground fleshy structures called bulbs that grow into clones, e.g. garlic.

You need to reproduce facts in the exam...

The main messages on this page are that: 1) sexual reproduction needs two parents and forms cells that are genetically different to the parents, so there's lots of genetic variation. And 2) asexual reproduction needs just one parent to make genetically identical cells (clones), so there's no genetic variation in the offspring.

Genetic Diagrams

Genetic diagrams are really handy for working out how characteristics move from one generation to the next.

The Combination of Alleles Determines the Phenotype

When you've got two copies of a gene, usually only one of them can be expressed in the phenotype:

1) As I've said before, alleles are different versions of the same gene.

2) Most of the time you have two of each gene (i.e. two alleles) — one from each parent.

3) If you're homozygous for a trait, you have two alleles the same for that particular gene. If you're heterozygous for a trait, you have two different alleles for that particular gene.

4) Alleles can be dominant or recessive. If you have two dominant alleles for a gene or one dominant and one recessive allele, only the characteristic that's caused by the dominant allele will be shown.

5) To show the characteristic that's caused by the recessive allele, both alleles for a gene have to be recessive.

6) In genetic diagrams, letters are used to represent alleles. Alleles that produce dominant characteristics are always shown with a capital letter, and alleles that produce recessive characteristics with a small letter.

See page 34 for more on phenotypes.

Genetic Diagrams Show How Alleles are Inherited

Imagine you're cross-breeding hamsters, and that some have a normal, boring disposition while others have a leaning towards crazy acrobatics. And suppose you know the behaviour is due to one gene...

Let's say that the allele which causes the crazy nature is recessive — so use a 'b'.
And normal (boring) behaviour is due to a dominant allele — call it 'B'.

1) A crazy hamster must have the alleles 'bb' (i.e. it must be homozygous for this trait).

2) However, a normal hamster could be BB (homozygous) or Bb (heterozygous), because the dominant allele (B) overrules the recessive one (b).

3) The genetic diagram below shows what could happen when two normal hamsters (Bb) are crossed:

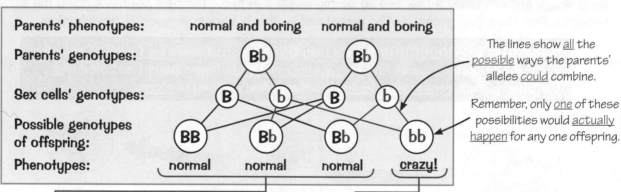

The lines show all the possible ways the parents' alleles could combine.

Remember, only one of these possibilities would actually happen for any one offspring.

There's a 75% chance of having a normal hamster, and a 25% chance of a crazy one.

4) Knowing how inheritance works can help you to interpret a family tree.

5) The case of the new hamster in the family tree is just the same as in the genetic diagram above.

6) Both of its parents have the alleles Bb — so there's a 75% chance the hamster could be normal (BB or Bb) and a 25% chance that it'll be crazy (bb).

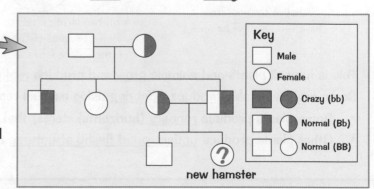

Key
- ☐ Male
- ○ Female
- ■ ● Crazy (bb)
- ◧ ◐ Normal (Bb)
- ☐ ○ Normal (BB)

new hamster

It's not just hamsters that have the crazy allele...

... my sister has it too. Remember, 'results' like this are only probabilities. It doesn't mean it'll actually happen.

Genetic Diagrams and Sex Chromosomes

Just when you thought you'd finished with genetic diagrams these things called Punnett squares march into view. Oh well, at least you can cheer yourself up by also finding out exactly why you are a boy or a girl.

Punnett Squares are Another Type of Genetic Diagram

Another way of working out a genetic cross is by using Punnett squares. They are basically just grids — so don't panic.

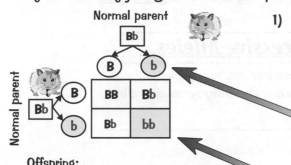

Normal parent

Normal parent

Offspring:
One BB genotype and two Bb genotypes, so there's a 75% chance of having a normal, boring hamster. One bb genotype, so there's a 25% chance of having a crazy hamster.

1) The diagram on the left shows how you would draw the hamster cross from the previous page using a Punnett square.

2) The first bit's the same as a normal genetic diagram — you work out what alleles the sex cells would have from the parents' genotypes.

3) Then you just write the sex cells' alleles (from one parent) along the left-hand side of the square, and along the top of the square (from the other parent).

4) Then you pair them up in the boxes to see the different possible combinations of alleles in the offspring.

Your Chromosomes Control Whether You're Male or Female

There are 23 pairs of chromosomes in every human body cell. The 23rd pair are labelled XY. These are sex chromosomes — they decide whether you turn out male or female.

> All men have an X and a Y chromosome: XY
> The Y chromosome causes male characteristics.
>
> All women have two X chromosomes: XX
> The lack of a Y chromosome causes female characteristics.

female parent

male parent

Offspring:
Two XX genotypes and two XY genotypes, so there's a 50% chance of having either a girl or a boy.

Like all other characteristics, sex is determined by a gene. The Y chromosome carries a gene which makes an embryo develop into a male as it grows. Females, who always have two X chromosomes, don't have this gene and so they develop in a different way.

The genetic diagram for sex inheritance is fairly similar to a bog-standard one. It just shows the sex chromosomes rather than different alleles.

One Gene Determines Which Sex Organs You Develop

1) The gene that makes an embryo into a male causes a specific protein to be produced.

2) When the embryo's reproductive system begins to develop, this protein causes the development of testes (instead of ovaries).

3) The testes then produce male sex hormones, which in turn make the rest of the male reproductive system develop.

4) In females the protein is not produced, so the embryo develops ovaries and the rest of a female reproductive system.

I thought it was all to do with crisps and cereal...

I have a theory that the two big differences between boys and girls are that boys eat crisps more than one at a time and they mix different types of cereal together in the same bowl. It's just a theory though.

Genetic Disorders

The alleles of some genes can be <u>faulty</u> which can cause some pretty <u>nasty</u> disorders.
Since the disorders are a genetic problem, they can be <u>passed on</u> from parents to children.

Genetic Disorders Are Caused by Faulty Alleles

1) Some <u>disorders</u> are <u>inherited</u> — one or both parents carry a <u>faulty allele</u> and pass it on to their children.

2) <u>Cystic fibrosis</u> and <u>Huntington's disease</u> are both caused by a faulty allele of a <u>single gene</u>.

Some Genetic Disorders Are Caused by Recessive Alleles...

Most of the <u>defective alleles</u> that are responsible for genetic disorders are <u>recessive</u>.
<u>Cystic fibrosis</u> is a <u>genetic disorder</u> of the <u>cell membranes</u> caused by a faulty recessive allele.
It <u>results</u> in some pretty nasty symptoms:

- <u>Thick sticky mucus</u> in the <u>air passages</u>, <u>gut</u> and <u>pancreas</u>.
- <u>Breathing difficulty</u>.
- <u>Chest infections</u> (lots of painful coughing).
- <u>Difficulty in digesting food</u> (sufferers are often short and skinny as a result).

1) The allele which causes cystic fibrosis is a <u>recessive allele</u>, 'f', carried by about <u>1 person in 25</u>.

2) Because it's recessive, people with only <u>one copy</u> of the allele <u>won't</u> show the symptoms of the disorder — they're known as <u>carriers</u>.

3) For a child to have a chance of inheriting the disorder, <u>both parents</u> must be <u>carriers</u> or <u>sufferers</u>.

4) As the diagram shows, there's a <u>1 in 4 chance</u> of a child having the disorder if <u>both</u> parents are <u>carriers</u>.

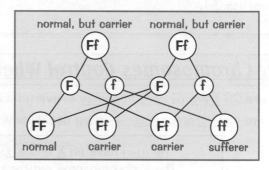

normal, but carrier   normal, but carrier

Ff   Ff

F f F f

FF   Ff   Ff   ff

normal   carrier   carrier   sufferer

...Others Are Caused by Dominant Alleles

Remember that Punnett squares are just another way of drawing genetic diagrams (see page 36).

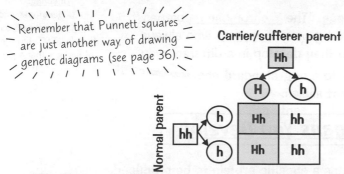

Carrier/sufferer parent

Hh

H   h

Normal parent

hh

h | Hh | hh |

h | Hh | hh |

Offspring

Two Hh genotypes so 50% of the offspring will be carriers/sufferers. Two hh genotypes so the other 50% of the offspring will be normal.

So, if one parent is a sufferer, there's a 50% chance of each of their children having the disorder.

1) Unlike cystic fibrosis, <u>Huntington's disease</u> is caused by a <u>dominant</u> allele.

2) The disorder causes <u>tremors</u> (shaking), <u>clumsiness</u>, <u>memory loss</u>, <u>mood changes</u> and <u>poor concentration</u>. There's <u>no cure</u>.

3) The dominant allele means there's a <u>50%</u> chance of each child inheriting the disorder if just one parent is a carrier. These are <u>seriously grim</u> odds.

4) The "carrier" parent will of course be a <u>sufferer</u> too since the allele is <u>dominant</u>, but the disease has a <u>late onset</u> — the symptoms do not usually appear until after the age of 40, by which time the allele has been <u>passed on</u> to children and even grandchildren. Hence the disorder persists.

Unintentional mooning — caused by faulty genes...

We <u>all</u> have defective genes in us somewhere — but usually they don't cause us a problem (as they're often <u>recessive</u>, so if you have a healthy <u>dominant</u> allele too, you'll be fine). At the moment scientists are looking at new ways of treating genetic disorders, but it'll be a while until these diseases are a thing of the past.

Cloning

We can clone plants and animals in several different ways. Cool. But some of them have potential problems...

Plants Can Be Cloned from Cuttings and by Tissue Culture

CUTTINGS

1) Gardeners can take cuttings from good parent plants, and then plant them to produce genetically identical copies (clones) of the parent plant.

2) These plants can be produced quickly and cheaply.

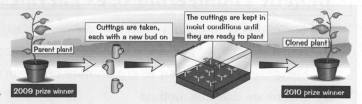
Parent plant | Cuttings are taken, each with a new bud on | The cuttings are kept in moist conditions until they are ready to plant | Cloned plant
2009 prize winner | 2010 prize winner

TISSUE CULTURE

This is where a few plant cells are put in a growth medium with hormones, and they grow into new plants — clones of the parent plant. These plants can be made very quickly, in very little space, and be grown all year.

You Can Make Animal Clones Using Embryo Transplants

Farmers can produce cloned offspring from their best bull and cow — using embryo transplants.

1) Sperm cells are taken from a prize bull and egg cells are taken from a prize cow. The sperm are then used to artificially fertilise an egg cell. The embryo that develops is then split many times (to form clones) before any cells become specialised.

2) These cloned embryos can then be implanted into lots of other cows where they grow into baby calves (which will all be genetically identical to each other).

3) Hundreds of "ideal" offspring can be produced every year from the best bull and cow.

Adult Cell Cloning is Another Way to Make a Clone

1) Adult cell cloning involves taking an unfertilised egg cell and removing its genetic material (the nucleus). A complete set of chromosomes from an adult body cell (e.g. skin cell) is inserted into the 'empty' egg cell.

2) The egg cell is then stimulated by an electric shock — this makes it divide, just like a normal embryo.

3) When the embryo is a ball of cells, it's implanted into an adult female (the surrogate mother) to grow into a genetically identical copy (clone) of the original adult body cell.

4) This technique was used to create Dolly — the famous cloned sheep.

Egg cell | Adult body cell
Nucleus removed | Nucleus removed
Electric shock
Embryo
Implanted into surrogate mother
Live animal

There are Many Issues Surrounding Cloning

1) Cloning quickly gets you lots of "ideal" offspring. But you also get a "reduced gene pool" — this means there are fewer different alleles in a population. If a population are all closely related and a new disease appears, they could all be wiped out — there may be no allele in the population giving resistance to the disease.

2) But the study of animal clones could lead to greater understanding of the development of the embryo, and of ageing and age-related disorders.

3) Cloning could also be used to help preserve endangered species.

4) However, it's possible that cloned animals might not be as healthy as normal ones, e.g. Dolly the sheep had arthritis, which tends to occur in older sheep (but the jury's still out on if this was due to cloning).

5) Some people worry that humans might be cloned in the future. If it was allowed, any success may follow many unsuccessful attempts, e.g. children born severely disabled.

Thank goodness they didn't do that with my little brother...

Cloning can be a controversial topic — especially when it's to do with cloning animals (and especially humans). More large-scale, long-term studies into cloned animals are needed to find out what the dangers are.

Genetic Engineering

Scientists can now <u>change</u> an organism's <u>genes</u> to alter its characteristics. This is a new science with exciting possibilities, but there might be <u>dangers</u> too...

Genetic Engineering Uses Enzymes to Cut and Paste Genes

The basic idea is to copy a <u>useful gene</u> from one organism's chromosome into the cells of another...

1) A useful gene is "<u>cut</u>" from one organism's chromosome using <u>enzymes</u>.

2) <u>Enzymes</u> are then used to <u>cut</u> another organism's chromosome and then to <u>insert</u> the useful gene.

3) Scientists use this method to do all sorts of things — for example, the human insulin gene can be inserted into <u>bacteria</u> to <u>produce human insulin</u>:

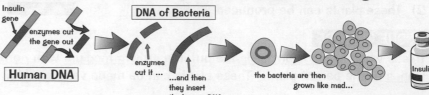

Insulin gene — enzymes cut the gene out — Human DNA — DNA of Bacteria — enzymes cut it ... ...and then they insert the human DNA — the bacteria are then grown like mad... — Insulin — ...and the insulin produced is purified and used by people with diabetes.

Genes can be Transferred into Animals and Plants

The same method can be used to <u>transfer useful genes</u> into <u>animals</u> and <u>plants</u> at the <u>very early stages</u> of their development (i.e. shortly after <u>fertilisation</u>). This means they'll develop <u>useful characteristics</u>, e.g:

1) <u>Genetically modified</u> (<u>GM</u>) <u>crops</u> have had their genes modified, e.g. to make them <u>resistant to viruses</u>, <u>insects</u> or <u>herbicides</u> (chemicals used to kill weeds).

2) <u>Sheep</u> have been genetically engineered to produce substances, like drugs, in their <u>milk</u> that can be used to treat <u>human diseases</u>.

3) <u>Genetic disorders</u> like cystic fibrosis are caused by faulty genes. Scientists are trying to treat these disorders by <u>inserting working genes</u> into sufferers. This is called <u>gene therapy</u>.

But Genetic Engineering is a Controversial Topic...

1) Genetic engineering is an <u>exciting new area in science</u> which has the <u>potential</u> for solving many of our problems (e.g. treating diseases, more efficient food production etc.) but not everyone thinks it's a great idea.

2) There are <u>worries</u> about the long-term effects of genetic engineering — that changing a person's genes might <u>accidentally</u> create unplanned <u>problems</u>, which could then get passed on to <u>future generations</u>.

It's the Same with GM Crops — There Are Pros and Cons...

1) Some people say that growing GM crops will affect the number of <u>weeds</u> and <u>flowers</u> (and so the population of <u>insects</u>) that live in and around the crops — <u>reducing</u> farmland <u>biodiversity</u>.

2) Not everyone is convinced that GM crops are <u>safe</u>. People are worried they may develop <u>allergies</u> to the food — although there's probably no more risk for this than for eating usual foods.

3) A big concern is that <u>transplanted genes</u> may get out into the <u>natural environment</u>. For example, the <u>herbicide resistance</u> gene may be picked up by weeds, creating a new '<u>superweed</u>' variety.

4) On the plus side, GM crops can <u>increase the yield</u> of a crop, making more food.

5) People living in developing nations often lack <u>nutrients</u> in their diets. GM crops could be <u>engineered</u> to contain the nutrient that's <u>missing</u>. For example, they're testing 'golden rice' that contains beta-carotene — lack of this substance causes <u>blindness</u>.

6) GM crops are already being grown elsewhere in the world (not the UK) often <u>without any problems</u>.

If only there was a gene to make revision easier...

At the end of the day, it's up to the <u>Government</u> to weigh up all the <u>evidence</u> for the pros and cons before <u>making a decision</u> on how this scientific knowledge is used. All scientists can do is make sure the Government has all the information it needs to make the decision. Anyway, let's not get too bogged down in politics...

Adaptations

Organisms survive in many <u>different environments</u> because they have <u>adapted</u> to them.

Desert Animals <u>Have Adapted to Save Water</u> <u>and Keep Cool</u>

LARGE SURFACE AREA COMPARED TO VOLUME	This lets desert animals <u>lose more body heat</u> — which helps to stop them overheating.
EFFICIENT WITH WATER	1) Desert animals <u>lose less water</u> by producing small amounts of <u>concentrated urine</u>. 2) They also make very little <u>sweat</u>. Camels are able to do this by tolerating <u>big changes</u> in <u>body temperature</u>, while kangaroo rats live in <u>burrows</u> underground where it's <u>cool</u>.
GOOD IN HOT CONDITIONS	Desert animals have very <u>thin layers</u> of <u>body fat</u> and a <u>thin coat</u> to help them <u>lose</u> body heat. E.g. camels keep nearly all their fat in their <u>humps</u>.
CAMOUFLAGE	A <u>sandy colour</u> gives <u>good camouflage</u> — to help them <u>avoid predators</u>, or <u>sneak up on prey</u>.

Arctic Animals <u>Have Adapted to Reduce Heat Loss</u>

SMALL SURFACE AREA COMPARED TO VOLUME	Animals living in <u>cold</u> conditions have a <u>compact</u> (rounded) shape to keep their <u>surface area</u> to a minimum — this <u>reduces heat loss</u>.

WELL INSULATED	1) They also have a thick layer of <u>blubber</u> for <u>insulation</u> — this also acts as an <u>energy store</u> when food is scarce. 2) <u>Thick hairy coats</u> keep body heat in, and <u>greasy fur</u> sheds water (this <u>prevents cooling</u> due to evaporation).
CAMOUFLAGE	Arctic animals have <u>white fur</u> to help them <u>avoid predators</u>, or <u>sneak up on prey</u>.

Desert Plants <u>Have Adapted to Having Little Water</u>

SMALL SURFACE AREA COMPARED TO VOLUME	1) Plants <u>lose water vapour</u> from the surface of their leaves. Cacti have <u>spines instead of leaves</u> — to <u>reduce water loss</u>. 2) They also have a <u>small surface area</u> compared to their size (about 1000 times smaller surface area than normal plants), which also <u>reduces water loss</u>.
WATER STORAGE TISSUES	For example, a cactus <u>stores water</u> in its thick stem.
MAXIMISING WATER ABSORPTION	Some cacti have <u>shallow</u> but <u>extensive roots</u> to <u>absorb</u> water quickly over a large area. Others have <u>deep roots</u> to access <u>underground water</u>.

Some Plants <u>and</u> Animals <u>Are Adapted to Deter Predators</u>

There are various <u>special features</u> used by animals and plants to help <u>protect</u> them against being <u>eaten</u>:
1) Some plants and animals have <u>armour</u> — like roses (<u>thorns</u>), cacti (<u>sharp spines</u>) and tortoises (<u>shells</u>).
2) Others produce <u>poisons</u> — like bees and poison ivy.
3) And some have amazing <u>warning colours</u> to scare off predators — like wasps.

Microorganisms <u>Have a Huge Variety of Adaptations...</u>

...so that they can live in a <u>wide range</u> of environments, for example:

Some <u>microorganisms</u> (e.g. bacteria) are known as <u>extremophiles</u> — they're adapted to live in seriously <u>extreme conditions</u> like super <u>hot</u> volcanic vents, in very <u>salty</u> lakes or at <u>high pressure</u> on the sea bed.

<u>In a nutshell, it's horses for courses...</u>

By looking at an animal or plant's <u>characteristics</u>, you should be able to have a pretty good guess at the kind of <u>environment</u> it lives in (or vice versa). Why does it have a large/small surface area... what are those spines for..?

Variation

You'll probably have noticed that not all people are identical. There are reasons for this.

Organisms of the Same Species Have Differences

A SPECIES is a group of organisms that can breed together to produce fertile offspring.

1) Different species look... well... different — my dog definitely doesn't look like a daisy.

2) But even organisms of the same species will usually look at least slightly different — e.g. in a room full of people you'll see different colour hair, individually shaped noses, a variety of heights etc.

3) These differences are called the variation within a species — and there are two types of variation: genetic variation and environmental variation.

Different Genes Cause Genetic Variation

1) All plants and animals have characteristics that are in some ways similar to their parents' (e.g. I've got my dad's nose, apparently).

2) This is because an organism's characteristics are determined by the genes inherited from their parents. (Genes are the codes inside your cells that control how you're made — more about these on page 34).

3) These genes are passed on in sex cells (gametes), which the offspring develop from (see page 35).

4) Most animals (and quite a lot of plants) get some genes from the mother and some from the father.

5) This combining of genes from two parents causes genetic variation — no two of the species are genetically identical (other than identical twins).

6) Some characteristics are determined only by genes (e.g. violet flower colour). In animals these include: eye colour, blood group and inherited disorders (e.g. haemophilia or cystic fibrosis).

Characteristics are also Influenced by the Environment

1) The environment that organisms live and grow in also causes differences between members of the same species — this is called environmental variation.

2) Environmental variation covers a wide range of differences — from losing your toes in a piranha attack, to getting a suntan, to having yellow leaves (never happened to me yet though), and so on.

A plant grown on a nice sunny windowsill would grow luscious and green.

The same plant grown in darkness would grow tall and spindly and its leaves would turn yellow — these are environmental variations.

3) Basically, any difference that has been caused by the conditions something lives in, is an environmental variation.

Most Characteristics are Due to Genes AND the Environment

1) Most characteristics (e.g. body weight, height, skin colour, condition of teeth, academic or athletic prowess, etc.) are determined by a mixture of genetic and environmental factors.

2) For example, the maximum height that an animal or plant could grow to is determined by its genes. But whether it actually grows that tall depends on its environment (e.g. how much food it gets).

My mum's got no trousers — cos I've got her jeans...

So, you are the way you are partly because of the genes you inherited off your folks. But you can't blame it all on your parents, since your environment then takes over and begins to mould you in all sorts of ways. In fact, it's often really tricky to decide which factor is more influential, your genes or the environment — a good way to study this is with identical twins.

Evolution

> **THEORY OF EVOLUTION:** More than 3 billion years ago, life on Earth began as simple organisms from which all the more complex organisms evolved (rather than just popping into existence).

All Organisms are Related... even if Only Distantly

Looking at the <u>similarities</u> and <u>differences</u> between organisms allows us to <u>classify</u> them into groups. E.g:

1) <u>Plants</u> make their <u>own food</u> (by photosynthesis) and are <u>fixed</u> in the ground.
2) <u>Animals move</u> about the place and <u>can't</u> make their own food.
3) <u>Microorganisms</u> are different to plants and animals, e.g. bacteria are <u>single-celled</u>.

Studying the similarities and differences between organisms also help us to understand how <u>all</u> living things are <u>related</u> (<u>evolutionary relationships</u>) and how they <u>interact</u> with each other (<u>ecological relationships</u>):

EVOLUTIONARY

1) Species with similar characteristics often have <u>similar genes</u> because they share a <u>recent common ancestor</u>, so they're <u>closely related</u>. They often look very <u>alike</u> and tend to live in similar types of <u>habitat</u>, e.g. whales and dolphins.

2) Occasionally, <u>genetically different</u> species might <u>look alike</u> too. E.g. dolphins and sharks look pretty similar because they've both <u>adapted</u> to living in the same habitat. But they're <u>not</u> <u>closely related</u> — they've evolved from <u>different ancestors</u>.

3) <u>Evolutionary trees</u> show common ancestors and relationships between organisms. The more <u>recent</u> the common ancestor, the more <u>closely related</u> the two species.

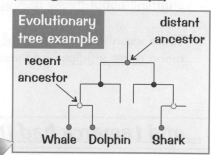

Whales and dolphins have a recent common ancestor so are closely related. They're both more distantly related to sharks.

ECOLOGICAL

1) If we see organisms in the same environment with <u>similar characteristics</u> (e.g. dolphins and sharks) it suggests they might be in <u>competition</u> (e.g for the same food source).

2) <u>Differences</u> between organisms in the same environment (e.g. dolphins swim in small groups, but herring swim in giant shoals) can show <u>predator-prey relationships</u> (e.g. dolphins hunt herring).

Natural Selection Explains How Evolution Occurs

<u>Charles Darwin</u> came up with the idea of <u>natural selection</u>. It works like this...

> Genetic differences are caused by sexual reproduction (see page 35) and mutations (see below).

1) Individuals within a species show <u>variation</u> because of the differences in their <u>genes</u>, e.g. some rabbits have big ears and some have small ones.

2) Individuals with characteristics that make them <u>better adapted</u> to the environment have a <u>better chance of survival</u> and so are more likely to <u>breed</u> successfully. E.g. big-eared rabbits are more likely to hear a fox sneaking up on them, and so are more likely to live and have millions of babies. Small-eared rabbits are more likely to end up as fox food.

3) So, the <u>genes</u> that are responsible for the useful characteristics are more likely to be <u>passed on</u> to the <u>next generation</u>. E.g. all the baby rabbits are born with big ears.

Evolution can Occur Due To Mutations

1) A mutation is a <u>change</u> in an organism's <u>DNA</u>.

2) Most of the time mutations have <u>no effect</u>, but occasionally they can be <u>beneficial</u> by producing a <u>useful</u> <u>characteristic</u>. This characteristic may give the organism a better chance of <u>surviving</u> and <u>reproducing</u>.

3) If so, the beneficial mutation is more likely to be passed on to <u>future generations</u> by <u>natural selection</u>.

4) Over time, the beneficial mutation will <u>accumulate</u> in a population, e.g. some species of bacteria have become <u>resistant to antibiotics</u> due to a mutation (see page 31).

"Natural selection" — sounds like vegan chocolates...

Natural selection's all about the organisms with the <u>best characteristics</u> surviving to <u>pass on their genes</u> so that the whole species ends up <u>adapted</u> to its environment. It doesn't happen overnight though.

More About Evolution

There's a lot of evidence for the theory of evolution by natural selection.
But back in the day, poor Charlie Darwin didn't have half as much evidence to convince people.

Not Everyone Agreed with Darwin...

Darwin's idea was very controversial at the time — for various reasons...

1) It went against common religious beliefs about how life on Earth developed — it was the first plausible explanation for our own existence without the need for a "Creator" (God).

2) Darwin couldn't give a good explanation for why these new, useful characteristics appeared or exactly how individual organisms passed on their beneficial characteristics to their offspring. But then he didn't know anything about genes or mutations — they weren't discovered 'til 50 years after his theory was published.

3) There wasn't enough evidence to convince many scientists, because not many other studies had been done into how organisms change over time.

...and Lamarck had Different Ideas

There were different scientific hypotheses about evolution around at the same time, such as Lamarck's:

1) Lamarck (1744-1829) argued that if a characteristic was used a lot by an organism then it would become more developed during its lifetime. E.g. if a rabbit used its legs to run a lot (to escape predators), then its legs would get longer.

2) Lamarck believed that these acquired characteristics would be passed on to the next generation, e.g. the rabbit's offspring would have longer legs.

Scientists can Develop Different Hypotheses from Similar Observations

1) Often scientists come up with different hypotheses to explain similar observations.

2) Scientists might develop different hypotheses because they have different beliefs (e.g. religious) or they have been influenced by different people (e.g. other scientists and their way of thinking)... or they just darn well think differently.

There's more about how science works on pages 1-8.

3) The only way to find out whose hypothesis is right is to find evidence to support or disprove each one.

4) For example, Lamarck and Darwin both had different hypotheses to explain how evolution happens. In the end...

- Lamarck's hypothesis was eventually rejected because experiments didn't support his hypothesis. You can see it for yourself, e.g. if you dye a hamster's fur bright pink (not recommended), its offspring will still be born with the normal fur colour because the new characteristic won't have been passed on.
- The discovery of genetics supported Darwin's idea because it provided an explanation of how organisms born with beneficial characteristics can pass them on (i.e. via their genes).

5) There's so much evidence for Darwin's idea that it's now an accepted hypothesis (a theory).

Did you know that exams evolved from the Spanish Inquisition...

This is a good example of how scientific hypotheses come about — someone observes something and then tries to explain it. Their hypothesis will then be tested by other scientists — if their evidence supports the hypothesis, it gains in credibility. If not, it's rejected. Darwin's theory hasn't been rejected yet.

Competition and Environmental Change

It's tough in the wild — there's always competition for food and other resources. So if the environment changes, e.g. there's not enough food or it's too hot, that can be the last straw and populations can decline.

Organisms Compete for Resources to Survive

Organisms need things from their <u>environment</u> and from <u>other organisms</u> in order to <u>survive</u> and <u>reproduce</u>:

1) <u>Plants</u> need <u>light</u>, <u>space</u>, <u>water</u> and <u>minerals (nutrients)</u> from the soil.

2) <u>Animals</u> need <u>space (territory)</u>, <u>food</u>, <u>water</u> and <u>mates</u>.

Organisms <u>compete with other species</u> (and members of their own species) for the <u>same resources</u>. E.g. red and grey <u>squirrels</u> live in the same habitat and eat the same food. Competition with the grey squirrels for these resources means there's not enough food for the reds — so the <u>population</u> of red squirrels is <u>decreasing</u>.

Environmental Changes are Caused by Different Factors

The <u>environment</u> in which plants and animals live <u>changes all the time</u>. These changes are caused by <u>living</u> and <u>non-living</u> factors, such as:

A change could be an increase or a decrease.

LIVING FACTORS	

1) A change in the occurrence of <u>infectious diseases</u>.

2) A change in the number of <u>predators</u>.

3) A change in the number of <u>prey</u> or the availability of <u>food sources</u>.

4) A change in the number or types of <u>competitors</u>.

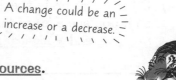

NON-LIVING FACTORS	

1) A change in average <u>temperature</u>.

2) A change in average <u>rainfall</u>.

3) A change in the level of <u>air or water pollution</u>.

Environmental Changes Affect Populations in Different Ways

Environmental changes can affect animals and plants in these <u>three ways</u>:

1) Population SIZE INCREASES

E.g. if the number of <u>prey increases</u>, then there's <u>more food</u> available for predators, so more predators survive and reproduce, and their numbers <u>increase</u> too.

2) Population SIZE DECREASES

E.g. the number of bees in the US is <u>falling rapidly</u>.
Experts aren't sure why but they <u>think</u> it could be because:

1) Some <u>pesticides</u> may be having a negative effect on bees.

2) There's <u>less food</u> available — there aren't as many <u>nectar-rich plants</u> around any more.

3) There's <u>more disease</u> — bees are being killed by new pathogens or parasites.

3) Population DISTRIBUTION CHANGES A change in distribution means a change in <u>where</u> an organism <u>lives</u>.

For example, the distribution of <u>bird species</u> in Germany is changing because of a rise in average <u>temperature</u>. E.g. the <u>European Bee-Eater</u> bird is a <u>Mediterranean</u> species but it's now present in parts of <u>Germany</u>.

I compete with my brother for the front seat of the car...

In the exam you might be given some <u>data</u> and asked about the change in distribution of <u>any</u> organism. But don't panic — just think about what that organism would need to <u>survive</u> and any <u>environmental changes</u> that have occurred. And remember, if things are in <u>limited supply</u> then there's going to be <u>competition</u>.

Measuring Environmental Change

There are lots of different ways to gauge just how much the environments changing — here are a few of 'em.

Environmental Changes can be Measured Using Living Indicators...

1) Some organisms are very sensitive to changes in their environment and so can be studied to see the effect of human activities — these organisms are known as indicator species.

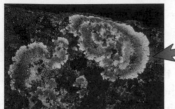

2) For example, air pollution can be monitored by looking at particular types of lichen that are very sensitive to the concentration of sulfur dioxide in the atmosphere (and so can give a good idea about the level of pollution from car exhausts, power stations, etc.). The number and type of lichen at a particular location will indicate how clean the air is (e.g. the air is clean if there are lots of lichen).

3) If raw sewage is released into a river, the bacterial population in the water increases and uses up the oxygen. Some invertebrate animals, like mayfly larvae, are good indicators for water pollution because they're very sensitive to the concentration of dissolved oxygen in the water. If you find mayfly larvae in a river, it indicates that the water is clean.

4) Other invertebrate species have adapted to live in polluted conditions — so if you see a lot of them you know there's a problem. E.g. rat-tailed maggots and sludgeworms indicate a very high level of water pollution.

...and Non-Living Indicators

To find out about environmental change, scientists are busy collecting data about the environment.

1) They use satellites to measure the temperature of the sea surface and the amount of snow and ice cover. These are modern, accurate instruments and give us a global coverage.

2) Automatic weather stations tell us the atmospheric temperature at various locations. They contain thermometers that are sensitive and accurate — they can measure to very small fractions of a degree.

3) They measure rainfall using rain gauges, to find out how much the average rainfall changes year on year.

4) They use dissolved oxygen meters, which measure the concentration of dissolved oxygen in water, to discover how the level of water pollution is changing.

Both Ways of Looking at Pollution Level Have Their Weaknesses

	Advantages	Disadvantages
Living methods (indicator species)	• Using living methods is a relatively quick, cheap and easy way of saying whether an area is polluted or not. No expensive equipment or highly trained workers are needed.	• Factors other than pollution (e.g. temperature) can influence the survival of indicator species so living methods aren't always reliable.
Non-living methods	• Directly measuring the pollutants gives reliable, numerical data that's easy to compare between different sites. • The exact pollutants can be identified too.	• Non-living methods often require more expensive equipment and trained workers than methods that use indicator species.

Teenagers are an indicator species — not found in clean rooms...

In your exam, you might get given some data about lichen or mayfly larvae as an indirect measure of pollution — and you'll have to figure out what the data means. It'll be a lot easier than it looks. Just remember that lots of lichen indicates clean air, whereas lots of mayfly larvae indicates clean water. Nothing to it.

Pyramids of Biomass and Number

A <u>trophic level</u> is a <u>feeding</u> level. It comes from the Greek word <u>trophe</u> meaning 'nourishment'. So there.

You Need to Be Able to Construct Pyramids of Biomass

There's <u>less energy</u> and <u>less biomass</u> every time you move <u>up</u> a stage (<u>trophic level</u>) in a food chain.
There are usually <u>fewer organisms</u> every time you move up a level too:

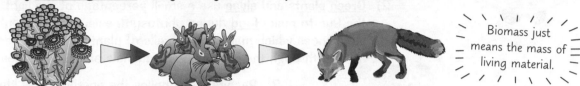

Biomass just means the mass of living material.

<u>100</u> dandelions... feed... <u>10</u> rabbits... which feed... <u>one</u> fox.

This <u>isn't</u> always true though — for example, if <u>500 fleas</u> are feeding on the fox, the number of organisms has <u>increased</u> as you move up that stage in the food chain. So a better way to look at the food chain is often to think about <u>biomass</u> instead of number of organisms. You can use information about biomass to construct a <u>pyramid of biomass</u> to represent the food chain:

1) Each bar on a <u>pyramid of biomass</u> shows the <u>mass of living material</u> at that stage of the food chain — basically how much all the organisms at each level would "<u>weigh</u>" if you put them <u>all together</u>.

2) So the one fox above would have a <u>big biomass</u> and the <u>hundreds of fleas</u> would have a <u>very small biomass</u>. Biomass pyramids are practically <u>always pyramid-shaped</u> (unlike number pyramids):

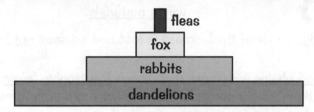

You need to be able to <u>construct</u> pyramids of biomass. Luckily it's pretty simple — they'll give you <u>all</u> the <u>information</u> you need to do it in the exam.

The big bar along the bottom of the pyramid always represents the <u>producer</u> (i.e. a plant).
The next bar will be the <u>primary consumer</u> (the animal that eats the plant), then the <u>secondary consumer</u> (the animal that eats the primary consumer) and so on up the food chain. Easy.

Pyramids of Biomass and Pyramids of Numbers can be Different Shapes

<u>Pyramids of numbers</u> are similar to <u>pyramids of biomass</u>, but each bar on a <u>pyramid of numbers</u> shows the <u>number of organisms</u> at that stage of the food chain — <u>not</u> their <u>mass</u>.

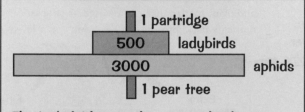

PYRAMID OF NUMBERS

1 partridge
500 ladybirds
3000 aphids
1 pear tree

The 'aphids' bar on this pyramid is <u>longer</u> than the 'pear tree' bar, because <u>one</u> pear tree can feed a <u>huge number</u> of aphids...

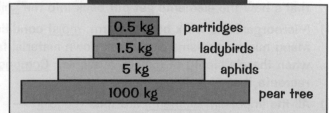

PYRAMID OF BIOMASS

0.5 kg partridges
1.5 kg ladybirds
5 kg aphids
1000 kg pear tree

...but the <u>biomass</u> of the pear tree is much <u>bigger</u> than the biomass of the aphids — which is why the biomass pyramid is the right shape.

Constructing pyramids is a breeze — just ask the Egyptians...

There are actually a couple of exceptions where pyramids of <u>biomass</u> aren't quite pyramid-shaped. It happens when the producer has a very short life but reproduces loads, like with plankton at certain times of year. But it's <u>rare</u>, and you <u>don't</u> need to know about it. Forget I ever mentioned it. Sorry.

Energy Transfer and Decay

So now you need to learn <u>why</u> there's <u>less energy</u> and <u>biomass</u> each time you move up a trophic level.

All That Energy Just Disappears Somehow...

1) Energy from the <u>Sun</u> is the source of energy for <u>nearly all</u> life on Earth.

2) <u>Green plants</u> and <u>algae</u> use a small percentage of the light energy from the Sun to make <u>food</u> during photosynthesis. This energy's stored in the substances which make up the cells of plants and algae, and then works its way through the food chain as animals eat them and each other.

Material and energy are both lost at each stage of the food chain.

HEAT LOSS

MATERIALS LOST IN ANIMAL'S WASTE

3) <u>Respiration</u> supplies the energy for all life processes, including <u>movement</u>. Most of the energy is eventually <u>lost</u> to the surroundings as <u>heat</u>. This is especially true for <u>mammals</u> and <u>birds</u>, whose bodies must be kept at a <u>constant temperature</u> which is normally higher than their surroundings.

4) Some of the material which makes up plants and animals is <u>inedible</u> (e.g. bone), so it <u>doesn't pass</u> to the next stage of the food chain. <u>Material</u> and <u>energy</u> are also lost from the food chain in the organisms' <u>waste materials</u>.

5) This explains why you get <u>biomass pyramids</u>. Most of the biomass is lost and so does <u>not</u> become biomass in the <u>next level up</u>.

6) It also explains why you hardly ever get <u>food chains</u> with more than about <u>five trophic levels</u>. So much <u>energy</u> is <u>lost</u> at each stage that there's not enough left to support more organisms after four or five stages.

Elements are Cycled Back to the Start of the Food Chain by Decay

1) <u>Living things</u> are made of materials they take from the world around them.

2) <u>Plants</u> take elements like <u>carbon</u>, <u>oxygen</u>, <u>hydrogen</u> and <u>nitrogen</u> from the <u>soil</u> or the <u>air</u>. They turn these elements into the <u>complex compounds</u> (carbohydrates, proteins and fats) that make up living organisms, and these then pass through the <u>food chain</u>.

3) These elements are <u>returned</u> to the environment in <u>waste products</u> produced by the organisms, or when the organisms <u>die</u>. These materials decay because they're <u>broken down</u> (digested) by <u>microorganisms</u> — that's how the elements get put back into the <u>soil</u>.

4) Microorganisms work best in <u>warm</u>, <u>moist</u> conditions. Many microorganisms also break down material faster when there's plenty of <u>oxygen</u> available. <u>Compost bins</u> recreate these <u>ideal conditions</u>.

5) All the important <u>elements</u> are thus <u>recycled</u> — they return to the soil, ready to be <u>used</u> by new <u>plants</u> and put back into the <u>food chain</u> again.

6) In a <u>stable community</u> the materials <u>taken out</u> of the soil and <u>used</u> are <u>balanced</u> by those that are put <u>back in</u>. There's a constant <u>cycle</u> happening.

<u>A Compost Bin</u> — Kitchen waste (e.g. food peelings) can be made into compost. Compost is decayed remains of animal and plant matter that can be used as fertiliser. It recycles nutrients back into the soil — giving you a lovely garden.

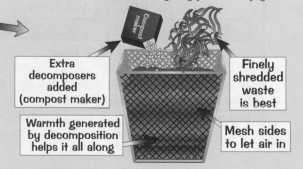

Extra decomposers added (compost maker)

Warmth generated by decomposition helps it all along

Finely shredded waste is best

Mesh sides to let air in

So when revising, put the fire on and don't take toilet breaks...

No, I'm being silly, go if you have to. But do your bit on the way — put your kitchen waste in the compost and your garden waste (e.g. hedge trimmings) into a green bin (then the council can do the composting for you).

The Carbon Cycle

As you've seen, all the <u>nutrients</u> in our environment are constantly being <u>recycled</u> — there's a nice balance between what <u>goes in</u> and what <u>goes out</u> again. This page is all about the recycling of <u>carbon</u>.

The Carbon Cycle Shows How Carbon is Recycled

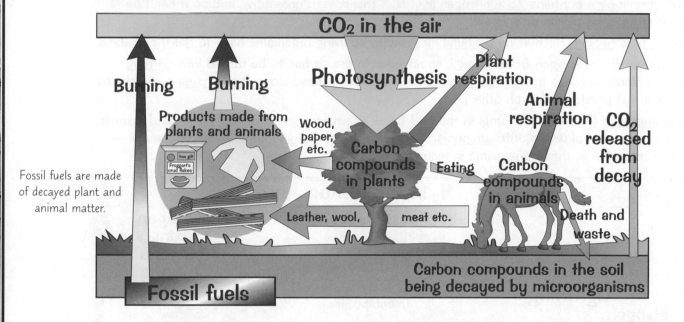

That can look a bit complicated at first, but it's actually pretty simple.
<u>Learn</u> these important points:

The <u>energy</u> that green plants and algae get from photosynthesis is <u>transferred up</u> the food chain.

1) There's only <u>one arrow</u> going <u>down</u> from the atmosphere.
   The whole thing is "powered" by <u>photosynthesis</u>. <u>CO$_2$</u> is removed from
   the <u>atmosphere</u> by green plants and algae, and the carbon is used to make
   <u>carbohydrates</u>, <u>fats</u> and <u>proteins</u> in the plants and algae.

2) Some of the carbon is <u>returned</u> to the atmosphere as CO$_2$ when the <u>plants and algae</u>
   <u>respire</u>. Some of the carbon becomes part of the <u>fats</u> and <u>proteins</u> in <u>animals</u> when
   the plants and algae are <u>eaten</u>. The carbon then moves through the <u>food chain</u>.

3) Some of the carbon is <u>returned</u> to the atmosphere as CO$_2$ when the <u>animals respire</u>.

4) When plants, algae and animals <u>die</u>, other animals (called <u>detritus feeders</u>)
   and <u>microorganisms</u> feed on their remains. When these organisms <u>respire</u>,
   CO$_2$ is <u>returned</u> to the atmosphere.

5) Animals also produce <u>waste</u>, and this too is broken down by <u>detritus feeders</u>
   and <u>microorganisms</u>. Compounds in the waste are taken up from the <u>soil</u> by plants
   as <u>nutrients</u> — they're put back into the <u>food chain</u> again.

6) Some useful plant and animal <u>products</u>, e.g. wood and fossil fuels,
   are <u>burnt</u> (<u>combustion</u>). This also <u>releases CO$_2$</u> back into the air.

7) So the carbon is constantly being <u>cycled</u> — from the <u>air</u>, through <u>food chains</u>
   and eventually back out into the <u>air</u> again.

What goes around comes around...

Carbon is very <u>important</u> for living things — it's the basis for all the <u>organic molecules</u> (fats, proteins, carbohydrates, etc.) in our bodies. In sci-fi films the aliens are sometimes <u>silicon-based</u>... but then by the end they've usually been defeated by some Bruce Willis type, so I don't really think they're onto a winner.

The Nitrogen Cycle

Nitrogen, just like carbon, is constantly being <u>recycled</u>. So the nitrogen in your proteins might once have been in the <u>air</u>. And before that it might have been in a <u>plant</u>. Or even in some <u>horse wee</u>. Nice.

Nitrogen is Recycled in the Nitrogen Cycle

1) The <u>atmosphere</u> contains <u>78% nitrogen gas</u>, N_2. This is <u>very unreactive</u> and so it can't be used <u>directly</u> by plants or animals.

2) <u>Nitrogen</u> is <u>needed</u> for making <u>proteins</u> for growth, so living organisms have to get it somehow.

3) Plants get their nitrogen from the <u>soil</u>, so nitrogen in the air has to be turned into <u>nitrates</u> before plants can use it. <u>Nitrogen compounds</u> are then passed along <u>food chains</u> and <u>webs</u> as animals eat plants (and each other).

4) <u>Decomposers</u> (bacteria and fungi in the soil) break down <u>proteins</u> in rotting plants and animals, and <u>urea</u> in animal waste, into <u>ammonia</u>. This returns the nitrogen compounds to the soil — so the nitrogen in these organisms is <u>recycled</u>.

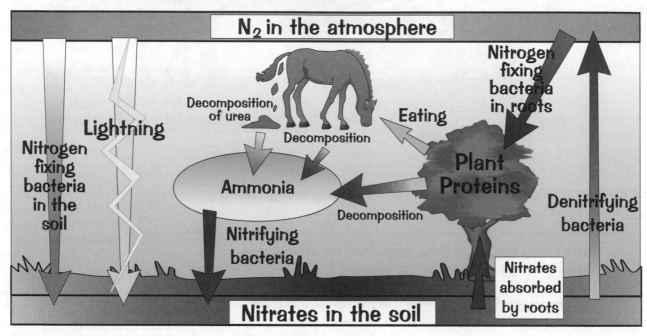

5) <u>Nitrogen fixation</u> isn't an obsession with nitrogen — it's the process of turning <u>N_2 from the air</u> into <u>nitrogen compounds</u> in the soil which <u>plants can use</u>. There are <u>two main ways</u> that this happens:
   a) <u>Lightning</u> — there's so much <u>energy</u> in a bolt of lightning that it's enough to make nitrogen <u>react with oxygen</u> in the air to give nitrates.
   b) <u>Nitrogen-fixing bacteria</u> in roots and soil (see below).

6) There are <u>four</u> different types of <u>bacteria</u> involved in the nitrogen cycle:
   a) <u>DECOMPOSERS</u> — decompose <u>proteins</u> and <u>urea</u> and turn them into <u>ammonia</u>.
   b) <u>NITRIFYING BACTERIA</u> — turn <u>ammonia</u> in decaying matter into <u>nitrates</u>.
   c) <u>NITROGEN-FIXING BACTERIA</u> — turn <u>atmospheric N_2</u> into <u>nitrogen compounds</u> that plants can use.
   d) <u>DENITRIFYING BACTERIA</u> — turn <u>nitrates</u> back into <u>N_2 gas</u>. This is of no benefit to living organisms.

7) Some <u>nitrogen-fixing bacteria</u> live in the <u>soil</u>. Others live in <u>nodules</u> on the roots of <u>legume plants</u> (e.g. peas and beans). This is why legume plants are so good at putting nitrogen <u>back into the soil</u>. The plants have a <u>mutualistic relationship</u> with the bacteria — the bacteria get <u>food</u> (sugars) from the plant, and the plant gets <u>nitrogen compounds</u> from the bacteria to make into <u>proteins</u>. So the relationship benefits <u>both</u> of them.

It's the cyyyycle of liiiiife...

People sometimes forget that when we breathe in, we're breathing in mainly <u>nitrogen</u>. It's a pretty <u>boring</u> gas, colourless and with no taste or smell. But nitrogen is <u>vital</u> to living things, because the <u>amino acids</u> that join together to make <u>proteins</u> (like enzymes) all contain nitrogen.

Revision Summary for Section 3

There's a lot to remember from this section and some of the topics are controversial, like cloning and genetic engineering. You need to know all sides of the story, as well as all the facts... so, here are some questions to help you figure out what you know. If you get any wrong, go back and learn the stuff.

1) What are alleles?
2) How do genes control the different characteristics we develop?
3) The table below compares sexual and asexual reproduction.
Complete the table by ticking whether each statement is true for sexual or asexual reproduction.

	Sexual reproduction	Asexual reproduction
Reproduction involves two parents.		
Offspring are clones of the parent.		
There is variation in the offspring.		
There is no fusion of gametes.		

4) What's the difference between homozygous and heterozygous?
5)* Draw a genetic diagram for the possible inheritance of an allele for loving Aston Villa (the football club). The allele is dominant and one parent is homozygous (AA) and one is heterozygous (Aa).
6)* Now draw a Punnett square diagram for the inheritance of the same allele where one parent is homozygous (aa) and one is heterozygous (Aa).
7) How does a gene on one of the human sex chromosomes cause embryos to develop into males?
8) What are the symptoms of cystic fibrosis?
9) What is the chance of a child inheriting Huntington's disease if one of their parents has one copy of the faulty allele?
10) How would you make a plant clone using tissue culture?
11) State two examples of useful applications of genetic engineering.
12) Why are some people concerned about genetic engineering?
13) Name four ways in which a desert animal may be adapted to its environment.
14) State three ways that plants and animals might be adapted to deter predators.
15) Name three animal characteristics that are determined only by genes.
16) Name three animal characteristics that are determined by a mixture of genes and the environment.
17) Explain Darwin's theory of natural selection.
18) Why was Darwin's idea very controversial at the time?
19) Explain how Lamarck's hypothesis was different from Darwin's.
20) Name three things that: a) plants compete for, b) animals compete for.
21) Give two examples of non-living factors that can cause environmental changes.
22) Explain how lichen can be used as an indicator of air pollution.
23) Name an organism that can be used as an indicator of water pollution.
24) What does each bar on a pyramid of biomass represent?
25) Give two ways that energy is lost from a food chain.
26) Give one way that carbon dioxide from the air enters a food chain.
27) Give three ways that carbon compounds in a food chain become carbon dioxide in the air again.
28) Explain the role that decomposers play in the nitrogen cycle.
29) What role do nitrogen-fixing bacteria play in the nitrogen cycle?

* Answers on page 140.

Section 3 — Genetics, Evolution and the Environment

Atoms and Elements

Atoms are the building blocks of <u>everything</u> — and I mean everything.
They're <u>amazingly tiny</u> — you can only see them with an incredibly powerful microscope.

Atoms have a Small Nucleus Surrounded by Electrons

There are quite a few different (and equally useful) models of the atom — but chemists tend to like this <u>nuclear model</u> best. You can use it to explain pretty much the whole of Chemistry... which is nice.

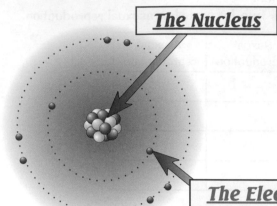

The Nucleus

1) It's in the <u>middle</u> of the atom.
2) It contains <u>protons</u> and <u>neutrons</u>.
3) <u>Protons</u> are <u>positively charged</u>.
4) <u>Neutrons</u> have <u>no charge</u> (they're neutral).
5) So the nucleus has a <u>positive charge</u> overall because of the protons.
6) But size-wise it's <u>tiny</u> compared to the rest of the atom.

The Electrons

1) Move <u>around</u> the nucleus.
2) They're <u>negatively charged</u>.
3) They're <u>tiny</u>, but they cover <u>a lot of space</u>.
4) They occupy <u>shells</u> around the nucleus.
5) These shells explain <u>the whole of Chemistry</u>.

Number of Protons Equals Number of Electrons

1) Atoms have <u>no charge</u> overall. They are neutral.
2) The <u>charge</u> on the electrons is the <u>same</u> size as the charge on the <u>protons</u> — but <u>opposite</u>.
3) This means the <u>number</u> of <u>protons</u> always equals the <u>number</u> of <u>electrons</u> in an <u>atom</u>.
4) If some electrons are <u>added or removed</u>, the atom becomes <u>charged</u> and is then an <u>ion</u>.

Elements Consist of One Type of Atom Only

1) Atoms can have different numbers of protons, neutrons and electrons.
   It's the number of <u>protons</u> in the nucleus that decides what <u>type</u> of atom it is.
2) For example, an atom with <u>one proton</u> in its nucleus is <u>hydrogen</u> and an atom with <u>two protons</u> is <u>helium</u>.
3) If a substance only contains <u>one type</u> of atom it's called an <u>element</u>.
4) There are about <u>100 different elements</u> — quite a lot of everyday substances are elements:

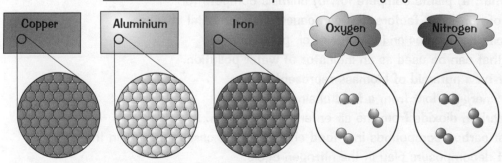

Copper   Aluminium   Iron   Oxygen   Nitrogen

So <u>all the atoms</u> of a particular <u>element</u> (e.g. nitrogen) have the <u>same number</u> of protons...

...and <u>different elements</u> have atoms with <u>different numbers</u> of protons.

Number of protons = number of electrons...

This stuff might seem a bit useless at first, but it should be permanently engraved into your mind.
You need to <u>know these basic facts</u> — then you'll have a better chance of understanding the rest of Chemistry.

The Periodic Table

Chemistry would be <u>really messy</u> if it was all <u>big lists</u> of names and properties. So instead they've come up with a kind of <u>shorthand</u> for the names, and made a beautiful table to organise the elements — like a big <u>filing system</u>. Might not be much fun, but it makes life (and <u>exam questions</u>) much, much <u>easier</u>.

Atoms Can be Represented by Symbols

Atoms of each element can be represented by a <u>one or two letter symbol</u> — it's a type of <u>shorthand</u> that saves you the bother of having to write the full name of the element.

Some make <u>perfect sense</u>, e.g.

| C = carbon | O = oxygen | Mg = magnesium |

Others seem to make about as much sense as an apple with a handle.

E.g.

| Na = sodium | Fe = iron | Pb = lead |

Most of these odd symbols actually come from the Latin names of the elements.

The Periodic Table Puts Elements with Similar Properties Together

1) The periodic table is laid out so that elements with <u>similar properties</u> form <u>columns</u>.

2) These <u>vertical columns</u> are called <u>groups</u> and Roman numerals are often used for them.

3) All of the elements in a <u>group</u> have the <u>same number</u> of <u>electrons</u> in their <u>outer shell</u>.

4) This is why <u>elements</u> in the same group have <u>similar properties</u>. So, if you know the <u>properties</u> of <u>one element</u>, you can <u>predict</u> properties of <u>other elements</u> in that group.

5) For example, the <u>Group 1</u> elements are Li, Na, K, Rb, Cs and Fr. They're all <u>metals</u> and they <u>react the same way</u>. E.g. they all react with water to form an <u>alkaline solution</u> and <u>hydrogen gas</u>, and they all react with oxygen to form an <u>oxide</u>.

6) The elements in the final column (<u>Group 0</u>) are the noble gases. They all have <u>eight electrons</u> in their <u>outer shell</u>, apart from helium (which has two). This means that they're <u>stable</u> and <u>unreactive</u>.

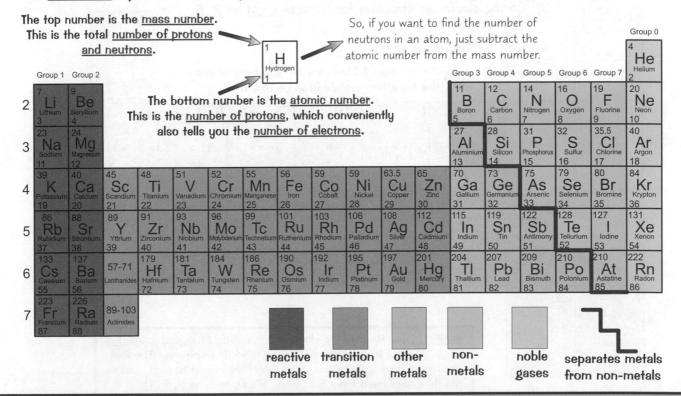

The top number is the <u>mass number</u>. This is the total <u>number of protons and neutrons</u>.

So, if you want to find the number of neutrons in an atom, just subtract the atomic number from the mass number.

The bottom number is the <u>atomic number</u>. This is the <u>number of protons</u>, which conveniently also tells you the <u>number of electrons</u>.

reactive metals | transition metals | other metals | non-metals | noble gases | separates metals from non-metals

I'm in a chemistry band — I play the symbols...

Scientists keep making <u>new elements</u> and feeling well chuffed with themselves. The trouble is, these new elements only last for <u>a fraction of a second</u> before falling apart. It could be really handy knowing that elements in the same group have <u>similar properties</u>. If you're told, for example, that fluorine (Group 7) forms <u>two-atom molecules</u>, it's a fair guess that chlorine, bromine, iodine and astatine <u>do too</u>. Astounding.

Electron Shells

The fact that electrons occupy "shells" around the nucleus is what causes the whole of chemistry. Remember that, and watch how it applies to each bit of it. It's ace.

Electron Shell Rules:

1) Electrons always occupy <u>shells</u> (sometimes called <u>energy levels</u>).

2) The <u>lowest</u> energy levels are <u>always filled first</u> — these are the ones closest to the nucleus.

3) Only <u>a certain number</u> of electrons are allowed in each shell:
   <u>1st shell:</u> 2   <u>2nd shell:</u> 8   <u>3rd shell:</u> 8

4) Atoms are much <u>happier</u> when they have <u>full electron shells</u> — like the <u>noble gases</u> in <u>Group 0</u>.

5) In most atoms the <u>outer shell</u> is <u>not full</u> and this makes the atom want to <u>react</u> to fill it.

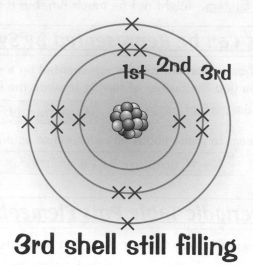

1st 2nd 3rd

3rd shell still filling

Follow the Rules to Work Out Electronic Structures

Hope you enjoyed those electron shell rules above, because you <u>aren't done</u> with them yet. You can use them to work out <u>electronic structures</u>. For a quick example, take nitrogen. <u>Follow the steps...</u>

1) The periodic table tells us nitrogen has <u>seven</u> protons... so it must have <u>seven</u> electrons.

2) Follow the 'Electron Shell Rules' above. The <u>first</u> shell can only take 2 electrons and the <u>second</u> shell can take a <u>maximum</u> of 8 electrons.

3) So the electronic structure for nitrogen <u>must</u> be <u>2, 5</u>. Easy peasy.

4) Now <u>you</u> try it for argon.

The periodic table has a big gap here where the transition metals fit in on row four.

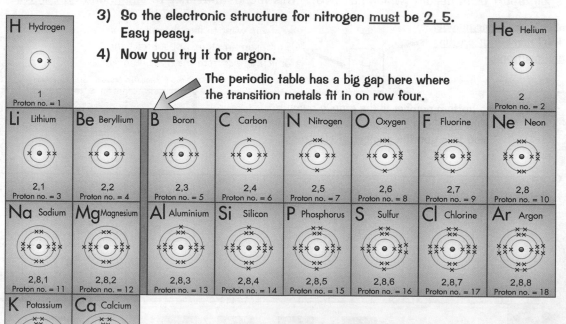

Answer... To calculate the electronic structure of argon, <u>follow the rules</u>. It's got 18 protons, so it <u>must</u> have 18 electrons. The first shell must have <u>2</u> electrons, the second shell must have <u>8</u>, and so the third shell must have <u>8</u> as well. It's as easy as <u>2, 8, 8</u>.

One little duck and two fat ladies — 2, 8, 8...

This electron shells business is <u>pretty important</u>. Believe me, I didn't say it "causes the whole of chemistry" for nothing. There are <u>only a few rules</u> to learn though — once you've got those down it'll be a breeze.

Section 4 — Atoms, Elements and Compounds

Compounds

Life'd be oh so simple if you only had to worry about elements, even if there are a hundred or so of them. But you can mix and match elements to make lots of compounds, which complicates things no end.

Atoms Join Together to Make Compounds

1) When _different elements react_, atoms form _chemical bonds_ with other atoms to form _compounds_. It's _usually difficult_ to _separate_ the two original elements out again.

2) _Making bonds_ involves atoms giving away, taking or sharing _electrons_. Only the _electrons_ are involved — it's nothing to do with the nuclei of the atoms at all.

3) A compound which is formed from a _metal_ and a _non-metal_ consists of _ions_. The _metal_ atoms _lose_ electrons to form _positive ions_ and the non-metal atoms _gain_ electrons to form _negative ions_. The _opposite charges_ (positive and negative) of the ions mean that they're strongly _attracted_ to each other. This is called _IONIC_ bonding.

E.g. NaCl

A sodium atom _gives_ an electron to a chlorine atom.

4) A compound formed from _non-metals_ consists of _molecules_. Each atom _shares_ an _electron_ with another atom — this is called a _COVALENT_ bond. Each atom has to make enough covalent bonds to _fill up_ its _outer shell_.

E.g. HCl

A hydrogen atom bonds with a chlorine atom by _sharing_ an electron with it.

5) The _properties_ of a compound are _totally different_ from the properties of the _original elements_. For example, if iron (a lustrous magnetic metal) and sulfur (a nice yellow powder) react, the compound formed (_iron sulfide_) is a _dull grey solid lump_, and doesn't behave _anything like_ either iron or sulfur.

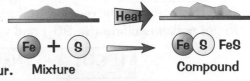

Fe + S → Fe S FeS
Mixture   Compound

6) Compounds can be _small molecules_ like water, or _great whopping lattices_ like sodium chloride (when I say whopping I'm talking in atomic terms).

a water molecule

Part of a sodium chloride lattice
● sodium ion
● chloride ion

A Formula Shows What Atoms are in a Compound

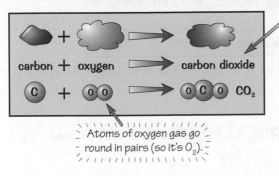

carbon + oxygen ⟹ carbon dioxide

C + O O ⟹ O C O CO_2

Atoms of oxygen gas go round in pairs (so it's O_2).

1) Carbon dioxide, CO_2, is a _compound_ formed from a _chemical reaction_ between carbon and oxygen. It contains 1 carbon atom and 2 oxygen atoms.

2) Here's another example: the formula of _sulfuric acid_ is H_2SO_4. So, each molecule contains 2 hydrogen atoms, 1 sulfur atom and 4 oxygen atoms.

3) There might be _brackets_ in a formula, e.g. calcium hydroxide is $Ca(OH)_2$. The little number outside the bracket applies to _everything_ inside the brackets. So in $Ca(OH)_2$ there is 1 calcium atom, 2 oxygen atoms and 2 hydrogen atoms.

Not learning this stuff will only compound your problems...

So, it turns out that _atoms_ can be very caring and _sharing_ little things when it comes to _forming compounds_. In fact, I know some people who could learn a lot from them. You know, just the other day...

Balancing Equations

Equations need a lot of practice if you're going to get them right — don't just skate over this stuff.

Atoms Aren't Lost or Made in Chemical Reactions

1) During chemical reactions, things don't appear out of nowhere and things don't just disappear.

2) You still have the same atoms at the end of a chemical reaction as you had at the start. They're just arranged in different ways.

3) Balanced symbol equations show the atoms at the start (the reactant atoms) and the atoms at the end (the product atoms) and how they're arranged. For example:

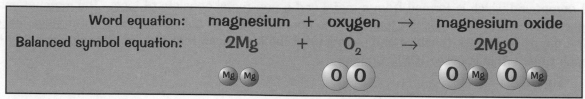

Word equation: magnesium + oxygen → magnesium oxide
Balanced symbol equation: $2Mg$ + O_2 → $2MgO$

4) Because atoms aren't gained or lost, the mass of the reactants equals the mass of the products. So, if you completely react 6 g of magnesium with 4 g of oxygen, you'd end up with 10 g of magnesium oxide.

Balancing the Equation — Match Them Up One by One

1) There must always be the same number of atoms of each element on both sides — they can't just disappear.

2) You balance the equation by putting numbers in front of the formulas where needed. Take this equation for reacting sulfuric acid (H_2SO_4) with sodium hydroxide (NaOH) to get sodium sulfate (Na_2SO_4) and water (H_2O):

$$H_2SO_4 + NaOH \rightarrow Na_2SO_4 + H_2O$$

The formulas are all correct but the numbers of some atoms don't match up on both sides. E.g. there are 3 Hs on the left, but only 2 on the right. You can't change formulas like H_2O to H_3O. You can only put numbers in front of them:

Method: Balance Just ONE Type of Atom at a Time

The more you practise, the quicker you get, but all you do is this:

1) Find an element that doesn't balance and pencil in a number to try and sort it out.

2) See where it gets you. It may create another imbalance — if so, just pencil in another number and see where that gets you.

3) Carry on chasing unbalanced elements and it'll sort itself out pretty quickly.

I'll show you. In the equation above you soon notice we're short of H atoms on the RHS (Right-Hand Side).

1) The only thing you can do about that is make it $2H_2O$ instead of just H_2O:
$$H_2SO_4 + NaOH \rightarrow Na_2SO_4 + 2H_2O$$

2) But that now causes too many H atoms and O atoms on the RHS, so to balance that up you could try putting 2NaOH on the LHS (Left-Hand Side):
$$H_2SO_4 + 2NaOH \rightarrow Na_2SO_4 + 2H_2O$$

3) And suddenly there it is! Everything balances. And you'll notice the Na just sorted itself out.

Balancing equations — weigh it up in your mind...

Remember — a number in front of a formula applies to the entire formula. So, $3Na_2SO_4$ means three lots of Na_2SO_4. The little numbers in the middle or at the end of a formula only apply to the atom or brackets immediately before. So the 4 in Na_2SO_4 just means 4 Os, not 4 Ss. Difficult, I know, but that's chemistry.

Materials and Properties

Not all materials are the <u>same</u>, as you'll find out if you try to make a hat out of spaghetti hoops...

Different Materials Have Different Properties

MELTING POINT

Most materials that are pure chemicals have a <u>unique melting point</u>. This is the temperature where the <u>solid</u> material turns to <u>liquid</u>. E.g. the melting point of <u>water</u> is <u>0 degrees Celsius</u> (0°C).

STRENGTH

<u>Strength</u> is how good a material is at <u>resisting</u> a <u>force</u>. You can judge how strong it is by how much force is needed to either <u>break</u> it or <u>permanently</u> change its <u>shape</u> (<u>deform</u> it). There are <u>two</u> types of strength you need to know about:

<u>TENSILE (OR TENSION) STRENGTH</u> — how much a material can resist a <u>pulling force</u>. Things like <u>ropes</u> and <u>cables</u> need a high tensile strength, or they'd snap.
<u>COMPRESSIVE STRENGTH</u> — how much a material can resist a <u>pushing force</u>. Building materials like <u>bricks</u> need good compressive strength, or they'd be <u>squashed</u> by the weight of the bricks above them.

Some things, like <u>cross beams</u> in roofs, need to be made of materials with good compressive <u>and</u> tensile strength — they get both pushed and pulled.

STIFFNESS

A <u>stiff</u> material is good at <u>not bending</u> when a force is applied to it. This <u>isn't</u> the same as strength — a bendy material can still be strong if a big force doesn't <u>permanently</u> deform it.

1) Materials like <u>steel</u> are very difficult to <u>bend</u> — they're very stiff.
2) Some kinds of rubber are very <u>strong</u> but they <u>bend and stretch</u> very easily — they're <u>not</u> stiff.

HARDNESS

The hardness of a material is how <u>difficult</u> it is to <u>cut</u> into.

1) The <u>hardest</u> material found in <u>nature</u> is <u>diamond</u>.
2) The only material that can <u>cut</u> a diamond is another diamond.
3) Diamonds can cut <u>most</u> other materials — many <u>industrial drills</u> have <u>diamond tips</u>.

DENSITY

Density is a material's <u>mass per unit volume</u> (e.g. <u>g/cm³</u>). Don't confuse <u>density</u> with <u>mass</u> or <u>weight</u>.

1) <u>Air</u> is <u>not</u> very dense. You'd need a <u>huge volume</u> of it to make up 1 kg in <u>mass</u>.
2) <u>Gold</u> is very <u>dense</u>. A <u>small volume</u> of gold would make up 1 kg in mass.
3) Objects that are <u>less dense</u> than water will float (like <u>ice</u>). Objects that are <u>more dense</u> than water will <u>sink</u>.

Substance	Density g/cm³
gold	19.3
iron	7.9
PVC	1.3
water	1.0
ice	0.97
air	0.001

'Cos diamonds are an industrial drill's best friend...

Make sure you're clear about what <u>density</u> is and why it's <u>NOT</u> the same as mass. Measure out 1 kg of loose change and 1 kg of breakfast cereal and <u>compare</u> the different volumes — same mass, but different densities...

58

Materials, Properties and Uses

Every material has a different set of properties, which makes it perfect for some jobs, and totally useless for others. That probably explains why chocolate teapots have never really caught on...

The Possible Uses for a Material Depend on Its Properties

When you're choosing a material to use in a product, you need to think about its properties, e.g.

PLASTICS
- Can be fairly hard, strong and stiff
- Some are fairly low density (good for lightweight goods)
- Some are mouldable (easily made into things)

E.g. cases for televisions, computers and kettles

RUBBER
- Strong but soft and flexible
- Mouldable

E.g. rubber car tyres

NYLON FIBRES
- Soft and flexible
- Good tensile strength

E.g. ropes and clothing fabric

A Product's Properties Depend on the Materials It's Made From

The effectiveness of a product is how good it is at the job it's supposed to do. A product's effectiveness depends on the materials it's made from. Materials also affect a product's durability — how long it will last.

1) Gramophone records 100 years ago were made of a mixture of materials like paper, slate and wax. There aren't many of these records left because they broke very easily — they weren't strong.

2) More modern records are made of polyvinyl chloride (PVC) or 'vinyl'. This material is strong and flexible so it's less likely to break. DJs sometimes still use vinyl records in clubs.

3) Most people these days own compact discs (CDs). These are made of a very tough, flexible plastic called polycarbonate. It's quite strong and hard (it's used in bulletproof glass) and should last even longer than PVC — but we'll have to wait a while to find out...

You Can Assess the Suitability of Different Materials

The properties of a material can be used to work out what sort of purposes the material might be suitable for, e.g.

1) Cooking utensils must be made from something with a high melting point that's non-toxic.

2) Material to make a toy car must be non-toxic and should be strong, stiff and low density — e.g. some kinds of plastic.

3) Clothing fabric mustn't be stiff, but needs a good tensile strength (so it can be made into fibres) and high flame-resistance, especially if it's for nightwear or children's clothes.

It's not rocket science — that's 'cos it's materials science...

It's all fairly straightforward stuff on this page — looking at the properties of materials and what they're suitable for just needs a bit of common sense. Don't think that any of the materials are totally useless — their properties will probably be ideal for something. My properties are tired and sleepy, so I should have a nap.

Properties of Metals

Metals are all the <u>same</u> but slightly <u>different</u>. They have some <u>basic properties</u> in common, but each has its own <u>specific combination</u> of properties, which mean you use different ones for different purposes.

Metals are Strong and Bendy and They're Great Conductors

1) <u>Most of the elements</u> are <u>metals</u> — so they cover most of the periodic table. In fact, <u>only</u> the elements on the <u>far right</u> are <u>non-metals</u>.

2) All metals have some fairly similar <u>basic properties</u>:

- Metals are <u>strong</u> (hard to break), but they can be <u>bent or hammered</u> into different shapes.
- They're great at <u>conducting heat</u>.
- They <u>conduct electricity well</u>.

The coloured elements are metals
Just look at 'em all
— there's loads of 'em!

Transition Metals

3) Metals (and especially <u>transition metals</u>, which are found in the <u>centre block</u> of the periodic table) have loads of <u>everyday</u> uses because of these properties...

- Their strength and 'bendability' makes them handy for making into things like <u>bridges</u> and <u>car bodies</u>.
- Metals are ideal if you want to make something that heat needs to travel through, like a <u>saucepan base</u>.
- And their conductivity makes them great for making things like <u>electrical wires</u>.

A Metal's Exact Properties Decide How It's Best Used

1) The properties above are <u>typical properties</u> of metals. Not all metals are the same though...

<u>Copper</u> is a <u>good conductor</u> of <u>electricity</u>, so it's ideal for drawing out into electrical wires. It's <u>hard</u> and <u>strong</u> but can be <u>bent</u>. It also <u>doesn't react with water</u>.

<u>Aluminium</u> is <u>corrosion-resistant</u> and has a <u>low density</u>. Pure aluminium <u>isn't</u> very strong, but it forms hard, strong alloys (see page 60).

2) <u>Different metals</u> are chosen for <u>different uses</u> because of their specific properties. For example:

- If you were doing some <u>plumbing</u>, you'd pick a metal that could be <u>bent</u> to make pipes and tanks, and is below hydrogen in the reactivity series so it <u>doesn't react with water</u>. <u>Copper</u> is great for this.
- If you wanted to make an <u>aeroplane</u>, you'd probably use metal as it's <u>strong</u> and can be <u>bent into shape</u>. But you'd also need it to be <u>light</u>, so <u>aluminium</u> would be a good choice.

Metals are Good — but Not Perfect

1) Metals are very useful <u>structural materials</u>, but some <u>corrode</u> when exposed to air and water, so they need to be <u>protected</u>, e.g. by painting. If metals corrode, they lose their strength and hardness.

When <u>iron</u> corrodes, it's combining with oxygen (and also water). The iron <u>gains oxygen</u> to form <u>iron(III) oxide</u>. Water then becomes loosely bonded to the iron(III) oxide and the result is <u>hydrated iron(III) oxide</u> — which most people call <u>rust</u>.

iron + oxygen + water → hydrated iron(III) oxide

2) Metals can get 'tired' when stresses and strains are repeatedly put on them over time. This is known as <u>metal fatigue</u> and leads to metals breaking, which can be very <u>dangerous</u>, e.g. in planes.

Metal fatigue? — yeah, I've had enough of this page too...

So, all metals <u>conduct electricity and heat</u> and can be <u>bent into shape</u>. But lots of them have <u>special properties</u> too. You have to decide what properties you need and use the metal with those properties.

Section 4 — Atoms, Elements and Compounds

Making Metals More Useful

Pure metals often aren't quite right for certain jobs. Scientists don't just make do, oh no my friend... they mix two metals together (or mix a metal with a non-metal) — creating an alloy with the properties they want.

Pure Iron Tends to be a Bit Too Bendy

1) 'Iron' straight from the blast furnace is only 96% iron. The other 4% is impurities such as carbon.

2) This impure iron is used as cast iron. It's handy for making ornamental railings, but it doesn't have many other uses because it's brittle.

3) So all the impurities are removed from most of the blast furnace iron. This pure iron has a regular arrangement of identical atoms. The layers of atoms can slide over each other, which makes the iron soft and easily shaped. This iron is far too bendy for most uses.

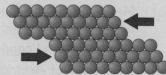

Most Iron is Converted into Steel — an Alloy

Most of the pure iron is changed into alloys called steels. Steels are formed by adding small amounts of carbon and sometimes other metals to the iron.

TYPE OF STEEL	PROPERTIES	USES
Low carbon steel (0.1% carbon)	easily shaped	car bodies
High carbon steel (1.5% carbon)	very hard, inflexible	blades for cutting tools, bridges
Stainless steel (chromium added, and sometimes nickel)	rust-resistant	cutlery, containers for corrosive substances

Alloys are Harder Than Pure Metals

1) Different elements have different sized atoms. So when an element such as carbon is added to pure iron, the smaller carbon atom will upset the layers of pure iron atoms, making it more difficult for them to slide over each other. So alloys are harder.

2) Many metals in use today are actually alloys. E.g.:

BRONZE = COPPER + TIN Bronze is harder than copper. It's good for making medals and statues from.

CUPRONICKEL = COPPER + NICKEL This is hard and corrosion resistant. It's used to make "silver" coins.

GOLD ALLOYS ARE USED TO MAKE JEWELLERY Pure gold is too soft. Metals such as zinc, copper, silver, palladium and nickel are used to harden the "gold".

ALUMINIUM ALLOYS ARE USED TO MAKE AIRCRAFT Aluminium has a low density, but it's alloyed with small amounts of other metals to make it stronger.

3) In the past, the development of alloys was by trial and error. But nowadays we understand much more about the properties of metals, so alloys can be designed for specific uses.

Some Alloys are Smart

1) Nitinol is the name given to a family of alloys of nickel and titanium that have shape memory.

2) This means they "remember" their original shape, and go back to it even after being bent and twisted.

3) This has increased the number of uses for alloys. You can get specs with Nitinol frames — these can be bent and even sat on and they still go back into their original shape.

A brass band — harder than Iron Maiden...

Hmm, so scientists can faff about with metals until they can make them do exactly what they want. Well, I'd like a gold ring that can cook meals, do the washing up and tidy rooms. And buy chocolate. Thanks.

Getting Metals from Rocks

A few unreactive metals like gold are found in the Earth as the metal itself, rather than as a compound. The rest of the metals we get by extracting them from rocks — and I bet you're just itching to find out how...

Ores Contain Enough Metal to Make Extraction Worthwhile

1) A metal ore is a rock which contains enough metal to make it worthwhile extracting the metal from it.

2) In many cases the ore is an oxide of the metal. For example, the main aluminium ore is called bauxite — it's aluminium oxide (Al_2O_3).

3) Most metals need to be extracted from their ores using a chemical reaction.

4) The economics (profitability) of metal extraction can change over time. For example:

- If the market price of a metal drops a lot, it might not be worth extracting it. If the price increases a lot then it might be worth extracting more of it.
- As technology improves, it becomes possible to extract more metal from a sample of rock than was originally possible. So it might now be worth extracting metal that wasn't worth extracting in the past.

Metals Are Extracted From their Ores Chemically

1) A metal can be extracted from its ore chemically — by reduction (see below) or by electrolysis (splitting with electricity, see page 62).

2) Some ores may have to be concentrated before the metal is extracted — this just involves getting rid of the unwanted rocky material.

3) Electrolysis can also be used to purify the extracted metal (see page 62).

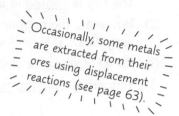

Occasionally, some metals are extracted from their ores using displacement reactions (see page 63).

Some Metals can be Extracted by Reduction with Carbon

1) A metal can be extracted from its ore chemically by reduction using carbon.

2) When an ore is reduced, oxygen is removed from it, e.g.

$2Fe_2O_3$	+	$3C$	$\rightarrow$	$4Fe$	+	$3CO_2$
iron(III) oxide	+	carbon	$\rightarrow$	iron	+	carbon dioxide

3) The position of the metal in the reactivity series determines whether it can be extracted by reduction with carbon.

a) Metals higher than carbon in the reactivity series have to be extracted using electrolysis, which is expensive.

b) Metals below carbon in the reactivity series can be extracted by reduction using carbon. For example, iron oxide is reduced in a blast furnace to make iron.

This is because carbon can only take the oxygen away from metals which are less reactive than carbon itself is.

Extracted using Electrolysis

Extracted by reduction using carbon

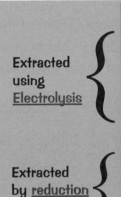

The Reactivity Series

Potassium	K	more reactive
Sodium	Na	
Calcium	Ca	
Magnesium	Mg	
Aluminium	Al	
CARBON	C	
Zinc	Zn	
Iron	Fe	
Tin	Sn	less reactive
Copper	Cu	

Learn how metals are extracted — ore else...

Extracting metals isn't cheap. You have to pay for special equipment, energy and labour. Then there's the cost of getting the ore to the extraction plant. If there's a choice of extraction methods, a company always picks the cheapest, unless there's a good reason not to (e.g. to increase purity). They're not extracting it for fun.

Getting Metals from Rocks

You may think you know all you could ever want to know about how to get metals from rocks, but no — there's <u>more</u> of it. Think of each of the facts on this page as a little <u>gold nugget</u>. Or, er, a copper one.

Some Metals have to be Extracted by Electrolysis

1) Metals that are <u>more reactive</u> than carbon (see previous page) have to be extracted using electrolysis of <u>molten compounds</u>.

2) An example of a metal that has to be extracted this way is <u>aluminium</u>.

3) However, the process is <u>much more expensive</u> than reduction with carbon (see previous page) because it <u>uses a lot of energy</u>.

> <u>FOR EXAMPLE</u>: a <u>high temperature</u> is needed to <u>melt</u> aluminium oxide so that <u>aluminium</u> can be extracted — this requires a lot of <u>energy</u>, which makes it an <u>expensive</u> process.

Copper is Purified by Electrolysis

1) Copper can be easily extracted by <u>reduction with carbon</u> (see previous page). The ore is <u>heated</u> in a <u>furnace</u> — this is called <u>smelting</u>.

2) However, the copper produced this way is <u>impure</u> — and impure copper <u>doesn't</u> conduct electricity very well. This <u>isn't</u> very <u>useful</u> because a lot of copper is used to make <u>electrical wiring</u>.

3) So <u>electrolysis</u> is also used to <u>purify</u> it, even though it's quite <u>expensive</u>.

4) This produces <u>very pure</u> copper, which is a <u>much better conductor</u>.

> You could <u>extract</u> copper straight from its ore by electrolysis if you wanted to, but it's more expensive than using reduction with carbon.

Electrolysis Means "Splitting Up with Electricity"

1) <u>Electrolysis</u> is the <u>breaking down</u> of a substance using <u>electricity</u>.

2) It requires a <u>liquid</u> to <u>conduct</u> the <u>electricity</u>, called the <u>electrolyte</u>.

3) Electrolytes are often <u>metal salt solutions</u> made from the ore (e.g. copper sulfate) or <u>molten metal oxides</u>.

4) The electrolyte has <u>free ions</u> — these <u>conduct</u> the electricity and allow the whole thing to work.

5) Electrons are <u>taken away</u> by the <u>(positive) anode</u> and <u>given away</u> by the <u>(negative) cathode</u>. As ions gain or lose electrons they become atoms or molecules and are released.

> Here's how electrolysis is used to get <u>copper</u>:
> 1) <u>Electrons</u> are <u>pulled off</u> copper atoms at the <u>anode</u>, causing them to go into solution as Cu^{2+} ions.
> 2) Cu^{2+} ions near the <u>cathode</u> gain electrons and turn back into <u>copper atoms</u>.
> 3) The <u>impurities</u> are dropped at the <u>anode</u> as a <u>sludge</u>, whilst <u>pure copper atoms</u> bond to the <u>cathode</u>.

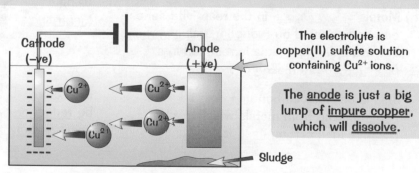

The <u>cathode</u> starts as a <u>thin</u> piece of <u>pure copper</u> and more pure copper <u>adds</u> to it.

Cathode (−ve)

Anode (+ve)

The electrolyte is copper(II) sulfate solution containing Cu^{2+} ions.

The <u>anode</u> is just a big lump of <u>impure copper</u>, which will <u>dissolve</u>.

Sludge

Someone robbed your metal? — call a copper...

The skin of the <u>Statue of Liberty</u> is made of copper — about 80 tonnes of it in fact. Its surface reacts with gases in the air to form <u>copper carbonate</u> — which is why it's that pretty shade of <u>green</u>.

Getting Metals from Rocks

Don't stop now — there's still a bit more about copper extraction... sigh, it's a hard life.

You Can Extract Copper From a Solution Using a Displacement Reaction

1) More reactive metals react more vigorously than less reactive metals.

2) If you put a reactive metal into a solution of a dissolved metal compound, the reactive metal will replace the less reactive metal in the compound.

3) This is because the more reactive metal bonds more strongly to the non-metal bit of the compound and pushes out the less reactive metal.

4) For example, scrap iron can be used to displace copper from solution — this is really useful because iron is cheap but copper is expensive. If some iron is put in a solution of copper sulfate, the more reactive iron will "kick out" the less reactive copper from the solution. You end up with iron sulfate solution and copper metal.

| copper sulfate + iron → iron sulfate + copper |

5) If a piece of silver metal is put into a solution of copper sulfate, nothing happens. The more reactive metal (copper) is already in the solution.

Copper-rich Ores are in Short Supply

1) The supply of copper-rich ores is limited, so it's important to recycle as much copper as possible.

2) The demand for copper is growing and this may lead to shortages in the future.

3) Scientists are looking into new ways of extracting copper from low-grade ores (ores that only contain small amounts of copper) or from the waste that is currently produced when copper is extracted.

4) Examples of new methods to extract copper are bioleaching and phytomining:

Bioleaching

This uses bacteria to separate copper from copper sulfide. The bacteria get energy from the bond between copper and sulfur, separating out the copper from the ore in the process. The leachate (the solution produced by the process) contains copper, which can be extracted, e.g. by filtering.

Phytomining

This involves growing plants in soil that contains copper.
The plants can't use or get rid of the copper so it gradually builds up in the leaves. The plants can be harvested, dried and burned in a furnace.
The copper can be collected from the ash left in the furnace.

5) Traditional methods of copper mining are pretty damaging to the environment (see next page). These new methods of extraction have a much smaller impact, but the disadvantage is that they're slow.

Personally, I'd rather be pound rich than copper rich...

Pure copper is expensive but very useful stuff. Just think where we'd be without good quality copper wire to conduct electricity (hmmm... how would I live without my electric pineapple corer). The fact that copper-rich ore supplies are dwindling means that scientists have to come up with ever-more-cunning methods to extract it.

Impacts of Extracting Metals

Metals are very useful. Just imagine if all knives and forks were made of plastic instead — there'd be prongs snapping all over the place at dinner time. However, metal extraction uses a lot of <u>energy</u> and is <u>bad</u> for the <u>environment</u>. And that's where recycling comes in handy.

Metal Extraction can be Bad for the Environment

People have to balance the <u>social</u>, <u>economic</u> and <u>environmental</u> effects of mining the ores.

Mining metal ores is <u>good</u> because it means that <u>useful</u> <u>products</u> can be made. It also provides local people with <u>jobs</u> and brings <u>money</u> into the area. This means services such as <u>transport</u> and <u>health</u> can be improved.

But mining ores is <u>bad for the environment</u> as it causes noise, scarring of the landscape and loss of habitats. Deep mine shafts can also be <u>dangerous</u> for a long time after the mine has been abandoned.

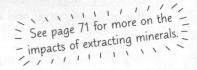

See page 71 for more on the impacts of extracting minerals.

Recycling Metals is Important

1) Mining and extracting metals takes lots of <u>energy</u>, most of which comes from burning <u>fossil fuels</u>.

2) Fossil fuels are <u>running out</u> so it's important to <u>conserve</u> them. Not only this, but burning them contributes to <u>acid rain</u>, (p.84) <u>global dimming</u> (p.84) and <u>climate change</u> (p.85).

3) Recycling metals only uses a <u>small fraction</u> of the energy needed to mine and extract new metal. E.g. recycling copper only takes 15% of the energy that's needed to mine and extract new copper.

4) Energy doesn't come cheap, so recycling <u>saves money</u> too.

5) Also, there's a <u>finite amount</u> of each <u>metal</u> in the Earth. Recycling conserves these resources.

6) Recycling metal cuts down on the amount of rubbish that gets sent to <u>landfill</u>. Landfill takes up space and <u>pollutes</u> the surroundings. If all the aluminium cans in the UK were recycled, there'd be 14 million fewer dustbins to empty each year.

Get back on your bike again — recycle...

Recycling metals saves <u>natural resources</u> and <u>money</u> and reduces <u>environmental problems</u>. It's great. There's no limit to the number of times metals like aluminium, copper and steel can be recycled. So your humble little drink can may one day form part of a powerful robot who takes over the galaxy.

Nanotechnology

Just time to squeeze in something really small before the end of the section...

Nanomaterials Are Really Really Really Really Tiny

...smaller than that.

1) Really tiny particles, 1–100 nanometres across, are called 'nanoparticles'.
2) Nanotechnology is the branch of technology dealing with the making and use of these nanoparticles.

$$1 \text{ nm} = 0.000\ 000\ 001 \text{ m}$$

3) Some of the structures that are dealt with in nanotechnology are only as big as some molecules, so nanotechnology involves understanding how to control matter on a very small scale.

Nanomaterials are Often Designed for a Specific Use

Most nanomaterials are made using nanotechnology, but some nanoscale materials occur naturally or are produced by accident. For example:

- Seaspray — The sea produces nanoscale salt particles which are present in the atmosphere.
- Combustion — When fuels are burnt, nanoscale soot particles are produced.

Nanoparticles are Often Used to Modify the Properties of Materials

Nanoparticles can be added to materials to give them different properties.

For example:

Nanoparticles are added to plastics in sports equipment, e.g. tennis rackets, golf clubs and golf balls. They make the plastic much stronger and more durable, and they don't add weight.

Silver nanoparticles are added to polymer fibres used to make surgical masks and wound dressings. This gives the fibres antibacterial properties.

Nanoparticles are much smaller than larger particles of the same material. This means they have a larger surface area-to-volume ratio, which is what gives them different properties and makes them super useful. Silver nanoparticles, for example, can kill bacteria, making them suitable for wound dressings. Normal silver particles are much bigger, have a smaller surface area to volume ratio and can't kill bacteria. Not so useful. Well, not for wound dressings anyway.

The Effects of Nanoparticles on Health are Not Fully Understood

1) Although nanoparticles are useful, the way they affect the body isn't fully understood, so it's important that any new products are tested thoroughly to minimise the risks.
2) Some people are worried that products containing nanoparticles have been made available before the effects on human health have been investigated properly, and that we don't know what the long-term impacts on health will be.
3) As the long-term impacts aren't known, many people believe that products containing nanoscale particles should be clearly labelled, so that consumers can choose whether or not to use them.

Carbon nanoparticles — bit of a fancy name for soot...

Some nanoparticles have really unexpected properties. Gold nanoparticles aren't gold-coloured, for example — they're either red or purple. Now that's definitely unexpected. But not all that useful. But others, such as antibacterial silver nanoparticles, are both unexpected and useful. Hurrah for unexpectedly useful properties.

Revision Summary for Section 4

There wasn't anything too ghastly in this section, and a few bits were even quite interesting I reckon. But you've got to make sure the facts are all firmly embedded in your brain and that you really understand what's going on. These questions will let you see what you know and what you don't. If you get stuck on any, you need to look at that stuff again. Keep going till you can do them all without coming up for air.

1) Sketch an atom. Label the nucleus and the electrons.

2) What are the symbols for: a) calcium, b) carbon, c) sodium?

3)* Which element's properties are more similar to magnesium's: calcium or iron?

4) Describe how you would work out the electronic structure of an atom given its atomic number.

5) Describe the process of ionic bonding.

6) What is covalent bonding?

7)* Say which of the diagrams on the right show:
   a) an element   and   b) a compound
   Suggest what elements or compounds could be in each.

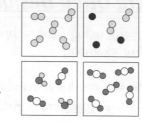

8)* Balance these equations:
   a) $CaCO_3 + HCl \rightarrow CaCl_2 + H_2O + CO_2$ b) $Ca + H_2O \rightarrow Ca(OH)_2 + H_2$

9) What's the difference between strength and stiffness?

10) What's the hardest material found in nature?

11) Give a definition of density.

12) Name two properties of each of the following materials that make them useful in manufacturing:
   a) plastic   b) rubber   c) nylon

13) Give three properties of metals.

14) Briefly describe two problems with metals.

15) What is the problem with using a) iron straight from the blast furnace, b) very pure iron?

16) Give two examples of alloys and say what's in them.

17) Give an example of a smart alloy. What is it used for?

18) What's the definition of an ore?

19) Explain why zinc can be extracted by reduction with carbon but magnesium can't.

20) Give a reason why aluminium is an expensive metal.

21) What is electrolysis?

22) Describe the process of purifying copper by electrolysis.

23) Describe how scrap iron is used to displace copper from solution.

24) What is the name of the method where plants are used to extract metals from soil?

25) Give three reasons why it's good to recycle metal.

26) What is nanotechnology?

27) Give two examples of uses of nanomaterials.

* Answers on page 140

Section 4 — Atoms, Elements and Compounds

The Earth's Structure

No one accepted the theory of <u>plate tectonics</u> for ages. Almost everyone does now. How times change.

The Earth Has a Crust, Mantle, Outer and Inner Core

The Earth is <u>almost spherical</u> and it has a <u>layered</u> structure, a bit like a scotch egg. Or a peach.

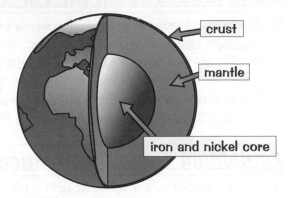

1) The bit we live on, the <u>crust</u>, is very <u>thin</u> (it varies between 5 km and 50 km) and is surrounded by the <u>atmosphere</u>.

2) Below that is the <u>mantle</u>. The <u>mantle</u> has all the properties of a <u>solid</u>, except that it can flow very <u>slowly</u>.

3) Within the mantle, <u>radioactive decay</u> takes place. This produces a lot of <u>heat</u>, which causes the mantle to <u>flow</u> in <u>convection currents</u>.

4) At the centre of the Earth is the <u>core</u>, which we think is made of <u>iron and nickel</u>.

The Earth's Surface is Made Up of Tectonic Plates

1) The crust and the upper part of the mantle are cracked into a number of large pieces called <u>tectonic plates</u>. These plates are a bit like <u>big rafts</u> that 'float' on the mantle.

2) The plates don't stay in one place though. That's because the <u>convection currents</u> in the mantle cause the plates to <u>drift</u>.

3) The map shows the <u>edges</u> of the plates as they are now, and the <u>directions</u> they're moving in (red arrows).

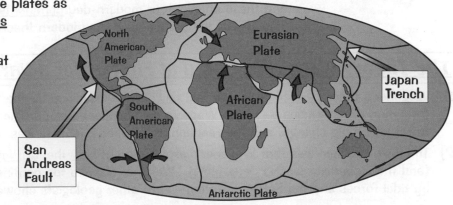

4) Most of the plates are moving at speeds of <u>a few cm per year</u> relative to each other.

5) Occasionally, the plates move very <u>suddenly</u>, causing an <u>earthquake</u>.

6) <u>Volcanoes</u> and <u>earthquakes</u> often occur at the boundaries between two tectonic plates.

Scientists Can't Predict Earthquakes and Volcanic Eruptions

1) Tectonic plates can stay more or less put for a while and then <u>suddenly</u> lurch forwards. It's <u>impossible to predict</u> exactly when they'll move.

2) Scientists are trying to find out if there are any <u>clues</u> that an earthquake might happen soon — things like strain in underground rocks. Even with these clues they'll only be able to say an earthquake's <u>likely</u> to happen, not <u>exactly when</u> it'll happen.

3) There are some <u>clues</u> that say a volcanic eruption might happen soon. Before an eruption, molten rock rises up into chambers near the surface, causing the ground surface to bulge slightly. This causes <u>mini-earthquakes</u> near the volcano.

4) But sometimes molten rock cools down instead of erupting, so mini-earthquakes can be a <u>false alarm</u>.

A few cm a year — that's as fast as your fingernails grow...

There's a mixture of <u>plain facts</u> and <u>scientific thinking</u> here. Learn the details of the Earth's structure, and make sure you can explain how tectonic plates move and what happens at plate boundaries. It's important to remember that earthquakes are unpredictable even with the best equipment.

Plate Tectonics

The idea that the Earth's surface is made up of <u>moving plates of rock</u> has been around since the early twentieth century. But it took a while to <u>catch on</u>.

Observations About the Earth Hadn't Been Explained

1) For years, fossils of <u>very similar</u> plants and animals had been found on <u>opposite sides</u> of the Atlantic Ocean. Most people thought this was because the continents had been <u>linked</u> by '<u>land bridges</u>', which had <u>sunk</u> or been <u>covered</u> by water as the Earth <u>cooled</u>. But not everyone was convinced, even back then.

2) Other things about the Earth puzzled people too — like why the <u>coastlines</u> of <u>Africa</u> and <u>South America</u> fit together and why there are fossils of <u>sea creatures</u> in the Alps.

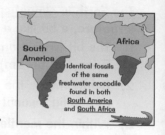

Identical fossils of the same freshwater crocodile found in both <u>South America</u> and <u>South Africa</u>

Explaining These Observations Needed a Leap of Imagination

What was needed was a scientist with a bit of <u>insight</u>... a smidgeon of <u>creativity</u>... a touch of <u>genius</u>...

1) In 1914 <u>Alfred Wegener</u> hypothesised that Africa and South America had previously been <u>one</u> continent which had then <u>split</u>. He started to look for more evidence to <u>back up</u> his hypothesis. He found it...

2) E.g. there were <u>matching layers</u> in the <u>rocks</u> on different continents, and similar <u>earthworms</u> living in <u>both</u> South America and South Africa.

3) Wegener's theory of '<u>continental drift</u>' supposed that about 300 million years ago there had been just one '<u>supercontinent</u>' — which he called Pangaea. According to Wegener, Pangaea broke into smaller chunks, and these chunks (our modern-day <u>continents</u>) are still slowly 'drifting' apart. This idea is the basis behind the modern theory of <u>plate tectonics</u>.

The Theory Wasn't Accepted at First — for a Variety of Reasons

1) Wegener's theory <u>explained</u> things that <u>couldn't</u> be explained by the 'land bridge' theory (e.g. the formation of <u>mountains</u> — which Wegener said happened as continents <u>smashed into</u> each other). But it was a big change, and the reaction from other scientists was <u>hostile</u>.

2) The main problem was that Wegener's explanation of <u>how</u> the '<u>drifting</u>' happened wasn't convincing (and the movement wasn't <u>detectable</u>). Wegener claimed the continents' movement could be caused by tidal forces and the Earth's rotation — but other geologists showed that this was <u>impossible</u>.

Eventually, the Evidence Became Overwhelming

1) In the 1960s, scientists investigated the <u>Mid-Atlantic ridge</u>, which runs the <u>whole length</u> of the Atlantic.

2) They found evidence that <u>magma</u> (molten rock) <u>rises up</u> through the sea floor, <u>solidifies</u> and forms underwater mountains that are <u>roughly symmetrical</u> either side of the ridge. The evidence suggested that the sea floor was <u>spreading</u> — at about 10 cm per year.

3) Even better evidence that the continents are moving apart came from the <u>magnetic orientation</u> of the rocks. As the liquid magma erupts out of the gap, <u>iron particles</u> in the rocks tend to <u>align themselves</u> with the Earth's <u>magnetic field</u> — and as it cools they <u>set</u> in position. Now then... every half million years or so the Earth's magnetic field <u>swaps direction</u> — and the rock on <u>either side</u> of the ridge has <u>bands</u> of <u>alternate magnetic polarity</u>, <u>symmetrical</u> about the ridge.

4) This was convincing evidence that new sea floor was being created... and <u>continents</u> were <u>moving apart</u>.

5) All the evidence collected by other scientists <u>supported Wegener's theory</u> — so it was gradually <u>accepted</u>.

Plate Tectonics — it's a smashing theory...

Wegener wasn't right about everything, but his <u>main idea</u> was <u>correct</u>. The scientific community was a bit slow to accept it, but once there was more <u>evidence</u> to support it, they got on board. That's science for you...

The Three Different Types of Rock

Scientists classify rocks according to how they're formed. The three different types are: <u>sedimentary</u>, <u>metamorphic</u> and <u>igneous</u>. Sedimentary rocks are generally pretty soft, while igneous rocks are well hard.

There are Three Steps in the Formation of Sedimentary Rock

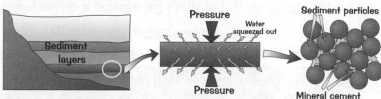

1) <u>Sedimentary rocks</u> are formed from <u>layers of sediment</u> laid down in <u>lakes</u> or <u>seas</u>.

2) Over <u>millions of years</u> the layers get <u>buried</u> under more layers and the <u>weight</u> pressing down <u>squeezes out</u> the water.

3) Fluids flowing through the pores deposit natural mineral <u>cement</u>.

4) <u>Limestone</u> is a sedimentary rock made from <u>calcium carbonate</u> (see next page).

Metamorphic Rocks are Formed from Other Rocks

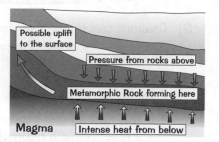

1) <u>Metamorphic rocks</u> are formed by the action of <u>heat and pressure</u> on <u>sedimentary</u> (or even <u>igneous</u>) rocks over <u>long periods</u> of time.

2) The <u>mineral structure</u> and <u>texture</u> may be different, but the chemical composition is often the same.

3) So long as the rocks don't actually <u>melt</u> they're classed as <u>metamorphic</u>. If they <u>melt</u> and turn to <u>magma</u>, they're <u>gone</u> (though they may eventually resurface as igneous rocks).

Marble is a Metamorphic Rock Formed from Limestone

1) Marble is another form of <u>calcium carbonate</u>.

2) Very high temperatures and pressures <u>break down</u> the limestone and it reforms as <u>small crystals</u>.

3) This gives marble a <u>more even texture</u> and makes it <u>much harder</u>.

Igneous Rock is Formed by Volcanic Activity

1) Volcanoes occur when <u>molten rock</u> (<u>magma</u>) from the <u>mantle</u> emerges through the Earth's crust.

2) Magma rises up (through the crust) and 'boils over' where it can — sometimes quite violently if the pressure is released suddenly.

When the molten rock is <u>below</u> the surface of the Earth it's called <u>magma</u> — but when it <u>erupts</u> from a volcano it's called <u>lava</u>.

3) <u>Igneous rocks</u> are formed when <u>magma</u> cools.

4) They contain various <u>different minerals</u> in <u>randomly arranged</u> interlocking <u>crystals</u> — this makes them very <u>hard</u>.

5) Granite is a <u>very hard</u> igneous rock (even harder than marble). It's ideal for <u>steps</u> and <u>buildings</u>.

Igneous rocks are real cool — or they're magma...

There are a few scientific terms on this page, but there's nothing too tricky to get your head round. Just remember that <u>limestone</u> is a <u>sedimentary rock</u>, <u>marble</u> is a <u>metamorphic rock</u> and <u>granite</u> is an <u>igneous rock</u>. And that's why granite is harder than marble, which is harder than limestone. Job's a good 'un.

Using Limestone

Limestone's often formed from sea shells, so you might not expect that it'd be useful as a building material...

Limestone is Mainly Calcium Carbonate

Limestone's quarried out of the ground — it's great for making into blocks for building with. Fine old buildings like cathedrals are often made purely from limestone blocks. It's pretty sturdy stuff, but don't go thinking it doesn't react with anything.

St Paul's Cathedral is made from limestone.

1) Limestone is mainly calcium carbonate — $CaCO_3$.
2) When it's heated it thermally decomposes to make calcium oxide and carbon dioxide.

> calcium carbonate → calcium oxide + carbon dioxide
> $$CaCO_{3(s)} \rightarrow CaO_{(s)} + CO_{2(g)}$$

Thermal decomposition is when one substance chemically changes into at least two new substances when it's heated.

- When magnesium, copper, zinc and sodium carbonates are heated, they decompose in the same way. E.g. magnesium carbonate → magnesium oxide + carbon dioxide (i.e. $MgCO_3 \rightarrow MgO + CO_2$)
- However, you might have difficulty doing some of these reactions in class — a Bunsen burner can't reach a high enough temperature to thermally decompose some carbonates of Group I metals.

3) Calcium carbonate also reacts with acid to make a calcium salt, carbon dioxide and water. E.g.:

> calcium carbonate + sulfuric acid → calcium sulfate + carbon dioxide + water
> $$CaCO_3 + H_2SO_4 \rightarrow CaSO_4 + CO_2 + H_2O$$

- The type of salt produced depends on the type of acid. For example, a reaction with hydrochloric acid would make a chloride (e.g. $CaCl_2$).   *This reaction means that limestone is damaged by acid rain (see p. 84).*
- Other carbonates that react with acids are magnesium, copper, zinc and sodium.

Calcium Oxide Reacts with Water to Produce Calcium Hydroxide

1) When you add water to calcium oxide you get calcium hydroxide.

> calcium oxide + water ⟶ calcium hydroxide   or $CaO + H_2O \longrightarrow Ca(OH)_2$

2) Calcium hydroxide is an alkali which can be used to neutralise acidic soil in fields (see p. 76). Powdered limestone can be used for this too, but the advantage of calcium hydroxide is that it works much faster.
3) Calcium hydroxide can also be used in a test for carbon dioxide. If you make a solution of calcium hydroxide in water (called limewater) and bubble gas through it, the solution will turn cloudy if there's carbon dioxide in the gas. The cloudiness is caused by the formation of calcium carbonate.

> calcium hydroxide + carbon dioxide → calcium carbonate + water
> $$Ca(OH)_2 + CO_2 \rightarrow CaCO_3 + H_2O$$

Limestone is Used to Make Other Useful Things Too

1) Powdered limestone is heated in a kiln with powdered clay to make cement.
2) Cement can be mixed with sand and water to make mortar. Mortar is the stuff you stick bricks together with. You can also add calcium hydroxide to mortar.
3) Or you can mix cement with sand and aggregate (water and gravel) to make concrete.

Limestone — a sea creature's cementery...

Wow. It sounds like you can achieve pretty much anything with limestone, possibly apart from a bouncy castle. I wonder what we'd be using instead if all those sea creatures hadn't died and conveniently become rock?

Using Limestone

Limestone is <u>useful</u> for all sorts of things, but it ain't all hunky-dory I'm afraid — tearing it out of the ground and making stuff from it causes quite a few <u>problems</u>...

Quarrying Limestone Makes a Right Mess of the Landscape

Digging limestone out of the ground can cause environmental problems.

1) For a start, it makes <u>huge ugly holes</u> which permanently change the landscape.

2) <u>Quarrying</u> processes, like blasting rocks apart with explosives, make lots of <u>noise</u> and <u>dust</u> in quiet, scenic areas.

3) Quarrying <u>destroys the habitats</u> of animals and birds.

4) The limestone needs to be <u>transported away</u> from the quarry — usually in lorries. This causes more noise and pollution.

5) Waste materials produce unsightly <u>tips</u>.

Making Stuff from Limestone Causes Pollution Too

1) <u>Cement factories</u> make a lot of <u>dust</u>, which can cause <u>breathing problems</u> for some people.

2) <u>Energy</u> is needed to produce cement and quicklime. The energy is likely to come from burning <u>fossil fuels</u>, which causes pollution.

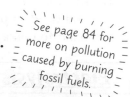

See page 84 for more on pollution caused by burning fossil fuels.

But on the Plus Side...

1) Limestone provides things that people want — like <u>houses</u> and <u>roads</u>. Chemicals used in making <u>dyes</u>, <u>paints</u> and <u>medicines</u> also come from limestone.

2) Limestone products are used to <u>neutralise acidic soil</u>. Acidity in lakes and rivers caused by <u>acid rain</u> is also <u>neutralised</u> by limestone products.

3) Limestone is also used in power station chimneys to <u>neutralise sulfur dioxide</u>, which is a cause of acid rain.

4) The quarry and associated businesses provide <u>jobs</u> for people and bring more money into the <u>local economy</u>. This can lead to <u>local improvements</u> in transport, roads, recreation facilities and health.

5) Once quarrying is complete, <u>landscaping</u> and <u>restoration</u> of the area is normally required as part of the planning permission.

Limestone Products Have Advantages and Disadvantages

Limestone and concrete (made from cement) are used as <u>building materials</u>. In some cases they're <u>perfect</u> for the job, but in other cases they're a bit of a compromise.

1) Limestone is <u>widely available</u> and is <u>cheaper</u> than granite or marble. It's also a fairly easy rock to <u>cut</u>.

2) Some limestone is more <u>hard-wearing</u> than marble, but it still looks <u>attractive</u>.

3) Concrete can be poured into <u>moulds</u> to make blocks or panels that can be joined together. It's a <u>very quick and cheap</u> way of constructing buildings — <u>and it shows</u>... — concrete has got to be the most <u>hideously unattractive</u> building material ever known.

4) Limestone, concrete and cement <u>don't rot</u> when they get wet like wood does. They can't be gnawed away by <u>insects</u> or <u>rodents</u> either. And to top it off, they're <u>fire-resistant</u> too.

5) Concrete <u>doesn't corrode</u> like lots of metals do. It does have a fairly <u>low tensile strength</u> though, and can crack. If it's <u>reinforced</u> with steel bars it'll be much stronger.

Tough revision here — this stuff's rock hard...

There's a <u>downside</u> to everything, including using limestone — ripping open huge quarries definitely <u>spoils the countryside</u>. But you have to find a <u>balance</u> between the environmental and ecological factors and the economic and social factors — is it worth keeping the countryside pristine if it means loads of people have nowhere to live because there's no stuff available to build houses with?

Salt

And now for a page all about <u>sodium chloride</u> (<u>NaCl</u>), or <u>salt</u> as it's known to its friends. In <u>hot countries</u> they get salt by pouring <u>sea water</u> into big flat open tanks and letting the <u>Sun</u> evaporate the water, leaving the salt behind. This is no good in a <u>cold country</u> like <u>Britain</u> though — there isn't enough sunshine.

Salt is Mined from Underneath Cheshire

1) In <u>Britain</u> salt is extracted from <u>underground deposits</u> left <u>millions of years</u> ago when <u>ancient seas</u> evaporated. There are huge deposits of this <u>rock salt</u> under <u>Cheshire</u>.

2) Rock salt is a mixture of <u>salt</u> and <u>impurities</u>. It's drilled, blasted and dug out and brought to the surface using machinery.

3) It can also be mined by <u>pumping hot water underground</u>. The <u>salt dissolves</u> and the salt solution is <u>forced to the surface</u> by the pressure of the water — this is called <u>solution mining</u>.

4) When the mining is finished, it's important to <u>fill in the holes</u> in the ground. If not, the land could <u>collapse</u> and <u>slide into the holes</u> — this is called <u>subsidence</u>.

5) Rock salt can be used in its <u>raw state</u> on roads to stop ice forming, or the salt can be separated out and used to preserve or enhance the flavour in <u>food</u> or for <u>making chemicals</u>. If salt's going to be used to make chemicals, usually the first thing they do is electrolyse it using the <u>chlor-alkali process</u>.

Electrolysis of Brine Gives Hydrogen, Chlorine and NaOH

<u>Concentrated brine</u> (sodium chloride solution) is <u>electrolysed</u> industrially using a set-up a bit like this one:

The electrodes are made of an <u>inert</u> material — this is so they won't react with the <u>electrolyte</u> or the <u>products</u> of the electrolysis.

There are <u>three</u> useful products:

a) <u>Hydrogen gas</u> is given off at the (–ve) cathode.

b) <u>Chlorine gas</u> is given off at the (+ve) anode.

c) <u>Sodium hydroxide</u> (NaOH) is formed from the ions left in solution.

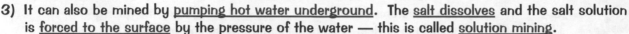

These are collected and used to make all sorts of things (see below).

The Half-Equations — Make Sure the Electrons Balance

The sodium chloride solution contains <u>four different ions</u>: Na^+, OH^-, Cl^- and H^+.

1) At the <u>cathode</u>, two hydrogen ions accept one electron each to become <u>one hydrogen molecule</u>.

$$\text{Cathode: } 2H^+ + 2e^- \rightarrow H_2$$

2) At the <u>anode</u>, two chloride (Cl^-) ions lose one electron each to become <u>one chlorine molecule</u>.

$$\text{Anode: } 2Cl^- - 2e^- \rightarrow Cl_2$$

<u>Oxidation</u> is the <u>loss of electrons</u>, and <u>reduction</u> is the <u>gain of electrons</u>. So the reaction at the <u>anode</u> is an <u>oxidation reaction</u>, and the reaction at the <u>cathode</u> is a <u>reduction reaction</u>.

The Electrolysis of Brine is Done by the Chlor-alkali Industry

1) The <u>products</u> of the chlor-alkali process are used for all kinds of things.

2) For example, the <u>hydrogen</u> gas is used to make <u>ammonia</u> (in the Haber process) and <u>margarine</u>.

3) The <u>chlorine</u> is used to <u>disinfect water</u>, to make <u>plastics</u> (e.g. <u>PVC</u>), <u>solvents</u> or <u>hydrochloric acid</u>.

4) The <u>sodium hydroxide</u> is used to make <u>soap</u>, or can be reacted with <u>chlorine</u> to make <u>household bleach</u>.

5) All of these uses of the <u>products</u> of the electrolysis of brine makes the chlor-alkali industry very important to the economy — lots of <u>new products</u> can be made and lots of <u>jobs</u> are created.

Salt — it's not just for chips any more...

Boy, that's a lot to take in about salt — read it through a <u>couple of times</u> if it was all a bit much first time round.

Chlorination

It's easy to take water for granted... turn on the tap, and there it is — nice clean water, thanks to chlorination.

Chlorine is Used in Water Treatment

1) In the UK, drinking water is treated to make it safe. Chlorine is an important part of water treatment:

- It kills disease-causing microorganisms.
- If the correct amount is added, enough chlorine remains in the water to kill bacteria that might enter the supply after treatment, further down the pipes.
- It prevents the growth of algae, gets rid of bad tastes and smells, and removes discolouration caused by organic compounds.

2) Not everyone has clean water. The World Health Organisation (WHO) and the United Nations estimated in 1995 that a billion people in the world don't have access to clean drinking water.

3) In many developing countries it's very expensive to get clean water. Some people in developing countries live in isolated rural areas, and have to walk miles to get any water at all.

4) It's a fact that the biggest increases in life expectancy in most countries' histories (including the UK's) are linked with the ability to supply clean water — not medicine or anything like that. It's that vital. In November 2004 the WHO said that improving drinking water quality could reduce diarrhoeal disease by up to 40%. Currently, 1.8 million people each year die from waterborne diseases like cholera, typhoid and dysentery because they have to drink dirty water.

Chlorine Can be Made from Hydrogen Chloride

1) Chlorine is found in lots of substances such as salt (sodium chloride) and hydrogen chloride (HCl), but it has to be separated out of these compounds before it can be used to treat drinking water.

2) This is because the properties of compounds are different from the properties of the elements from which they're made.

3) So although chlorine will kill microorganisms in water, compounds containing chlorine may not. In fact, adding sodium chloride to water will give you nothing more than salty water — not ideal for drinking.

4) Chlorine can be made by electrolysing brine (see p.72) or by oxidation of hydrogen chloride:

$$4HCl + O_2 \rightarrow 2Cl_2 + 2H_2O$$

There are Disadvantages to Chlorinating Water

Chlorination can have negative impacts on health:

- Water contains a variety of organic compounds, e.g. from the decomposition of plants. Chlorine reacts with these compounds to form chlorinated hydrocarbons, many of which are carcinogenic (cancer-causing). However, this increased cancer risk is small compared to the risks from untreated water — a cholera epidemic, say, could kill thousands of people.
- Chlorine gas is very harmful if it's breathed in — it irritates the respiratory system. Liquid chlorine on the skin or eyes causes severe chemical burns. Accidents involving chlorine during the chlorination process could be really serious, or fatal.

Some people object to the use of chlorine in drinking water. They feel that as we don't get a choice about having our water chlorinated it is in effect forced 'mass medication'.

Too much chlorine in swimming baths is a bit of a pain...

...but stinging eyes is a small price to pay for killing those germs. Another thing that's a small price to pay is the time spent learning this page, when you consider how smart it'll make you look and feel. And really, you'd probably regret wasting the day watching daytime TV anyway. There's never anything good on...

Impacts of Chemical Production

Time to look at some aspects of chemical production — including the times when things go wrong...

Lots of Products Can be Made Using Chemistry

A large number of chemicals are used in industry to make a wide range of products
These products include:

- <u>drugs</u>,
- chemicals such as <u>paints</u> and <u>dyes</u>,
- chemicals used in <u>industry</u>, e.g. <u>acids</u> and <u>alkalis</u>,
- chemicals used in the <u>home</u>, e.g. <u>bleach</u>, <u>toiletries</u>,

- <u>agricultural</u> chemicals, e.g. fertilisers,
- <u>plastics</u>,
- <u>metals</u>,
- <u>fuels</u>.

As there are so <u>many</u> chemicals, they <u>can't</u> all be <u>tested</u> as thoroughly as we'd like. This means there's <u>not enough data</u> to tell whether some chemicals are a risk to the environment or public health.

Some Chemicals Stay in the Environment for a Long Time

Toxic chemicals will stay in the environment if they're not <u>broken down</u>. Chemicals that end up in <u>waterways</u> or are eaten by <u>animals</u> may be carried over <u>long distances</u> and so spread over a <u>large area</u> as the water and animals move from place to place. They may also be passed along the <u>food chain</u> and cause harm to other animals and even <u>humans</u>. For example:

1) Chemicals such as <u>pesticides</u> are sprayed onto crops to kill the creatures that <u>damage</u> them.

2) They also tend to be <u>toxic</u> to creatures that aren't pests and there's a danger of the poison <u>passing on</u> through the food chain to other animals. There's even a risk that they could harm <u>humans</u>.

The build-up of toxic chemicals in the food chain is shown by the case of <u>otters</u>, which were almost <u>wiped out</u> in parts of southern England by a chemical called <u>DDT</u> in the early 1960s. The diagram shows how the pesticide ends up in the <u>otter</u>. DDT can't be <u>excreted</u>, so it <u>accumulates</u> and the <u>otter</u> ends up with <u>a lot</u> of the <u>DDT</u> collected by the other animals.

③ Each little tiny animal eats lots of small plants ⑤ Each eel eats lots of small fish

① Insecticide seeps into the river ② Small water plants take up a little insecticide ④ Each small fish eats lots of tiny animals ⑥ Each otter eats lots of eels

Plasticisers can Harm the Environment

1) PVC (polyvinyl chloride) is a very <u>common polymer</u> that contains <u>carbon</u>, <u>hydrogen</u> and <u>chlorine</u>. <u>Plasticisers</u> (see page 90) called PCBs used to be used to make PVC that had more heat and fire resistance for use in <u>electrical wiring</u>.

2) The PCBs can <u>leach out</u> of the plastic and into <u>water sources</u>. The PCBs are <u>toxic</u>, and in the same way as pesticides in water, can accumulate in animals like fish and end up being eaten by humans.

DDT, PVC, PCBs — NMP (No More Please)...

Impacts of Chemical Production — betcha knew straight off that we weren't going to be covering positive impacts. It's always the negative ones. What is it with that — like revision isn't depressing enough. ☹

Hazard Symbols, Acids and Bases

Well done, you've made it this far through the book. I hope you had a good journey and didn't get too lost along the way. My name is Ermintrude and I'll be your guide to the world of acids.

You Need to Learn the Common Hazard Symbols

Lots of the chemicals you'll meet in Chemistry can be bad for you or dangerous in some way. That's why the chemical containers will normally have symbols on them to tell you what the dangers are. Understanding these hazard symbols means that you'll be able to use suitable safe-working procedures in the lab.

Oxidising
Provides oxygen which allows other materials to burn more fiercely.
Example: Liquid oxygen.

Harmful
Like toxic but not quite as dangerous.
Example: Copper sulfate.

Highly Flammable
Catches fire easily.
Example: Petrol.

Irritant
Not corrosive but can cause reddening or blistering of the skin.
Examples: Bleach, children, etc.

Toxic
Can cause death either by swallowing, breathing in, or absorption through the skin.
Example: Hydrogen cyanide.

Corrosive
Attacks and destroys living tissues, including eyes and skin.
Example: Concentrated sulfuric acid.

Substances can be Acids, Bases or Neutral

An acid is a substance with a pH less than 7. A base is a substance with a pH greater than 7. An alkali is a base that dissolves in water.

There's a sliding scale from very strong acid to very strong base, with neutral water in the middle.

These are the colours you get when you add Universal indicator to an acid or an alkali.

pH numbers
0 1 2 3 4 5 6 7 8 9 10 11 12 13 14

ACIDS ← → ALKALIS

car battery acid, stomach acid
vinegar, lemon juice
acid rain
normal rain
NEUTRAL pure water
washing-up liquid
pancreatic juice
soap powder
ammonia
oven cleaner
caustic soda

An Indicator is a Dye That Changes Colour

1) The dye in an indicator changes colour depending on the pH of a substance.

2) Universal indicator is a combination of dyes. It changes colour gradually as the pH changes.

3) It's very useful for estimating the pH of a solution. You just add a drop of the indicator to your solution, then compare the colour it turns to a colour chart (like the one above) to work out the pH.

4) Some indicators change colour suddenly at a particular pH.
E.g. phenolphthalein changes suddenly from colourless to pink as the pH rises above 8.

This'll give you a firm base for Chemistry...

There's no getting away from acids and bases in Chemistry, or even in real life. They are everywhere — acids are found in loads of foods, like vinegar and fruit, and as food flavourings and preservatives, whilst alkalis (particularly sodium hydroxide) are used to help make all sorts of things from soaps to ceramics.

Reactions of Acids

When you mix an <u>acid</u> and a <u>base</u>, exactly what you end up with depends on which acid and base you use...

Metal Oxides and Metal Hydroxides are Bases

1) Some <u>metal oxides</u> and <u>metal hydroxides</u> dissolve in <u>water</u>. These soluble compounds are <u>alkalis</u>.

2) Even <u>bases</u> that <u>won't dissolve</u> in water will still react with acids.

3) So, all <u>metal oxides</u> and <u>metal hydroxides</u> react with <u>acids</u> to form a <u>salt</u> and <u>water</u>.

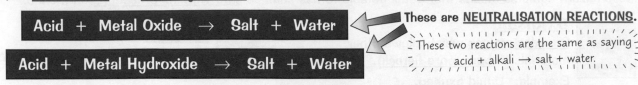

| Acid | + | Metal Oxide | → | Salt | + | Water |

| Acid | + | Metal Hydroxide | → | Salt | + | Water |

These are **NEUTRALISATION REACTIONS**.

These two reactions are the same as saying acid + alkali → salt + water.

hydrochloric acid	+	copper oxide	→	copper chloride	+	water
$2HCl$	+	CuO	→	$CuCl_2$	+	H_2O
sulfuric acid	+	potassium hydroxide	→	potassium sulfate	+	water
H_2SO_4	+	$2KOH$	→	K_2SO_4	+	$2H_2O$
nitric acid	+	sodium hydroxide	→	sodium nitrate	+	water
HNO_3	+	$NaOH$	→	$NaNO_3$	+	H_2O
phosphoric acid	+	sodium hydroxide	→	sodium phosphate	+	water
H_3PO_4	+	$3NaOH$	→	Na_3PO_4	+	$3H_2O$

Acids and Carbonates Produce Carbon Dioxide

These are very like the ones above — they just produce <u>carbon dioxide</u> as well.

| Acid | + | Carbonate | → | Salt | + | Water | + | Carbon dioxide |

hydrochloric acid	+	sodium carbonate	→	sodium chloride	+	water	+	carbon dioxide
$2HCl$	+	Na_2CO_3	→	$2NaCl$	+	H_2O	+	CO_2
sulfuric acid	+	calcium carbonate	→	calcium sulfate	+	water	+	carbon dioxide
H_2SO_4	+	$CaCO_3$	→	$CaSO_4$	+	H_2O	+	CO_2
phosphoric acid	+	sodium carbonate	→	sodium phosphate	+	water	+	carbon dioxide
$2H_3PO_4$	+	$3Na_2CO_3$	→	$2Na_3PO_4$	+	$3H_2O$	+	$3CO_2$

Acids and Ammonia Produce Ammonium Salts

And lastly...

| Acid | + | Ammonia | → | Ammonium salt |

If you're not sure how formulas or balanced equations work, have a look back at pages 55-56.

hydrochloric acid	+	ammonia	→	ammonium chloride
HCl	+	NH_3	→	NH_4Cl
sulfuric acid	+	ammonia	→	ammonium sulfate
H_2SO_4	+	$2NH_3$	→	$(NH_4)_2SO_4$
nitric acid	+	ammonia	→	ammonium nitrate
HNO_3	+	NH_3	→	NH_4NO_3

Acid + Revision → Insomnia Cure...

An acid and a metal oxide get together and fall in love. They decide to settle down and start a family. They have two lovely children named salt and water. The end. Ah, what a lovely story — who says science isn't touching?

The Evolution of the Atmosphere

The atmosphere wasn't always like it is today. It's <u>gradually evolved</u> over billions of years and <u>we</u> have evolved with it. All very slowly. Here's one theory for how the first 4.5 billion years have gone:

Phase 1 — Volcanoes Gave Out Steam and CO₂

The First Billion Years

1) The Earth's surface was originally <u>molten</u> for many millions of years. Any atmosphere <u>boiled away</u>.

2) Eventually it cooled and a <u>thin crust</u> formed, but <u>volcanoes</u> kept erupting, releasing gases from <u>inside the Earth</u>. This '<u>degassing</u>' released mainly <u>carbon dioxide</u>, but also <u>steam</u> and <u>ammonia</u>.

3) When things eventually settled down, the early atmosphere was <u>mostly CO₂</u> and water vapour (the water vapour later <u>condensed</u> to form the <u>oceans</u>). There was very little oxygen.

<u>Holiday report</u>: Not a nice place to be. Take strong walking boots and a good coat.

Phase 2 — Green Plants Evolved and Produced Oxygen

The Next Two Billion Years

<u>Holiday Report</u>: A bit slimy underfoot. Take wellies and a lot of suncream.

1) A lot of the early CO_2 <u>dissolved</u> into the oceans.

2) <u>Green plants</u> evolved over most of the Earth. As they photosynthesised, they <u>removed CO₂</u> and <u>produced O₂</u>.

3) Thanks to the plants the amount of O_2 in the air gradually <u>built up</u> and much of the CO_2 eventually got <u>locked up</u> in <u>fossil fuels</u> and <u>sedimentary rocks</u> (more about this on p.85).

4) <u>Nitrogen gas</u> (<u>N_2</u>) was put into the atmosphere in two ways — it was formed by ammonia reacting with oxygen, and was released by denitrifying bacteria.

5) N_2 isn't very <u>reactive</u>. So the amount of N_2 in the atmosphere <u>increased</u>, because it was being <u>made</u> but not <u>broken down</u>.

Phase 3 — Ozone Layer Allows Evolution of Complex Animals

The Last Billion Years or so

Nice safe OZONE, O₃

1) The build-up of <u>oxygen</u> in the atmosphere <u>killed off</u> early organisms that couldn't tolerate it.

2) But it did allow the <u>evolution</u> of more <u>complex</u> organisms that <u>made use</u> of the oxygen.

3) The oxygen also created the <u>ozone layer</u> (O_3), which <u>blocked</u> harmful rays from the Sun and <u>enabled</u> even <u>more complex</u> organisms to evolve.

4) There is virtually <u>no CO₂</u> left now.

<u>Holiday report</u>: A nice place to be. Get there before the crowds ruin it.

Today's Atmosphere is Just Right for Us

The <u>present composition</u> of Earth's atmosphere is:

78% nitrogen, 21% oxygen and 0.04% carbon dioxide
There are also: 1) Varying amounts of <u>water vapour</u>, 2) And <u>noble gases</u> (mainly argon).

4 billion years ago, it was a whole other world...

It's amazing how much the atmosphere of Planet Earth has changed. The <u>climate change</u> that we're all talking about nowadays is small beer in comparison (though it's massively important to <u>us</u> of course).

Life and the Atmosphere Today

Life on Earth began <u>billions of years</u> ago, but there's no way of knowing for definite how it all started.

Primordial Soup is Just One Theory of How Life was Formed

1) The primordial soup theory states that billions of years ago, the Earth's <u>atmosphere</u> was rich in <u>nitrogen</u>, <u>hydrogen</u>, <u>ammonia</u> and <u>methane</u>.

2) <u>Lightning</u> struck, causing a chemical reaction between the gases, resulting in the formation of <u>amino acids</u>.

3) The amino acids collected in a '<u>primordial soup</u>' — a body of water out of which life gradually crawled.

4) The amino acids gradually combined to produce <u>organic matter</u> which eventually evolved into simple <u>living organisms</u>.

5) In the 1950s, <u>Miller and Urey</u> carried out an experiment to prove this theory. They sealed the gases in their apparatus, heated them and applied an electrical charge for a week.

6) They found that <u>amino acids were made</u>, but not as many as there are on Earth. This suggests the theory could be along the <u>right lines</u>, but isn't quite right.

The Earth Has All the Resources Humans Need

The Earth's crust, oceans and atmosphere are the <u>ultimate source</u> of minerals and resources — we can get everything we need from them. For example, we can <u>fractionally distil air</u> to get a variety of products (e.g. nitrogen and oxygen) for use in <u>industry</u>:

1) Air is <u>filtered</u> to remove dust.

2) It's then <u>cooled</u> to around <u>-200 °C</u> and becomes a liquid.

3) During cooling <u>water vapour</u> condenses and is removed.

4) <u>Carbon dioxide</u> freezes and is removed.

5) The liquified air then enters the fractionating column and is <u>heated</u> slowly.

6) The remaining gases are separated by <u>fractional distillation</u>. Oxygen and argon come out together so <u>another</u> column is used to separate them.

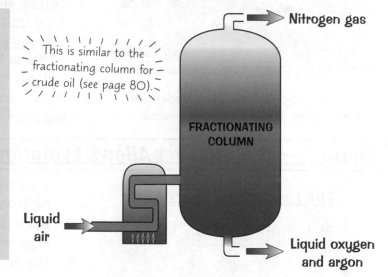

This is similar to the fractionating column for crude oil (see page 80).

Nitrogen gas

FRACTIONATING COLUMN

Liquid air

Liquid oxygen and argon

Increasing Carbon Dioxide Level Affects the Climate and the Oceans

<u>Burning fossil fuels</u> releases CO_2 — and as the world's become more industrialised, more fossil fuels have been burnt in power stations and in car engines. This CO_2 is thought to be altering our planet...

1) An increase in carbon dioxide is causing <u>global warming</u> — a type of <u>climate change</u> (see page 87).

2) The oceans are a <u>natural store</u> of CO_2 — they absorb it from the atmosphere. However the extra CO_2 we're releasing is making them too <u>acidic</u>. This is bad news for <u>coral</u> and <u>shellfish</u>, and also means that in the future they won't be able to absorb any more carbon dioxide.

Waiter, waiter, there's a primate in my soup...

No-one was around billions of years ago, so our theories about how life formed are just that — theories. We're also still <u>guessing</u> about the exact effects of global warming on things like the oceans.

Revision Summary for Section 5

The only way that you can tell if you've learned this section properly is to test yourself. Try these questions, and if there's something you don't know, it means you need to go back and learn it. Even if it's all those equations for the reactions of acids. Don't miss any questions out — you don't get a choice about what comes up on the exam so you need to be sure that you've learnt it all.

1) What can be found beneath the Earth's crust?

2) A geologist places a very heavy marker on the seabed in the middle of the Atlantic ocean. She records the marker's position over a period of four years. The geologist finds that the marker moves in a straight-line away from its original position. Her measurements are shown in the graph on the right.

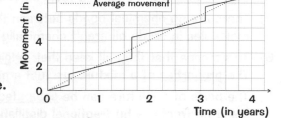

a) Explain the process that has caused the marker to move.

b)*What is the marker's average movement each year?

c)*On average, how many years will it take for the marker to move 7 cm?

3) Why can't scientists accurately predict volcanoes and earthquakes?

4) Describe the evidence that backs up Wegener's theory of continental drift.

5) Draw a diagram to show how metamorphic rocks form.

6) Give an example of a metamorphic rock and say what the material it formed from is.

7) Which material is hardest, granite, limestone or marble?

8) Write down the symbol equation showing the thermal decomposition of limestone.

9) What products are produced when limestone reacts with an acid?

10) What is calcium hydroxide used for?

11) Name three building materials made from limestone.

12) Plans to develop a limestone quarry and a cement factory on some hills next to your town are announced. Describe the views that the following might have:

    a) dog owners   b) a mother of young children

    c) the owner of a cafe   d) a beetle

13) Describe two ways that salt can be mined.

14) What are the three main products of brine electrolysis?

15) Why is chlorine added to water supplies?

16) What are chlorinated hydrocarbons?

17) What happens when chemicals like DDT get into rivers?

18) Give the meaning of this symbol:

19) Do acids have a pH greater or less than 7?

20)* Write a word equation for the reaction between phosphoric acid and potassium hydroxide.

21)* Write a balanced symbol equation for the reaction between sulfuric acid and sodium carbonate.

22) Write a balanced symbol equation for the reaction between nitric acid and ammonia.

23) 3 billion years ago, the Earth's atmosphere was mostly CO_2. Where did this CO_2 come from?

24) Today, there's mostly O_2 and N_2 in the Earth's atmosphere. What process produced the O_2? What two processes produced the N_2?

25) What is meant by 'primordial soup'?

26) Why do we fractionally distil air?

27) The burning of fossils fuels is causing a rise in the level of carbon dioxide in the atmosphere. How is this affecting the oceans and the climate?

* Answers on page 140

Section 5 — Chemicals and Rocks

Fractional Distillation of Crude Oil

Crude oil is formed from the buried remains of plants and animals — it's a <u>fossil fuel</u>. Over millions of years, the remains turn to crude oil, which can be extracted by drilling and pumping.

Crude Oil is a Mixture of Hydrocarbons

1) A mixture consists of <u>two</u> (or more) elements or compounds that <u>aren't chemically bonded</u> to each other.

2) <u>Crude oil</u> is a <u>mixture</u> of many different compounds. <u>Most</u> of the compounds are <u>hydrocarbon</u> molecules.

3) <u>Hydrocarbons</u> are basically <u>fuels</u> such as petrol and diesel. They're made of just <u>carbon</u> and <u>hydrogen</u>.

4) There are <u>no chemical bonds</u> between the different parts of a mixture, so the different hydrocarbon molecules in crude oil <u>aren't</u> chemically bonded to one another.

5) This means that they all keep their <u>original properties</u>, such as their condensing points. The <u>properties</u> of a mixture are just a <u>mixture</u> of the properties of the <u>separate parts</u>.

6) The parts of a mixture can be <u>separated</u> out by <u>physical methods</u>, e.g. crude oil can be split up into its separate <u>fractions</u> by <u>fractional distillation</u>. Each fraction contains molecules with a <u>similar number of carbon atoms</u> to each other (see next page).

Crude Oil is Split into Separate Groups of Hydrocarbons

The <u>fractionating column</u> works <u>continuously</u>, with heated crude oil piped in at the <u>bottom</u>. The vaporised oil rises up the column and the various <u>fractions</u> are <u>constantly tapped off</u> at the different levels where they <u>condense</u>.

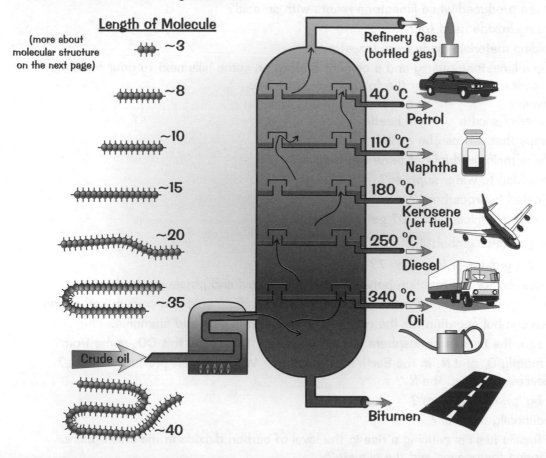

Length of Molecule
(more about molecular structure on the next page)

~3
~8 — 40 °C — Petrol
~10 — 110 °C — Naphtha
~15 — 180 °C — Kerosene (Jet fuel)
~20 — 250 °C — Diesel
~35 — 340 °C — Oil
~40

Refinery Gas (bottled gas)

Crude oil

Bitumen

Crude oil — it's always cracking dirty jokes...

It's amazing what you get from buried dead stuff. But it has had a <u>few hundred million years</u> with high <u>temperature</u> and <u>pressure</u> to get into the useful state it's in now. So if we use it all, we're going to have to wait an awful <u>long time</u> for more to form. <u>No one knows</u> exactly when oil will run out, but some scientists reckon that it could be within <u>this century</u>. The thing is, <u>technology</u> is advancing all the time, so one day it's likely that we'll be able to extract oil that's too difficult and expensive to extract at the moment.

Properties and Uses of Crude Oil

The different fractions of crude oil have different properties, and it's all down to their structure.

Crude Oil is Mostly Alkanes

1) All the fractions of crude oil are hydrocarbons called alkanes.
2) Alkanes are made up of chains of carbon atoms surrounded by hydrogen atoms. ⟹
3) Different alkanes have chains of different lengths.
4) The first four alkanes are methane (natural gas), ethane, propane and butane.

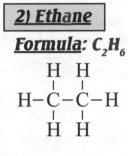

1) Methane
Formula: CH_4

$$H-C-H$$ (natural gas)

2) Ethane
Formula: C_2H_6

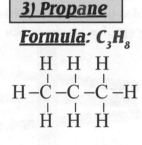

3) Propane
Formula: C_3H_8

4) Butane
Formula: C_4H_{10}

Each straight line shows a covalent bond.

5) Carbon atoms form four bonds and hydrogen atoms only form one bond. The diagrams above show that all the atoms have formed bonds with as many other atoms as they can — this means they're saturated.

6) Alkanes all have the general formula C_nH_{2n+2}. So if an alkane has 5 carbons, it's got to have $(2\times5)+2 = 12$ hydrogens.

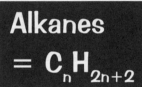

Alkanes $= C_nH_{2n+2}$

Learn the Basic Trends:

1) The shorter the molecules, the more runny the hydrocarbon is — that is, the less viscous (gloopy) it is.

2) The shorter the molecules, the more volatile they are. "More volatile" means they turn into a gas at a lower temperature. So, the shorter the molecules, the lower the temperature at which that fraction vaporises or condenses — and the lower its boiling point.

3) Also, the shorter the molecules, the more flammable (easier to ignite) the hydrocarbon is.

The Uses Of Hydrocarbons Depend on their Properties

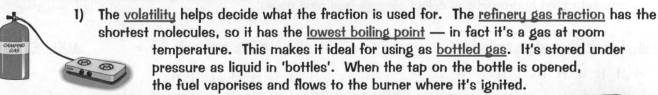

1) The volatility helps decide what the fraction is used for. The refinery gas fraction has the shortest molecules, so it has the lowest boiling point — in fact it's a gas at room temperature. This makes it ideal for using as bottled gas. It's stored under pressure as liquid in 'bottles'. When the tap on the bottle is opened, the fuel vaporises and flows to the burner where it's ignited.

2) The petrol fraction has longer molecules, so it has a higher boiling point. Petrol is a liquid which is ideal for storing in the fuel tank of a car. It can flow to the engine where it's easily vaporised to mix with the air before it is ignited.

3) The viscosity also helps decide how the hydrocarbons are used. The really gloopy, viscous hydrocarbons are used for lubricating engine parts and for covering roads.

Alkane ya if you don't learn this...

So short-chain hydrocarbons are less viscous, more volatile and easier to ignite than longer-chain hydrocarbons. If you learn the properties of short-chain hydrocarbons, you should be able to work out the properties of longer-chain ones. These properties decide how they're used. In the real world there's more demand for stuff like petrol than there is for long gloopy hydrocarbons like bitumen — I guess there's only so many roads that need covering.

Cracking Crude Oil

After the distillation of crude oil (see page 80), you've still got both short and long hydrocarbons, just not all mixed together. But there's <u>more demand</u> for some products, like <u>petrol</u>, than for others.

Cracking — Splitting Up Long-Chain Hydrocarbons

1) <u>Long-chain</u> hydrocarbons form <u>thick</u> gloopy liquids like <u>tar</u> which aren't all that useful.

2) The process called <u>cracking</u> turns them into <u>shorter</u> molecules which are <u>much</u> more useful.

3) <u>Cracking</u> is a form of <u>thermal decomposition</u>, which just means <u>breaking</u> molecules down into <u>simpler</u> molecules by <u>heating</u> them.

4) A lot of the longer molecules produced from fractional distillation are <u>cracked</u> into smaller ones because there's <u>more demand</u> for products like <u>petrol</u> than for diesel or lubricating oil.

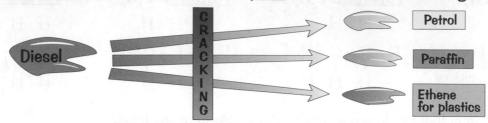

...by Passing Vapour Over a Hot Catalyst

1) <u>Cracking</u> is a <u>thermal decomposition</u> reaction — <u>breaking molecules down</u> by <u>heating</u> them.

2) The first step is to <u>heat</u> the long-chain hydrocarbon to <u>vaporise</u> it (turn it into a gas).

3) Then the <u>vapour</u> is passed over a <u>powdered catalyst</u> at a temperature of about <u>400 °C – 700 °C</u>.

4) <u>Aluminium oxide</u> is the catalyst used.

5) The <u>long-chain</u> molecules <u>split apart</u> or "crack" on the <u>surface</u> of the specks of catalyst.

Vaporised kerosene → Aluminium oxide → Octane + Ethene

~ An alternative way of cracking long-chain hydrocarbons is to mix the vapour with steam at a very high temperature. ~

6) Most of the <u>products</u> of cracking are <u>alkanes</u> (see previous page) and unsaturated hydrocarbons called <u>alkenes</u> (see next page)...

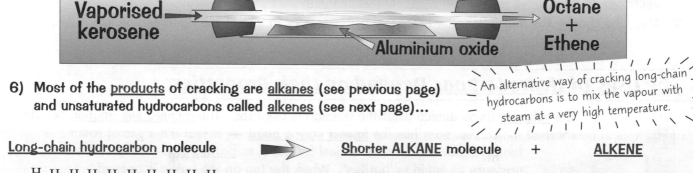

Long-chain hydrocarbon molecule	Shorter ALKANE molecule +	ALKENE
E.g. kerosene (ten C atoms) (Too much of this in crude oil)	octane (eight C atoms) (useful for petrol)	ethene (two C atoms) (for making plastics)

Get cracking — there's a lot to learn...

Crude oil is <u>useful stuff</u>, there's no doubt about it. But using it is not without its problems (see page 85 for more about fuels). For example, oil is shipped around the planet, which can lead to <u>slicks</u> if there's an accident. Also, burning oil is thought to cause <u>climate change</u>, <u>acid rain</u> and <u>global dimming</u>. Oil is going to start <u>running out</u> one day, which will lead to big difficulties.

Alkenes and Ethanol

Alkenes are very useful. You can use them to make all sorts of stuff.

Alkenes Have a C=C Double Bond

1) Alkenes are hydrocarbons which have a <u>double bond</u> between two of the <u>carbon</u> atoms in their chain.

2) They are known as <u>unsaturated</u> because they <u>can make more bonds</u> — the double bond can open up, allowing the two carbon atoms to bond with other atoms.

3) The first two alkenes are <u>ethene</u> (with two carbon atoms) and <u>propene</u> (three Cs).

4) <u>All alkenes</u> have the general formula: C_nH_{2n} — they have twice as many hydrogens as carbons.

1) Ethene
Formula: C_2H_4

$$\begin{array}{ccc} H & & H \\ \diagdown & & \diagup \\ C & = & C \\ \diagup & & \diagdown \\ H & & H \end{array}$$

Carbon atoms always make four bonds, but hydrogen atoms only make one.

This is a double bond — so each carbon atom is still making four bonds.

2) Propene
Formula: C_3H_6

$$\begin{array}{ccccc} & H & & H & \\ & | & & | & \\ H - & C & - & C & = C \diagup^H \\ & | & & & \diagdown_H \\ & H & & & \end{array}$$

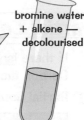

bromine water + alkene — decolourised

5) You can test for an alkene by adding the substance to <u>bromine water</u>. An alkene will <u>decolourise</u> the bromine water, turning it from <u>orange</u> to <u>colourless</u>. This is because the <u>double bond</u> has <u>opened</u> up and formed bonds with the bromine.

Ethene Can Be Reacted with Steam to Produce Ethanol

1) <u>Ethene</u> (C_2H_4) can be <u>hydrated</u> with <u>steam</u> (H_2O) in the presence of a catalyst to make <u>ethanol</u>.

2) At the moment this is a <u>cheap</u> process, because ethene's fairly <u>cheap</u> and <u>not much</u> of it is <u>wasted</u>.

3) The trouble is that ethene's produced from crude oil, which is a <u>non-renewable</u> resource that could start running out fairly soon. This means using ethene to make ethanol will become very <u>expensive</u>.

Ethanol Can Also Be Produced from Renewable Resources

The alcohol in beer and wine, etc. isn't made from ethene — it's made by <u>fermentation</u>.

1) The raw material for fermentation is <u>sugar</u>. This is converted into <u>ethanol</u> using yeast.

   The <u>word equation</u> for this is: | sugar → carbon dioxide + ethanol

2) This process needs a <u>lower temperature</u> and <u>simpler equipment</u> than when using ethene.

3) Another advantage is that the raw material is a <u>renewable resource</u>. <u>Sugar</u> is <u>grown</u> as a major crop in several parts of the world, including many poorer countries.

4) The ethanol produced this way can also be used as quite a cheap <u>fuel</u> in countries which don't have oil reserves for making <u>petrol</u> (see page 88 for more).

5) There are <u>disadvantages</u> though. The ethanol you get from this process <u>isn't very concentrated</u>, so if you want to increase its strength you have to <u>distil</u> it (as in whisky distilleries). It also needs to be <u>purified</u>.

Make ethanol — not war...

Don't get alkenes confused with alkanes — that one letter makes all the difference. Alkenes have a C=C bond, alkanes don't. The first parts of their names are the same though — "<u>eth-</u>" means "<u>two</u> C atoms", "<u>prop-</u>" means "<u>three</u> C atoms". And remember — alkenes decolourise <u>bromine water</u> and alkanes don't.

Burning Fuels

We get loads of fuels from oil. And then we burn them. But there's <u>burning</u> and there's <u>burning</u>...

Complete Combustion Happens When There's Plenty of Oxygen

1) When there's <u>plenty of oxygen</u> about, hydrocarbons burn to produce only <u>carbon dioxide</u> and <u>water</u>.

$$\text{hydrocarbon + oxygen} \longrightarrow \text{carbon dioxide + water} \quad (+ \text{ energy})$$

2) The <u>hydrogen</u> and <u>carbon</u> in the hydrocarbon have both been <u>oxidised</u>.

3) Many <u>gas room heaters</u> release these <u>waste gases</u> into the room, which is perfectly OK. As long as the gas heater is <u>working properly</u> and the room is <u>well ventilated</u>, there's no problem.

4) <u>Complete combustion</u> releases <u>lots of energy</u> and only produces those two <u>harmless waste products</u>. When there's <u>plenty of oxygen</u> and combustion is complete, the gas burns with a <u>clean blue flame</u>.

Lots of CO_2 isn't ideal, but the alternatives are worse (see below).

5) Here's the <u>equation</u> for the complete combustion of <u>methane</u> — a simple hydrocarbon fuel.

Natural gas is mostly methane (CH_4).

$$CH_4 + 2O_2 \rightarrow 2H_2O + CO_2$$

You can test for CO_2 by bubbling the gas through limewater. It turns limewater milky (see page 70).

Partial Combustion of Hydrocarbons is NOT Safe

Partial combustion is also called 'incomplete combustion'.

1) If there <u>isn't enough oxygen</u> the combustion will be <u>partial</u>. Carbon dioxide and water are still produced, but you can also get <u>carbon monoxide</u> (CO) and <u>carbon</u>.

2) Partial combustion means a <u>smoky yellow flame</u>, and <u>less energy</u> than complete combustion.

$$\text{hydrocarbon + oxygen} \longrightarrow \text{carbon + carbon monoxide + carbon dioxide + water}$$

3) The <u>carbon monoxide</u> is a <u>colourless</u>, <u>odourless</u> and very toxic (<u>poisonous</u>) gas. (+ energy)

4) Every year people are <u>killed</u> while they sleep due to <u>faulty</u> gas fires and boilers filling the room with <u>carbon monoxide</u> and nobody realising — this is why it's important to <u>regularly service gas appliances</u>. The black carbon given off produces <u>sooty marks</u> — a <u>clue</u> that the fuel is <u>not</u> burning fully.

5) So basically, you want <u>lots of oxygen</u> when you're burning fuel — you get <u>more energy</u> given out, and you don't get any <u>messy soot</u> or <u>poisonous gases</u>.

6) Here's an example of an <u>equation</u> for partial combustion too.

$$4CH_4 + 6O_2 \rightarrow C + 2CO + CO_2 + 8H_2O$$

This is just <u>one possibility</u>. The products depend on how much oxygen is present... ... e.g. you could also have: $4CH_4 + 7O_2 \rightarrow 2CO + 2CO_2 + 8H_2O$ — the important thing is that the equation is <u>balanced</u> (see p.56).

There's Lots to Consider When Choosing the Best Fuel

1) <u>Ease of ignition</u> — whether it <u>burns easily</u>. Fuels like gas burn more easily than diesel.

2) <u>Energy value</u> — the amount of energy released.

3) <u>Ash and smoke</u> — some fuels, like coal, leave behind a lot of <u>ash</u> that needs to be disposed of.

4) <u>Storage and transport</u> — gas needs to be stored in special <u>canisters</u> and coal needs to be kept <u>dry</u>. Fuels need to be transported <u>carefully</u> as gas leaks and oil spills can be dangerous.

Blue flame good, orange flame bad...

An ideal fuel would be <u>easy to ignite</u>, produce <u>no soot</u> or <u>toxic products</u>, release <u>loads of energy</u>, leave no <u>residue</u> (what's left after burning), and be capable of being <u>stored safely</u>. There should also be a <u>cheap</u> and <u>sustainable supply</u> of it. In reality, you have to go for the <u>best compromise</u>.

Section 6 — Chemicals from Oil

Using Crude Oil as a Fuel

Nothing as amazingly useful as crude oil would be without its problems. No, that'd be too good to be true.

Crude Oil Provides an Important Fuel for Modern Life

1) Crude oil fractions burn cleanly so they make good <u>fuels</u>. Most modern transport is fuelled by a crude oil fraction, e.g. cars, boats, trains and planes. Parts of crude oil are also burned in <u>central heating systems</u> in homes and in <u>power stations</u> to <u>generate electricity</u>.

2) There's a <u>massive industry</u> with scientists working to find oil reserves, take it out of the ground, and turn it into useful products. As well as fuels, crude oil also provides the raw materials for making various <u>chemicals</u>, including <u>plastics</u>.

3) Often, <u>alternatives</u> to using crude oil fractions as fuel are possible. E.g. electricity can be generated by <u>nuclear</u> power or <u>wind</u> power, there are <u>ethanol</u>-powered cars, and <u>solar</u> energy can be used to heat water.

4) But things tend to be <u>set up</u> for using oil fractions. For example, cars are designed for <u>petrol or diesel</u> and it's <u>readily available</u>. There are filling stations all over the country, with storage facilities and pumps specifically designed for these crude oil fractions. So crude oil fractions are often the <u>easiest and cheapest</u> thing to use.

5) Crude oil fractions are often <u>more reliable</u> too — e.g. solar and wind power won't work without the right weather conditions. Nuclear energy is reliable, but there are lots of concerns about its <u>safety</u> and the storage of radioactive waste.

But it Might Run Out One Day... Eeek

1) Most scientists think that oil will <u>run out</u> — it's a <u>non-renewable fuel</u>.

2) No one knows exactly when it'll run out but there have been heaps of <u>different predictions</u> — e.g. about 40 years ago, scientists predicted that it'd all be gone by the year 2000.

3) <u>New oil reserves</u> are discovered from time to time and <u>technology</u> is constantly improving, so it's now possible to extract oil that was once too <u>difficult</u> or <u>expensive</u> to extract.

4) In the <u>worst-case scenario</u>, oil may be pretty much gone in about 25 years — and that's not far off.

5) Some people think we should <u>immediately stop</u> using oil for things like transport, for which there are alternatives, and keep it for things that it's absolutely <u>essential</u> for, like some chemicals and medicines.

6) It will take time to <u>develop</u> alternative fuels that will satisfy all our energy needs (see page 88 for more info). It'll also take time to <u>adapt things</u> so that the fuels can be used on a wide scale. E.g. we might need different kinds of car engines, or special storage tanks built.

7) One alternative is to generate energy from <u>renewable</u> sources — these are sources that <u>won't run out</u>. Examples of renewable energy sources are <u>wind power</u>, <u>solar power</u> and <u>tidal power</u>.

8) So however long oil does last for, it's a good idea to start <u>conserving</u> it and finding <u>alternatives</u> now.

Crude Oil is NOT the Environment's Best Friend

1) <u>Oil spills</u> can happen as the oil is being transported by tanker — this spells <u>disaster</u> for the local environment. <u>Birds</u> get covered in the stuff and are <u>poisoned</u> as they try to clean themselves. Other creatures, like <u>sea otters</u> and <u>whales</u>, are poisoned too.

2) You have to <u>burn oil</u> to release the energy from it. But burning oil is thought to be a major cause of <u>global warming</u>, <u>acid rain</u> and <u>global dimming</u> — see pages 86 and 87.

If oil alternatives aren't developed, we might get caught short...

Crude oil is <u>really important</u> to our lives. Take <u>petrol</u> for instance — at the first whisper of a shortage, there's mayhem. Loads of people dash to the petrol station and start filling up their tanks. This causes a queue, which starts everyone else panicking. I don't know what they'll do when it runs out totally.

Environmental Problems

We burn fuels all the time to release the energy stored inside them — e.g. 90% of crude oil is used as fuel.

Burning Fossil Fuels Releases Gases and Particles

Remember — crude oil, coal and gas are fossil fuels.

1) Power stations burn huge amounts of fossil fuels to make electricity. Cars are also a major culprit in burning fossil fuels.

2) If the fuel contains sulfur impurities, the sulfur will be released as sulfur dioxide when the fuel is burnt.

3) Oxides of nitrogen will also form if the fuel burns at a high temperature.

Particles Cause Global Dimming

1) In the last few years, some scientists have been measuring how much sunlight is reaching the surface of the Earth and comparing it to records from the last 50 years.

2) They have been amazed to find that in some areas nearly 25% less sunlight has been reaching the surface compared to 50 years ago. They have called this global dimming.

3) They think that it is caused by particles of soot and ash that are produced when fossil fuels are burnt. These particles reflect sunlight back into space, or they can help to produce more clouds that reflect the sunlight back into space.

4) There are many scientists who don't believe the change is real and blame it on inaccurate recording equipment.

Sulfur Dioxide Causes Acid Rain

1) Sulfur dioxide is one of the gases that causes acid rain.

2) When the sulfur dioxide mixes with clouds it forms dilute sulfuric acid. This then falls as acid rain.

3) In the same way, oxides of nitrogen cause acid rain by forming dilute nitric acid in clouds.

4) Acid rain causes lakes to become acidic and many plants and animals die as a result.

5) Acid rain kills trees and damages limestone buildings and ruins stone statues. It's shocking.

6) Links between acid rain and human health problems have been suggested.

7) The benefits of electricity and travel have to be balanced against the environmental impacts. Governments have recognised the importance of this and international agreements have been put in place to reduce emissions of air pollutants such as sulfur dioxide.

You can Reduce Acid Rain by Reducing Sulfur Emissions

1) Most of the sulfur can be removed from fuels before they're burnt, but it costs more to do it.

2) Also, removing sulfur from fuels takes more energy. This usually comes from burning more fuel, which releases more of the greenhouse gas carbon dioxide.

3) However, petrol and diesel are starting to be replaced by low-sulfur versions.

4) Power stations now have Acid Gas Scrubbers to take the harmful gases out before they release their fumes into the atmosphere.

5) The other way of reducing acid rain is simply to reduce our usage of fossil fuels.

Eee, problems, problems — there's always summat goin' wrong...

Saving the planet's not just up to big industries and governments — there are loads of things you can do to reduce the amount of fossil fuels that are burnt. Maybe you could try sharing showers to save energy...

Carbon Dioxide in the Atmosphere

From driving around in gas guzzlers to lopping down trees, we're messing with natural CO_2 levels.

Carbon Dioxide is a Greenhouse Gas

See p.126 for more on the greenhouse effect.

1) The temperature of the Earth is a balance between the heat it gets from the Sun and the heat it radiates back out into space.

2) Gases in the atmosphere like carbon dioxide, methane and water vapour naturally act like an insulating layer. They are often called 'greenhouse gases'. They absorb most of the heat that would normally be radiated out into space, and re-radiate it in all directions — including back towards the Earth. This is called the greenhouse effect.

3) Human activity affects the amount of greenhouse gases in the atmosphere, e.g. deforestation (see below).

4) The Earth is gradually heating up (global warming). There's a correlation between this and the amount of carbon dioxide in the atmosphere. Although the Earth's temperature varies naturally, there's a scientific consensus that human activity is influencing this and causing climate change.

Carbon is Constantly Being Recycled

See p.49 for more on the carbon cycle.

Carbon is the key to the greenhouse effect — it exists in the atmosphere as carbon dioxide gas, and is also present in many other greenhouse gases (e.g. methane).

1) The carbon on Earth moves in a big cycle — the diagram on the right is a pretty good summary.

2) Respiration, combustion and decay of plants and animals add carbon dioxide to the air and remove oxygen.

3) Photosynthesis does the opposite — it removes carbon dioxide and adds oxygen.

4) These processes should all balance out. However, humans have upset the natural carbon cycle, which has affected the balance of gases in the atmosphere.

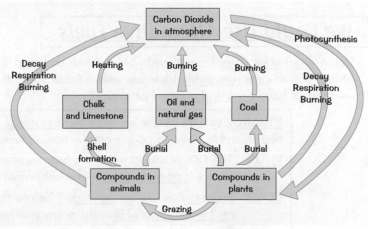

Human Activity Affects Carbon Dioxide Levels

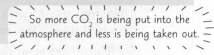

1) People around the world are cutting down large areas of forest (deforestation) for timber and to clear land for farming. This increases the level of carbon dioxide in the atmosphere (see p.127) because:

- Carbon dioxide is released when trees are burnt to clear land. (Carbon in wood is 'locked up' and doesn't contribute to atmospheric CO_2 — until it's released by burning.)

- Microorganisms feeding on bits of dead wood release CO_2 as a waste product of respiration.

- Because living trees use CO_2 for photosynthesis, removing these trees means less CO_2 is removed from the atmosphere.

So more CO_2 is being put into the atmosphere and less is being taken out.

2) Burning fossil fuels is another way humans are releasing 'locked up' carbon into the atmosphere as CO_2. The carbon was locked up in the fossil fuels when plants and animals were crushed over millions of years.

3) Scientists have been researching ways to restore the balance and limit the increase in CO_2 level in the atmosphere (see page 88).

Eeeek — the carbon cycle's got a puncture...

The consequences of global warming are pretty scary. But luckily there are some things that can be done...

Reducing Carbon Dioxide in the Atmosphere

It's not all doom and gloom... There are lots of ways we can help to <u>reduce</u> our carbon dioxide emissions.

We Could Remove CO₂ from the Air

There are a couple of ways we could do this:

IRON SEEDING

1) <u>Iron</u> is an element needed by plants for <u>photosynthesis</u>.
   Injecting iron into the upper ocean promotes the growth of <u>phytoplankton</u>.

2) These <u>blooms</u> of phytoplankton <u>absorb</u> CO₂ from the atmosphere for
   <u>photosynthesis</u>. This could help to get things back in balance.

3) It's a great idea in theory, only we have no way of controlling what plankton grows
   — some are <u>toxic</u>. Also, microorganisms which decompose dead plankton use up
   oxygen and this creates '<u>dead zones</u>' in the ocean — where nothing can live.

CONVERTING CARBON DIOXIDE INTO HYDROCARBONS

1) Chemists are researching the possibility of <u>converting</u> waste CO₂ into <u>hydrocarbons</u>.

2) Several different methods are being tested — most use <u>high pressure</u>, <u>high temperature</u> and a
   <u>metal catalyst</u>. <u>Short chain</u> hydrocarbons can be generated fairly <u>easily</u> but the <u>longer</u> hydrocarbons
   required for petrol are more <u>difficult</u> to produce.

3) This would make a <u>dent</u> in the excess of CO₂, but only if the conversion process used '<u>green</u>' energy.

We Could Use Alternative Fuels

Some <u>alternative fuels</u> have already been developed, and there are others in the pipeline (so to speak).
Many of them are <u>renewable</u> fuels so, unlike fossil fuels, they won't run out. However, none of them are perfect
— they all have <u>pros and cons</u>. For example:

> <u>ETHANOL</u> can be produced from <u>plant material</u> so is known as a <u>biofuel</u>. It's made by <u>fermentation</u> of
> plants and is used to power <u>cars</u> in some places. It's often mixed with petrol to make a better fuel.
>
> <u>PROS</u>: The CO₂ released when it's burnt was taken in by the plant as it grew,
>   so it's '<u>carbon neutral</u>'. The only other product is <u>water</u>.
>
> <u>CONS</u>: <u>Engines</u> need to be <u>converted</u> before they'll work with ethanol fuels. And ethanol fuel
>   <u>isn't widely available</u>. There are worries that as demand for it increases farmers will switch
>   from growing food crops to growing crops to make ethanol — this will <u>increase food prices</u>.

> <u>BIODIESEL</u> is another type of <u>biofuel</u>. It can be produced from <u>vegetable oils</u> such as rapeseed oil
> and soybean oil. Biodiesel can be mixed with ordinary diesel fuel and used to run a <u>diesel engine</u>.
>
> <u>PROS</u>: Biodiesel is '<u>carbon neutral</u>'. Engines <u>don't</u> need to be <u>converted</u>.
>   It produces much <u>less sulfur dioxide</u> and '<u>particulates</u>' than ordinary diesel or petrol.
>
> <u>CONS</u>: We <u>can't make enough</u> to completely replace diesel. It's <u>expensive</u> to make.
>   It could <u>increase food prices</u> like using more ethanol could (see above).

There's more on alternative fuels on pages 108-109.

> <u>HYDROGEN GAS</u> can also be used to power vehicles. You get the hydrogen from the
> <u>electrolysis of water</u> — there's plenty of water about but it takes <u>electrical energy</u>
> to split it up. This energy can come from a <u>renewable</u> source, e.g. solar.
>
> <u>PROS</u>: Hydrogen combines with oxygen in the air to form <u>just water</u> — so it's <u>very clean</u>.
>
> <u>CONS</u>: You need a <u>special, expensive engine</u> and hydrogen <u>isn't widely available</u>. You still
>   need to use <u>energy</u> from <u>another source</u> to make it. Also, hydrogen's hard to <u>store</u>.

My brother is a major source of air pollution...

<u>Alternative fuels</u> are the shining light at the end of a long tunnel of problems caused by burning fuels (and I mean
long). But <u>nothing's perfect</u> (except my quiff... and maybe my golf swing), so get learnin' those <u>disadvantages</u>.

Using Alkenes to Make Polymers

Before you get stuck in to the exciting world of <u>polymers</u>, it'll be a good idea to take a look back at page 83 and brush up on your <u>alkenes</u>. Polymers really are pretty useful things...

Alkenes Can Be Used to Make Polymers

1) Probably the most useful thing you can do with alkenes is <u>polymerisation</u>. This means joining together lots of <u>small alkene molecules</u> (<u>monomers</u>) to form <u>very large molecules</u> — these long-chain molecules are called <u>polymers</u>.

Polymers are often written without the brackets — e.g. polyethene.

2) For instance, many <u>ethene</u> molecules can be joined up to produce <u>poly(ethene)</u> or "polythene".

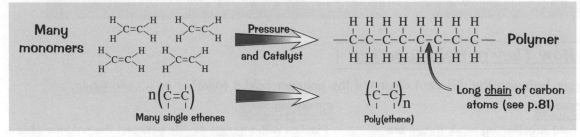

Many monomers → Pressure and Catalyst → Polymer — Long chain of carbon atoms (see p.81)

$n \left(\overset{|}{\underset{|}{C}} = \overset{|}{\underset{|}{C}} \right)$ Many single ethenes → $\left(\overset{|}{\underset{|}{C}} - \overset{|}{\underset{|}{C}} \right)_n$ Poly(ethene)

3) In the same way, if you join lots of <u>propene</u> molecules together, you've got <u>poly(propene)</u>.

Different Polymers Have Different Physical Properties...

1) The physical properties of a polymer depend on <u>what it's made from</u>. Polyamides are usually stronger than poly(ethene), for example.

2) A polymer's <u>physical properties</u> are also affected by the <u>temperature and pressure</u> of polymerisation. Poly(ethene) made at <u>200 °C</u> and <u>2000 atmospheres pressure</u> is <u>flexible</u>, and has <u>low density</u>. But poly(ethene) made at <u>60 °C</u> and a <u>few atmospheres pressure</u> with a <u>catalyst</u> is <u>rigid</u> and <u>dense</u>.

...Which Make Them Suitable for Various Different Uses

1) <u>Light, stretchable</u> polymers such as low density poly(ethene) are used to make plastic bags. <u>Elastic</u> polymer fibres are used to make super-stretchy <u>LYCRA® fibre</u> for tights.

2) <u>New uses</u> are developed all the time. <u>Waterproof</u> coatings for fabrics are made of polymers. <u>Dental polymers</u> are used in resin <u>tooth fillings</u>. Polymer <u>hydrogel wound dressings</u> keep wounds moist.

3) <u>New biodegradable packaging</u> materials made from polymers and <u>cornstarch</u> are being produced.

4) <u>Memory foam</u> is an example of a <u>smart material</u>. It's a polymer that gets <u>softer</u> as it gets <u>warmer</u>. Mattresses can be made of memory foam — they mould to your body shape when you lie on them.

Polymers Are Cheap, but Most Don't Rot — They're Hard to Get Rid Of

1) Most polymers aren't "<u>biodegradable</u>" — they're not broken down by microorganisms, so they <u>don't rot</u>.

2) It's difficult to get rid of them — if you bury them in a landfill site, they'll <u>still</u> be there <u>years later</u>. The best thing is to <u>re-use</u> them as many times as possible and then <u>recycle</u> them if you can.

3) Things made from polymers are usually <u>cheaper</u> than things made from metal. However, as <u>crude oil resources</u> get <u>used up</u>, the <u>price</u> of crude oil will rise. Crude oil products like polymers will get dearer.

4) It may be that one day there won't be <u>enough</u> oil for fuel AND plastics AND all the other uses. Choosing how to use the oil that's left means weighing up advantages and disadvantages on all sides.

Revision's like a polymer — you join lots of little facts up...

Polymers are <u>all over the place</u> — and I don't just mean all those plastic bags stuck in trees. There are <u>naturally occurring</u> polymers, like rubber and silk. That's quite a few clothing options, even without synthetic polymers like polyester and PVC. You've even got polymers <u>on the inside</u> — DNA's a polymer.

Structure and Properties of Polymers

You need to know how the <u>properties</u> of a polymer are affected by the <u>way it's made</u>.

A Polymer's Properties Depend on its Structure

Its Properties Depend on How the Molecules are Arranged...

A polymer's properties don't just depend on the <u>chemicals</u> it's made from (see previous page). The way the polymer chains are <u>arranged</u> has a lot to do with them too:

> If the polymer chains are packed close together, the material will have a high density.
>
> If the polymer chains are spread out, the material will have a low density.

...And How They're Held Together

The <u>forces</u> between the different chains of the polymer hold it together as a <u>solid mass</u>.

Weak Forces:
<u>Chains</u> held together by <u>weak forces</u> are free to <u>slide</u> over each other. This means the plastic can be <u>stretched easily</u>, and will have a <u>low melting point</u>.

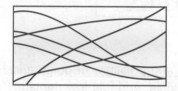

Strong Forces:
Plastics with <u>stronger bonds</u> between the polymer chains have <u>higher melting points</u> and <u>can't be easily stretched</u>, as the <u>crosslinks</u> hold the chains firmly together. Crosslinks are <u>chemical bonds</u> between the polymer chains (see below).

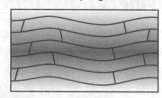

So, the <u>stronger</u> the bonds or forces between the polymer chains, the more <u>energy</u> is needed to break them apart, and the <u>higher</u> the <u>melting point</u>.

Polymers Can be Modified to Give Them Different Properties

You can <u>chemically modify</u> polymers to change their <u>properties</u>.

1) Polymers can be modified to <u>increase</u> their <u>chain length</u>. Polymers with <u>short</u> chains are <u>easy</u> to shape and have <u>lower</u> melting points. <u>Longer</u> chain polymers are <u>stiffer</u> and have <u>higher</u> melting points.

2) Polymers can be made stronger by adding <u>cross-linking agents</u>. These agents chemically <u>bond</u> the chains together, making the polymer <u>stiffer</u>, <u>stronger</u> and more <u>heat-resistant</u>.

3) <u>Plasticisers</u> can be added to a polymer to make it <u>softer</u> and easier to shape. Plasticisers work by getting in <u>between</u> the polymer chains and <u>reducing</u> the forces between them.

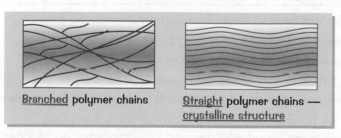

Branched polymer chains   Straight polymer chains — crystalline structure

4) The polymer can be made more <u>crystalline</u>. A crystalline polymer has straight chains with no branches so the chains can fit <u>close together</u>. Crystalline polymers have <u>higher density</u>, are <u>stronger</u> and have a <u>higher</u> melting point.

Choose your polymers wisely...

The molecules that make up a plastic affect the <u>properties</u> of the plastic, which also affects what the plastic can be used for. I know there's a lot of diagrams of lines on this page, but the <u>structure</u> of polymers is really important — it affects their properties, and it might even come up in the exam.

Plant Oils

If you squeeze a <u>walnut</u> really hard, out will ooze some <u>walnut oil</u>, which you could use to make <u>walnut mayonnaise</u>. Much better to just buy some oil from the shop though.

We Can Extract Oils from Plants

1) Some <u>fruits</u> and <u>seeds</u> contain a lot of <u>oil</u>. For example, avocados and olives are oily fruits. Brazil nuts, peanuts and sesame seeds are oily seeds (a nut is just a big seed really).
2) These oils can be extracted and used for <u>food</u> or for <u>fuel</u>.
3) To get the oil out, the plant material is <u>crushed</u>. The next step is to <u>press</u> the crushed plant material between metal plates and squash the oil out. This is the traditional method of producing <u>olive oil</u>.
4) Oil can be separated from crushed plant material by a <u>centrifuge</u> — rather like using a spin-dryer to get water out of wet clothes.
5) Or <u>solvents</u> can be used to get oil from plant material.
6) <u>Distillation</u> refines oil, and <u>removes water</u>, <u>solvents</u> and <u>impurities</u>.

Vegetable Oils Are Used in Food

1) Vegetable oils provide a lot of <u>energy</u> — they have a very high energy content.
2) There are other nutrients in vegetable oils. For example, oils from seeds contain <u>vitamin E</u>.
3) Vegetable oils contain <u>essential fatty acids</u>, which the body needs for many metabolic processes.

Vegetable Oils Have Benefits for Cooking

1) Vegetable oils have <u>higher boiling points</u> than water. This means they can be used to cook foods at higher temperatures and at <u>faster</u> speeds.
2) Cooking with vegetable oil gives food a <u>different flavour</u>. This is because of the oil's <u>own</u> flavour, but it's also down to the fact that many flavours come from chemicals that are <u>soluble</u> in oil. This means the oil '<u>carries</u>' the flavour, making it seem more <u>intense</u>.
3) Using oil to cook food <u>increases</u> the <u>energy</u> we get from eating it.

Vegetable Oils Can Be Used to Produce Fuels

1) Vegetable oils such as rapeseed oil and soybean oil can be <u>processed</u> and turned into <u>fuels</u>.
2) Because vegetable oils provide a lot of <u>energy</u> they're really suitable for use as fuels.
3) A particularly useful fuel made from vegetable oils is called <u>biodiesel</u>. Biodiesel has similar properties to ordinary diesel fuel — it burns in the same way, so you can use it to fuel a diesel engine.

That lippie fried a few sausages back in her heyday...

Plant oils have loads of different uses, from frying bacon to fuelling cars. Even <u>waste oil</u>, left over from manufacturing and cooking in fast food restaurants, ends up being used in <u>pet food</u> and <u>cosmetics</u>. Grim.

Plant Oils

Oils are usually quite runny at room temperature. That's fine for salad dressing, say, but not so good for spreading in your sandwiches. For that, you could hydrogenate the oil to make margarine...

Unsaturated Oils Contain C=C Double Bonds

1) Oils and fats contain long-chain molecules with lots of carbon atoms.
2) Oils and fats are either saturated or unsaturated.
3) Unsaturated oils contain double bonds between some of the carbon atoms in their carbon chains.
4) So, an unsaturated oil will decolourise bromine water (as the bromine opens up the double bond and joins on).
5) Monounsaturated fats contain one C=C double bond somewhere in their carbon chains. Polyunsaturated fats contain more than one C=C double bond.

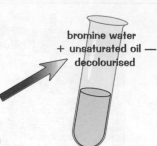
bromine water + unsaturated oil — decolourised

Unsaturated Oils Can Be Hydrogenated

1) Unsaturated vegetable oils are liquid at room temperature.
2) They can be hardened by reacting them with hydrogen in the presence of a nickel catalyst at about 60 °C. This is called hydrogenation. The hydrogen reacts with the double-bonded carbons and opens out the double bonds.
3) Hydrogenated oils have higher melting points than unsaturated oils, so they're more solid at room temperature. This makes them useful as spreads and for baking cakes and pastries.
4) Margarine is usually made from partially hydrogenated vegetable oil — turning all the double bonds in vegetable oil to single bonds would make margarine too hard and difficult to spread. Hydrogenating most of them gives margarine a nice, buttery, spreadable consistency.
5) Partially hydrogenated vegetable oils are often used instead of butter in processed foods, e.g. biscuits. These oils are a lot cheaper than butter and they keep longer. This makes biscuits cheaper and gives them a long shelf life.
6) But partially hydrogenating vegetable oils means you end up with a lot of so-called trans fats. And there's evidence to suggest that trans fats are very bad for you.

Vegetable Oils in Foods Can Affect Health

1) Vegetable oils tend to be unsaturated, while animal fats tend to be saturated.
2) In general, saturated fats are less healthy than unsaturated fats (as saturated fats increase the amount of cholesterol in the blood, which can block up the arteries and increase the risk of heart disease).
3) Natural unsaturated fats such as olive oil and sunflower oil reduce the amount of blood cholesterol. But because of the trans fats, partially hydrogenated vegetable oil increases the amount of cholesterol in the blood. So eating a lot of foods made with partially hydrogenated vegetable oils can actually increase the risk of heart disease.
4) Cooking food in oil, whether saturated, unsaturated or partially hydrogenated, makes it more fattening.

Double bonds — licensed to saturate...

This is tricky stuff. In a nutshell... there are saturated and unsaturated fats, which are generally bad and good for you (in that order) — easy enough. But... partially hydrogenated vegetable oil (which is unsaturated) is bad for you. Too much of the wrong types of fats can lead to heart disease. Got that...

Emulsions

Emulsions are all over the place in <u>foods</u>, <u>cosmetics</u> and <u>paint</u>. And maybe in your exams...

Emulsions Can Be Made from Oil and Water

1) Oils <u>don't dissolve in water</u>. So far so good...

2) However, you <u>can</u> mix an oil with water to make an <u>emulsion</u>. Emulsions are made up of lots of <u>droplets</u> of one liquid <u>suspended</u> in another liquid. You can have an oil-in-water emulsion (oil droplets suspended in water) or a water-in-oil emulsion (water droplets suspended in oil).

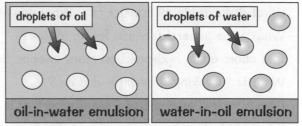

droplets of oil | droplets of water

oil-in-water emulsion | water-in-oil emulsion

3) Emulsions are <u>thicker</u> than either oil or water. E.g. mayonnaise is an emulsion of sunflower oil (or olive oil) and vinegar — it's thicker than either.

4) The physical properties of emulsions make them suited to <u>lots of uses</u> in food — e.g. as salad dressings and in sauces. For instance, a salad dressing made by shaking olive oil and vinegar together forms an <u>emulsion</u> that <u>coats</u> salad better than plain oil or plain vinegar.

5) Generally, the <u>more oil</u> you've got in an oil-in-water emulsion, the <u>thicker</u> it is. Milk is an oil-in-water emulsion with not much oil and a lot of water — there's about 3% oil in full-fat milk. Single cream has a bit more oil — about 18%. Double cream has lots of oil — nearly 50%.

6) <u>Whipped cream</u> and ice cream are oil-in-water emulsions with an extra ingredient — <u>air</u>. Air is whipped into cream to give it a <u>fluffy</u>, frothy consistency for use as a topping. Whipping air into ice cream gives it a <u>softer texture</u>, which makes it easier to scoop out of the tub.

7) Emulsions also have <u>non-food uses</u>. Most <u>moisturising lotions</u> are oil-in-water emulsions. The smooth texture of an emulsion makes it easy to rub into the skin.

Some Foods Contain Emulsifiers to Help Oil and Water Mix

Oil and water mixtures naturally <u>separate out</u>. But here's where emulsifiers come in...

1) Emulsifiers are molecules with one part that's <u>attracted to water</u> and another part that's <u>attracted to oil</u> or fat. The bit that's attracted to water is called <u>hydrophilic</u>, and the bit that's attracted to oil is called <u>hydrophobic</u>.

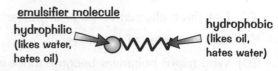

emulsifier molecule
hydrophilic (likes water, hates oil)
hydrophobic (likes oil, hates water)

2) The <u>hydrophilic</u> end of each emulsifier molecule latches onto <u>water molecules</u>.

3) The <u>hydrophobic</u> end of each emulsifier molecule cosies up to <u>oil molecules</u>.

4) When you shake oil and water together with a bit of emulsifier, the oil forms droplets, surrounded by a coating of emulsifier... <u>with the hydrophilic bit facing outwards</u>. Other oil droplets are <u>repelled</u> by the hydrophilic bit of the emulsifier, while water molecules latch on. So the emulsion won't separate out. Clever.

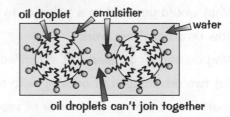

oil droplet | emulsifier | water

oil droplets can't join together

Using Emulsifiers Has Pros and Cons

1) Emulsifiers <u>stop</u> emulsions from <u>separating</u> out and this gives them a longer <u>shelf-life</u>.

2) Emulsifiers allow food companies to produce food that's <u>lower in fat</u> but that still has a <u>good texture</u>.

3) The <u>down side</u> is that some people are <u>allergic</u> to certain emulsifiers. For example, <u>egg yolk</u> is often used as an emulsifier — so people who are allergic to eggs need to <u>check</u> the <u>ingredients</u> very carefully.

Emulsion paint — spread mayonnaise all over the walls...

Before fancy stuff from abroad like olive oil, we fried our bacon and eggs in <u>lard</u>. Mmmm. Lard wouldn't be so good for making salad cream though. Emulsions like salad cream have to be made from shaking up two liquids — tiny droplets of one liquid are 'suspended' (NOT dissolved) in the other liquid.

Revision Summary for Section 6

Fractional distillation, global warming, polymers and plant oils — can they really belong in the same section, I almost hear you ask. Yes they can is the answer, and it'll be really helpful if you know them all inside out. Try these questions and see how much you really know:

1) What does crude oil consist of? What does fractional distillation do to crude oil?
2) What's the general formula for an alkane?
3) Is a short-chain hydrocarbon more viscous than a long-chain hydrocarbon? Is it more volatile?
4) What is "cracking"? Why is it done?
5) Give a typical example of a substance that is cracked, and the products that you get from cracking it.
6) What kind of carbon-carbon bond do alkenes have?
7) What is the general formula for alkenes?
8) Draw the chemical structure of ethene.
9) When ethene is hydrated with steam, what substance is formed?
10) What is produced during complete combustion of hydrocarbons?
11) Explain how incomplete combustion can be harmful to humans.
12) Give three things you might want to consider when deciding on the best fuel to use.
13)* You're going on holiday to a very cold place. The temperature will be about −10 °C. Which of the fuels shown on the right do you think will work best in your camping stove? Explain your answer.

Fuel	Boiling point (°C)
Propane	−42
Butane	−0.4
Pentane	36.2

14) Give two disadvantages of using crude oil as a fuel.
15) Name three pollutants released into the atmosphere when fuels are burned. What environmental problems are associated with each?
16) What are greenhouse gases?
17) List two ways in which human activity is increasing CO_2 levels.
18) List three alternative ways of powering cars. What are the pros and cons of each?
19) List four uses of polymers.
20) Why might polymers become more expensive in the future?
21) A polymer is easily stretched and has a low melting point. What can you say about the arrangement of its molecule chains and the forces holding them together?
22) What would you add to a polymer to make it stiffer and stronger?
23) How do plasticisers work?
24) Why do some oils need to be distilled after they have been extracted?
25) List two advantages of cooking with oil.
26) Apart from cooking, give a use of vegetable oils.
27) What kind of carbon-carbon bond do unsaturated oils contain?
28) What happens when you react unsaturated oils with hydrogen?
29) What is an emulsion? Give an example.
30) How do emulsifiers keep emulsions stable?
31) Suggest one problem of adding emulsifiers to food.

* Answers on page 140

Section 6 — Chemicals from Oil

Heat, Temperature and Kinetic Theory

When it starts to get a bit nippy, on goes the heating to warm things up a bit.
Heating is all about the <u>transfer of energy</u>. Here are a few useful definitions to begin with.

Heat is a Measure of Energy

1) When a substance is <u>heated</u>, its particles gain <u>kinetic energy</u> (<u>KE</u>). This energy makes the particles in a <u>gas or a liquid</u> move around <u>faster</u>. In a <u>solid</u>, the particles <u>vibrate more rapidly</u>.

2) This energy is measured on an <u>absolute scale</u>. (This means it can't go <u>lower</u> than <u>zero</u>, because there's a <u>limit</u> to how slow particles can move.) The unit of heat energy is the <u>joule (J)</u>.

Temperature is a Measure of Hotness

1) <u>Temperature</u> is a <u>measure</u> of the <u>average kinetic energy</u> of the <u>particles</u> in a substance.
The <u>hotter</u> something is, the <u>higher</u> its <u>temperature</u>, and the <u>higher</u> the <u>average KE</u> of its particles.

2) Temperature is usually measured in <u>°C</u> (degrees Celsius), but there are other temperature scales, like <u>°F</u> (degrees Fahrenheit). These are <u>not absolute</u> scales as they can go <u>below zero</u>.

3) <u>Energy</u> tends to <u>flow</u> from <u>hot objects</u> to <u>cooler</u> ones. E.g. warm radiators heat the cold air in your room — they'd be no use if heat didn't flow.

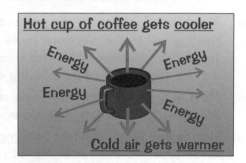

Hot cup of coffee gets cooler

Energy / Energy / Energy / Energy

Cold air gets warmer

> If there's a <u>DIFFERENCE IN TEMPERATURE</u> between two places, then <u>ENERGY WILL FLOW</u> between them.

4) The <u>greater</u> the <u>difference</u> in temperature, the <u>faster</u> the <u>rate of cooling</u> will be. E.g. a <u>hot</u> cup of coffee will cool down <u>quicker</u> in a <u>cold</u> room than in a <u>warm</u> room.

Kinetic Theory Can Explain the Three States of Matter

The <u>three states of matter</u> are <u>solid</u> (e.g. ice), <u>liquid</u> (e.g. water) and <u>gas</u> (e.g. water vapour). The <u>particles</u> of a particular substance in each state are <u>the same</u> — only the <u>arrangement</u> and <u>energy</u> of the particles are <u>different</u>.

SOLIDS — <u>strong forces</u> of attraction hold the particles <u>close together</u> in a <u>fixed</u>, <u>regular</u> arrangement. The particles don't have much <u>energy</u> so they <u>can</u> only <u>vibrate</u> about their <u>fixed</u> positions.

LIQUIDS — there are <u>weaker forces</u> of attraction between the particles. The particles are <u>close together</u>, but can <u>move past each other</u>, and form <u>irregular</u> arrangements. They have <u>more energy</u> than the particles in a <u>solid</u> — they move in <u>random directions</u> at <u>low speeds</u>.

GASES — There are <u>almost no</u> forces of attraction between the particles. The particles have <u>more energy</u> than those in <u>liquids</u> and <u>solids</u> — they are <u>free to move</u>, and travel in <u>random directions</u> and at <u>high speeds</u>.

When you <u>heat</u> a substance, you give its particles <u>more kinetic energy</u> so they <u>vibrate</u> or <u>move faster</u>, which eventually causes <u>solids</u> to <u>melt</u> and <u>liquids</u> to <u>boil</u>.

Physics makes me a bit hot under the collar...

So, the more <u>energy</u> something has, the <u>faster</u> it moves about (or <u>vibrates</u>). Makes sense. On the other hand, if you <u>cool</u> something down enough it <u>stops</u> moving altogether. The temperature this happens at is the <u>same</u> for everything and it's called '<u>absolute zero</u>', which is − 273°C. There isn't a limit to how <u>hot</u> something can be, but if you keep heating something it will eventually <u>disintegrate</u> and split into <u>tiny bits</u>. That could be bad.

Conduction and Convection

Mmmm... I do like being toasty warm. But keeping the heat where you want it is easier said than done — there are several ways that heat is 'lost'. <u>Convection</u> and <u>conduction</u> are up first.

Conduction Occurs Mainly in Solids

1) In a <u>solid</u>, the particles are held tightly together. So when one particle <u>vibrates</u>, it <u>bumps into</u> other particles nearby and quickly passes the vibrations on.

2) Particles which vibrate <u>faster</u> than others pass on their <u>extra kinetic energy</u> to <u>neighbouring particles</u>. These particles then vibrate faster themselves.

3) This process continues throughout the solid and gradually the extra kinetic energy (or <u>heat</u>) is spread all the way through the solid. This causes a <u>rise in temperature</u> at the <u>other side</u>.

> <u>CONDUCTION OF HEAT</u> is the process where <u>vibrating particles</u> pass on <u>extra kinetic energy</u> to <u>neighbouring particles</u>.

4) <u>Metals</u> conduct heat <u>really well</u> because some of their <u>electrons</u> are <u>free to move</u> inside the metal. <u>Heating</u> makes the electrons move <u>faster</u> and collide with other <u>free electrons</u>, <u>transferring energy</u>. These then pass on their extra energy to other electrons, etc. Because the electrons move <u>freely</u>, this is a much <u>faster way</u> of transferring energy than slowly passing it between jostling <u>neighbouring</u> atoms.

5) Most <u>non-metals</u> <u>don't</u> have free electrons, so warm up more <u>slowly</u>, making them good for <u>insulating</u> things — that's why <u>metals</u> are used for <u>saucepans</u>, but <u>non-metals</u> are used for saucepan <u>handles</u>.

6) <u>Liquids and gases</u> conduct heat <u>more slowly</u> than solids — the particles aren't held so tightly together, which prevents them bumping into each other so often. So <u>air</u> is a good insulator.

Convection Occurs in Liquids and Gases

1) When you heat up a liquid or gas, the particles move faster, and the fluid (liquid or gas) <u>expands</u>, becoming <u>less dense</u>.

2) The <u>warmer</u>, <u>less dense</u> fluid <u>rises</u> above its <u>colder</u>, <u>denser</u> surroundings, like a hot air balloon does.

3) As the <u>warm</u> fluid <u>rises</u>, cooler fluid takes its place. As this process continues, you actually end up with a <u>circulation</u> of fluid (<u>convection currents</u>). This is how <u>immersion heaters</u> work.

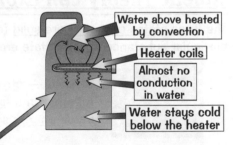

Water above heated by convection

Heater coils

Almost no conduction in water

Water stays cold below the heater

> <u>CONVECTION</u> occurs when the more energetic particles <u>move</u> from the <u>hotter region</u> to the <u>cooler region</u> — <u>and take their heat energy with them</u>.

4) <u>Radiators</u> in the home rely on convection to make the warm air <u>circulate</u> round the room.

5) Convection <u>can't happen in solids</u> because the <u>particles can't move</u> — they just vibrate on the spot.

6) To <u>reduce convection</u>, you need to <u>stop the fluid moving</u>. Clothes, blankets and cavity wall foam insulation all work by <u>trapping pockets of air</u>. The air can't move so the heat has to conduct <u>very slowly</u> through the pockets of air, as well as the material in between.

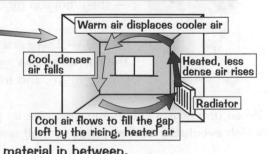

Warm air displaces cooler air

Cool, denser air falls

Heated, less dense air rises

Radiator

Cool air flows to fill the gap left by the rising, heated air

And the good old garden spade is a great example...

If a <u>garden spade</u> is left outside in cold weather, the metal bit will always feel <u>colder</u> than the wooden handle. But it <u>isn't</u> colder — it just <u>conducts heat away</u> from your hand quicker. The opposite is true if the spade is left out in the sunshine — it'll <u>feel</u> hotter because it conducts heat into your hand quicker.

Heat Radiation

As well as conduction and convection, heat energy can be transferred by <u>radiation</u>.

Thermal Radiation Involves Emission of Electromagnetic Waves

<u>Heat</u> (thermal) <u>radiation</u> consists purely of electromagnetic waves (see p.121) of a certain range of frequencies — <u>infrared radiation</u>. It's next to visible light in the <u>electromagnetic spectrum</u>.

1) <u>All objects</u> are <u>continually</u> emitting and absorbing <u>heat radiation</u>.

2) An object that's <u>hotter</u> than its surroundings <u>emits more radiation</u> than it <u>absorbs</u> (as it <u>cools</u> down). And an object that's <u>cooler</u> than its surroundings <u>absorbs more radiation</u> than it <u>emits</u> (as it <u>warms</u> up).

3) <u>Power</u> (see p.114) is the just the <u>rate of energy change</u> — that's energy ÷ time. For an object to stay at the <u>same</u> temperature, the <u>power</u> of heat <u>absorbed</u> needs to be the <u>same</u> as the power <u>emitted</u>.

4) You can <u>feel</u> this <u>heat radiation</u> if you stand near something <u>hot</u> like a fire or if you put your hand just above the bonnet of a recently parked car.

(recently parked car)

(after an hour or so)

Radiation Depends an Awful Lot on Surface Colour and Texture

1) <u>Dark matt</u> surfaces <u>absorb</u> heat radiation falling on them much <u>better</u> than <u>bright glossy</u> surfaces, such as <u>gloss white</u> or <u>silver</u>. They also <u>emit much more</u> heat radiation (at any given temperature).

2) <u>Silvered</u> surfaces <u>reflect</u> nearly all heat radiation falling on them.

Solar hot water panels

1) <u>Solar hot water panels</u> contain <u>water pipes</u> under a <u>black surface</u> (or black painted pipes under glass).

2) <u>Heat radiation</u> from the Sun is <u>absorbed</u> by the <u>black surface</u> to <u>heat the water</u> in the pipes.

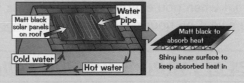

Survival Blankets

1) If someone gets injured halfway up a big snowy hill, it can be <u>crucial</u> to <u>keep them</u> as <u>warm</u> as possible till help arrives.

2) A <u>silver coloured blanket</u> helps to <u>stop</u> their body <u>heat radiating away</u> — and could save their life.

There Are Lots of Fairly Dull Experiments to Demonstrate This...

Here are two of the most gripping:

Leslie's Cube

The <u>matt black</u> side <u>emits most heat</u>, so it's that thermometer which gets <u>hottest</u>.

The Melting Wax Trick

The <u>matt black</u> surface <u>absorbs most heat</u>, so its wax <u>melts</u> first and the ball bearing <u>drops</u>.

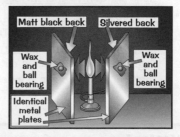

I know it's Leslie's Cube — but he said I could borrow it...

The key idea here is that <u>heat radiation</u> is affected by the <u>colour</u> and <u>texture</u> of surfaces. Thermal radiation questions often ask you <u>why</u> something's painted silver, or how you could <u>reduce the heat losses</u> from something.

Condensation and Evaporation

Changing from a gas to a liquid or a liquid to a gas has a lot to do with the energy of the particles.

Condensation is When Gas Turns to Liquid

1) When a gas cools, the particles in the gas slow down and lose kinetic energy (see p. 95). The attractive forces between the particles pull them closer together.

2) If the temperature gets cold enough and the gas particles get close enough together that condensation can take place, the gas becomes a liquid.

3) Water vapour in the air condenses when it comes into contact with cold surfaces e.g. drinks glasses.

4) The steam you see rising from a boiling kettle is actually invisible water vapour condensing to form tiny water droplets as it spreads into cooler air.

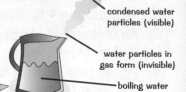

condensed water particles (visible)

water particles in gas form (invisible)

boiling water

Evaporation is When Liquid Turns to Gas

1) Evaporation is when particles escape from a liquid.

2) Particles can evaporate from a liquid at temperatures that are much lower than the liquid's boiling point.

3) Particles near the surface of a liquid can escape and become gas particles if:

> - The particles are travelling in the right direction to escape the liquid.
> - The particles are travelling fast enough (they have enough kinetic energy) to overcome the attractive forces of the other particles in the liquid.

4) The fastest particles (with the most kinetic energy) are most likely to evaporate from the liquid — so when they do, the average speed and kinetic energy of the remaining particles decreases.

5) This decrease in average particle energy means the temperature of the remaining liquid falls — the liquid cools.

6) This cooling effect can be really useful. For example, you sweat when you exercise or get hot. As the water from the sweat on your skin evaporates, it cools you down.

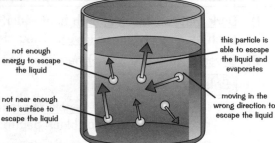

not enough energy to escape the liquid

not near enough the surface to escape the liquid

this particle is able to escape the liquid and evaporates

moving in the wrong direction to escape the liquid

Rates of Evaporation and Condensation can Vary

The RATE OF EVAPORATION will be faster if the...

- TEMPERATURE is higher — the average particle energy will be higher, so more particles will have enough energy to escape.
- DENSITY is lower — the forces between the particles will usually be weaker, so more particles will have enough energy to overcome these forces and escape the liquid.
- SURFACE AREA is larger — more particles will be near enough to the surface to escape the liquid.
- AIRFLOW over the liquid is greater — the lower the concentration of an evaporating substance in the air it's evaporating into, the higher the rate of evaporation. A greater airflow means air above the liquid is replaced more quickly, so the concentration in the air will be lower.

The RATE OF CONDENSATION will be faster if the...

- TEMPERATURE OF THE GAS is lower — the average particle energy in the gas is lower — so more particles will slow down enough to clump together and form liquid droplets.
- TEMPERATURE OF THE SURFACE THE GAS TOUCHES is lower.
- DENSITY is higher — the forces between the particles will be stronger. Fewer particles will have enough energy to overcome these forces and will instead clump together and form a liquid.
- AIRFLOW is less — the concentration of the substance in the air will be higher, and so the rate of condensation will be greater.

A little less condensation, a little more action...

The people who make adverts for drinks know what customers like to see — condensation on the outside of the bottle. It makes the drink look nice and cold and extra-refreshing. Mmmm. If it wasn't for condensation, you'd never be able to draw pictures on the bus window with your finger either — you've got a lot to be thankful for...

Rate of Heat Transfer

There are loads of factors that affect the <u>rate</u> of <u>heat transfer</u>.
Different objects can lose or gain heat much <u>faster</u> than others — even in the <u>same conditions</u>. Read on...

The Rate of Heat Energy Transfer Depends on Many Things

1) <u>Heat energy</u> is <u>radiated</u> from the <u>surface</u> of an object (see p. 97).

2) The <u>bigger</u> the <u>surface area</u>, the <u>more infrared waves</u> that can be <u>emitted</u> from (or absorbed by) the surface — so the <u>quicker</u> the <u>transfer of heat</u>. E.g. <u>radiators</u> have <u>large surface areas</u> to <u>maximise</u> the amount of heat they transfer.

3) This is why <u>car and motorbike engines</u> often have '<u>fins</u>' — they <u>increase</u> the <u>surface area</u> so heat is radiated away quicker. So the <u>engine cools quicker</u>.

4) <u>Heat sinks</u> are devices designed to transfer heat <u>away</u> from <u>objects</u> they're in <u>contact</u> with, e.g. computer components. They have <u>fins</u> and a large <u>surface area</u> so they can <u>emit heat</u> as <u>quickly</u> as possible.

Cooling fins on engines increase surface area to speed up cooling.

5) If two objects at the <u>same</u> temperature have the same surface area but <u>different</u> volumes, the object with the <u>smaller</u> volume will cool more <u>quickly</u> — as a higher proportion of the object will be in <u>contact</u> with its surroundings.

6) Other factors, like the <u>type</u> of material, affect the rate too. Objects made from good <u>conductors</u> (see p.96) transfer heat away more <u>quickly</u> than <u>insulating</u> materials, e.g. <u>plastic</u>. It also matters whether the materials in <u>contact</u> with it are <u>insulators</u> or <u>conductors</u>. If an object is in contact with a <u>conductor</u>, the heat will be conducted away <u>much faster</u> than if it is in contact with a good <u>insulator</u>.

Some Devices are Designed to Limit Heat Transfer

Products can be designed to <u>reduce</u> <u>heat transfer</u> — a <u>vacuum flask</u> is a good example of this.

Vacuum Flasks

1) The glass bottle is <u>double-walled</u> with a <u>vacuum</u> between the two walls. This stops <u>conduction</u> and <u>convection</u> through the <u>sides</u>.

2) The walls either side of the vacuum are <u>silvered</u> to keep heat loss by <u>radiation</u> to a <u>minimum</u>.

3) The bottle is supported using <u>insulating foam</u>. This minimises heat <u>conduction</u> to or from the <u>outer</u> glass bottle.

4) The <u>stopper</u> is made of <u>plastic</u> and filled with <u>cork</u> or <u>foam</u> to reduce any <u>heat conduction</u> through it.

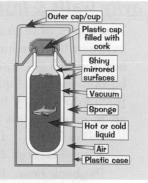

Outer cap/cup
Plastic cap filled with cork
Shiny mirrored surfaces
Vacuum
Sponge
Hot or cold liquid
Air
Plastic case

Humans and Animals Have Ways of Controlling Heat Transfer Too

1) In the <u>cold</u>, the hairs on your skin 'stand up' to trap a <u>thicker</u> layer of <u>insulating air</u> around the body. This limits the amount of heat loss by <u>convection</u>. Some animals do the same using <u>fur</u>.

2) When you're <u>too warm</u>, your body diverts more <u>blood</u> to flow near the surface of your skin so that more heat can be lost by <u>radiation</u> — that's why some people go <u>pink</u> when they get hot.

3) Generally, animals in <u>warm</u> climates have <u>larger</u> ears than those in <u>cold</u> climates to help <u>control</u> heat transfer.

For example, Arctic foxes have evolved <u>small ears</u>, with a small surface area to minimise <u>heat loss</u> by <u>radiation</u> and conserve body heat.

Desert foxes on the other hand have <u>huge ears</u> with a large surface area to allow them to <u>lose heat</u> by <u>radiation</u> easily and keep cool.

Don't call me 'Big Ears' — call me 'Large Surface Area'...

Examiners are like <u>small children</u> — they ask some <u>barmy questions</u>. If they ask you one about heat transfer, you must <u>always</u> say which form of heat transfer is involved at any point, either <u>conduction</u>, <u>convection</u> or <u>radiation</u>. You've got to show them that you know your stuff — it's the only way to get top marks.

Energy Efficiency in the Home

It's daft to keep paying for energy to heat your house only to let the heat escape straight out again.

Insulating Your House Saves Energy and Money

1) Energy in the home is emitted and transferred (or wasted) in different ways.

'Sources' can also waste energy if they're not very efficient.

2) Things that emit energy are called sources, e.g. radiators.
Things that transfer and waste or lose energy are called sinks, e.g. windows and computers.

3) To save energy, you can insulate your house so the sinks 'drain' less energy, e.g. use curtains to reduce energy loss. You can also make sources and sinks more efficient, so they waste less energy, e.g. use energy-saving light bulbs instead of normal ones.

4) It costs money to buy and install insulation, or buy more efficient appliances, but it also saves you money, because your energy bills are lower.

$$\text{payback time} = \frac{\text{initial cost}}{\text{annual saving}}$$

5) Eventually, the money you've saved on energy bills will equal the initial cost of installing the insulation — the time this takes is called the payback time.

6) If you subtract the annual saving from the initial cost repeatedly then eventually the one with the biggest annual saving must always come out as the winner, if you think about it.

7) But you might sell the house (or die) before that happens. If you look at it over, say, a five-year period then a cheap and cheerful hot water tank jacket wins over expensive double glazing.

Loft Insulation

Fibreglass 'wool' laid across the loft floor reduces conduction through the ceiling into the roof space.

Initial Cost: £200
Annual Saving: £100
Payback time: 2 years

Hot Water Tank Jacket

Reduces conduction.
Initial Cost: £60
Annual Saving: £15
Payback time: 4 years

These figures are rough. It'll vary from house to house.

Cavity Walls & Insulation

Two layers of bricks with a gap between them reduce conduction but you still get some energy lost by convection. Squirting insulating foam into the gap traps pockets of air to minimise this convection.

Initial Cost: £150
Annual Saving: £100
Payback time: 18 months

(Heat is still lost through the walls by radiation though. Also, if there are any spaces where air is not trapped there'll still be some convection too.)

Draught-proofing

Strips of foam and plastic around doors and windows stop hot air going out — reducing convection.
Initial Cost: £100
Annual Saving: £15
Payback time: 7 years

Double Glazing

Two layers of glass with an air gap between reduce conduction.
Initial Cost: £2400
Annual Saving: £80
Payback time: 30 years

Thick Curtains

Reduce conduction and radiation through the windows.
Initial Cost: £180
Annual Saving: £20
Payback time: 9 years

U-Values Show How Fast Heat can Transfer Through a Material

1) Heat transfers faster through materials with higher U-values than through materials with low U-values.

2) So the better the insulator (see p.96) the lower the U-value. E.g. The U-value of a typical duvet is about $0.75 \text{ W/m}^2\text{K}$, whereas the U-value of loft insulation material is around $0.15 \text{ W/m}^2\text{K}$.

It's payback time...

Payback time applies to other things too, like cars. Buying a more fuel-efficient car might sound like a great idea — but if it costs loads more than a clapped-out old fuel-guzzler, you might still end up out of pocket.
If it's cost-effectiveness you're thinking about, you always have to offset initial cost against annual savings.

Specific Heat Capacity

Specific heat capacity is one of those topics that puts people off just because it has a weird name. If you can get over that, it's actually not too bad — it sounds a lot harder than it is. Go on. Give it a second chance.

Specific Heat Capacity Tells You How Much Energy Stuff Can Store

1) It takes more heat energy to increase the temperature of some materials than others. E.g. you need 4200 J to warm 1 kg of water by 1 °C, but only 139 J to warm 1 kg of mercury by 1 °C.

2) Materials which need to gain lots of energy to warm up also release loads of energy when they cool down again. They can 'store' a lot of heat.

3) The measure of how much energy a substance can store is called its specific heat capacity.

4) Specific heat capacity is the amount of energy needed to raise the temperature of 1 kg of a substance by 1 °C. Water has a specific heat capacity of 4200 J/kg°C.

There's a Handy Formula for Specific Heat Capacity

If you have to do calculations involving specific heat capacity, this is the equation to learn:

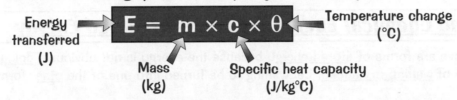

Energy transferred (J) → $E = m \times c \times \theta$ ← Temperature change (°C)

Mass (kg)   Specific heat capacity (J/kg°C)

EXAMPLE: How much energy is needed to heat 2 kg of water from 10 °C to 100 °C?

ANSWER: Energy needed = $2 \times 4200 \times 90 = \underline{756\ 000\ J}$

If you're not working out the energy, you'll have to rearrange the equation, so this formula triangle will come in dead handy.

You cover up the thing you're trying to find. The parts of the formula you can still see are what it's equal to.

$$\frac{E}{m \times c \times \theta}$$

EXAMPLE: An empty 200 g aluminium kettle cools down from 115 °C to 10 °C, losing 19 068 J of heat energy. What is the specific heat capacity of aluminium?

Remember — you need to convert the mass to kilograms first.

ANSWER: $SHC = \dfrac{Energy}{Mass \times Temp\ Ch} = \dfrac{19\ 068}{0.2 \times 105} = \underline{908\ J/kg°C}$

Heaters Have High Heat Capacities to Store Lots of Energy

1) The materials used in heaters usually have high specific heat capacities so that they can store large amounts of heat energy.

2) Water has a really high specific heat capacity. It's also a liquid, so it can easily be pumped around in pipes — ideal for central heating systems in buildings.

3) Electric storage heaters are designed to store heat energy at night (when electricity is cheaper), and then release it during the day. They store the heat using concrete or bricks, which (surprise surprise) have a high specific heat capacity (around 880 J/kg°C).

4) Some heaters are filled with oil, which has a specific heat capacity of around 2000 J/kg°C. Because this is lower than water's specific heat capacity, oil heating systems are often not as good as water-based systems. Oil does have a higher boiling point though, which usually means oil-filled heaters can safely reach higher temperatures than water-based ones.

I've just eaten five sausages — I have a high specific meat capacity...

I'm sure you'll agree that this isn't the most exciting part of GCSE physics — it's not about space travel, crashing cars or even using springs — but it might just come up in your exam. Sadly you just have to knuckle down and get that formula triangle learnt — then you'll be well on the way to breezing through this question in the exam.

Energy Transfer

Heat is just one type of <u>energy</u>, but there are lots more as well:

Learn These Nine Types of Energy

You should know all of these <u>well enough</u> to list them <u>from memory</u>, including the examples:

1) <u>ELECTRICAL</u> Energy.. — whenever a <u>current</u> flows.
2) <u>LIGHT</u> Energy... — from the <u>Sun</u>, <u>light bulbs</u>, etc.
3) <u>SOUND</u> Energy... — from <u>loudspeakers</u> or anything <u>noisy</u>.
4) <u>KINETIC</u> Energy, or <u>MOVEMENT</u> Energy......... — anything that's <u>moving</u> has it.
5) <u>NUCLEAR</u> Energy.. — released only from <u>nuclear reactions</u>.
6) <u>THERMAL</u> Energy or <u>HEAT</u> Energy................ — <u>flows</u> from <u>hot objects</u> to colder ones.
7) <u>GRAVITATIONAL POTENTIAL</u> Energy............... — possessed by anything which can <u>fall</u>.
8) <u>ELASTIC POTENTIAL</u> Energy......................... — stretched <u>springs</u>, <u>elastic</u>, <u>rubber bands</u>, etc.
9) <u>CHEMICAL</u> Energy... — possessed by <u>foods</u>, <u>fuels</u>, <u>batteries</u> etc.

Potential and Chemical Energy Are Forms of Stored Energy

The <u>last three</u> above are forms of <u>stored energy</u> because the energy is not obviously <u>doing</u> anything, it's kind of <u>waiting to happen</u>, i.e. waiting to be turned into one of the <u>other</u> forms.

Everything Obeys the Conservation of Energy Principle

There are plenty of different <u>types</u> of energy, but <u>they all obey the principle below</u>:

> **ENERGY CAN BE <u>TRANSFERRED</u> USEFULLY FROM ONE FORM TO ANOTHER,**
> **<u>STORED</u> OR <u>DISSIPATED</u> — BUT IT CAN NEVER BE <u>CREATED OR DESTROYED</u>.**

Dissipated is a fancy way of saying the energy is spread out and lost.

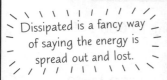

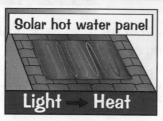
Light → Heat

Gravitational Potential → Kinetic

Here's another <u>important energy principle</u>:

> **Energy is <u>only useful</u> when it can be <u>converted</u> from one form to another.**

You Could Get Exam Questions on Energy Transfers

In the exam, they could ask you about <u>any device</u> or <u>energy transfer system</u> they feel like. If you understand a few different <u>examples</u>, it'll be easier to think through whatever they ask you about in the exam.

EXAMPLES:

<u>Electrical Devices, e.g. televisions</u>: Electrical energy ⟹ Light, sound and heat energy
<u>Batteries</u>: Chemical energy ⟹ Electrical and heat energy
<u>Electrical Generation, e.g. wind turbines</u>: Kinetic energy ⟹ Electrical and heat energy
<u>Potential Energy, e.g. firing a bow and arrow</u>: Elastic potential energy ⟹ Kinetic and heat energy

Energy can't be created or destroyed — only talked about a lot...

<u>Chemical</u> energy → <u>kinetic</u> energy → <u>electrical</u> energy → <u>kinetic</u> energy → <u>chemical</u> energy.
  (me thinking)   (me typing)   (my computer)   (printing machine)   (you reading this)

Efficiency of Machines

An open fire looks cosy, but a lot of its heat energy goes straight up the chimney, by <u>convection</u>, instead of heating up your living room. All this energy is 'wasted', so open fires aren't very efficient.

Machines Always Waste Some Energy

1) <u>Useful machines</u> are only <u>useful</u> because they <u>convert energy</u> from <u>one form</u> to <u>another</u>. Take cars for instance — you put in <u>chemical energy</u> (petrol or diesel) and the engine converts it into <u>kinetic (movement) energy</u>.

2) The <u>total energy output</u> is always the <u>same</u> as the <u>energy input</u>, but only some of the output energy is <u>useful</u>. So for every joule of chemical energy you put into your car you'll only get <u>a fraction of it</u> converted into useful kinetic energy.

3) This is because some of the <u>input energy</u> is always <u>lost</u> or <u>wasted</u>, often as <u>heat</u>. In the car example, the rest of the chemical energy is converted (mostly) into <u>heat and sound energy</u>. This is wasted energy — although you could always stick your dinner under the bonnet and warm it up on the drive home.

4) The <u>less energy</u> that is <u>wasted</u>, the <u>more efficient</u> the device is said to be.

More Efficient Machines Waste Less Energy

The <u>efficiency</u> of a machine (or anything else for that matter) is defined as:

$$\text{Efficiency} = \frac{\text{USEFUL Energy OUTPUT}}{\text{TOTAL Energy INPUT}} \ (\times 100\%)$$

1) To work out the efficiency of a machine, first find out the <u>Total Energy INPUT</u>. This is the energy supplied to the machine.

2) Then find how much <u>useful energy</u> the machine <u>delivers</u> — the <u>Useful Energy OUTPUT</u>. The question might tell you this directly, or it might tell you how much energy is <u>wasted</u> as heat/sound.

3) Then just <u>divide</u> the <u>smaller number</u> by the <u>bigger one</u> to get a value for <u>efficiency</u> somewhere between <u>0 and 1</u>. Easy. If your number is bigger than 1, you've done the division upside down.

Electric kettle
180 000 J of electrical energy supplied
9000 J of heat given out <u>to the room</u>
Think about it!

$$\text{Efficiency} = \frac{\text{Useful En. Out}}{\text{Total En. In}} = \frac{171\,000}{180\,000} = 0.95$$

4) You can convert the efficiency to a <u>percentage</u>, by multiplying it by 100. E.g. 0.6 = 60%.

5) In the exam you might be told the <u>efficiency</u> and asked to work out the <u>total energy input</u>, the <u>useful energy output</u> or the <u>energy wasted</u>. So you need to be able to <u>rearrange</u> the formula.

EXAMPLE: An ordinary light bulb is 5% efficient. If 1000 J of light energy is given out, how much energy is wasted?

ANSWER: Total Input = $\frac{\text{Useful Output}}{\text{Efficiency}} = \frac{1000\,\text{J}}{0.05} = 20\,000\,\text{J}$,

so Energy Wasted = 20 000 – 1000 = <u>19 000 J</u>

Shockingly inefficient, those ordinary light bulbs. Low-energy light bulbs are roughly 4 times more efficient, and last about 8 times as long. They're more expensive though.

6) You can use information like this to <u>draw</u> a <u>Sankey diagram</u>, or use the equation to work out the <u>efficiency</u> of something <u>from</u> a Sankey diagram — coming up on the next page.

Efficiency = pages learned ÷ cups of tea made...

Some 'waste' energy can be made useful again by a <u>heat exchanger</u>. These clever devices use wasted heat to heat a <u>fluid</u>, which traps some of the <u>energy</u>. The heat energy in the fluid can then be <u>converted</u> into a useful form again. For example, heat from a car's <u>engine</u> can be used to heat the <u>air</u> in the <u>passenger compartment</u>.

Energy Transformation Diagrams

This is another opportunity for a <u>MATHS</u> question. Fantastic. So best prepare yourself — here's what those <u>energy transformation diagrams</u> (also known as <u>Sankey</u> diagrams) are all about...

The Thickness of the Arrow Represents the Amount of Energy

The idea of <u>Sankey diagrams</u> is to make it <u>easy to see</u> at a glance how much of the <u>total energy in</u> is being <u>usefully employed</u> compared with how much is being <u>wasted</u>.

The <u>thicker the arrow</u>, the <u>more energy</u> it represents — so you see a big <u>thick arrow going in</u>, then several <u>smaller arrows going off</u> it to show the different energy transformations taking place.

You can have either a little <u>sketch</u> or a properly <u>detailed diagram</u> where the width of each arrow is proportional to the number of joules it represents.

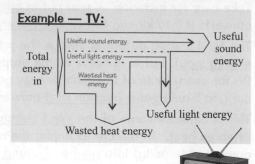

Example — TV:

Example — Sankey Diagram for a Simple Motor:

HERE'S THE SKETCH VERSION:

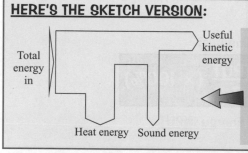

You don't know the actual amounts, but you can see that most of the energy is being wasted, and that it's mostly wasted as heat.

EXAM QUESTIONS:

With sketches, they're likely to ask you to compare two different devices and say which is more efficient. You generally want to be looking for the one with the thickest useful energy arrow(s).

AND HERE'S THE DETAILED ONE:

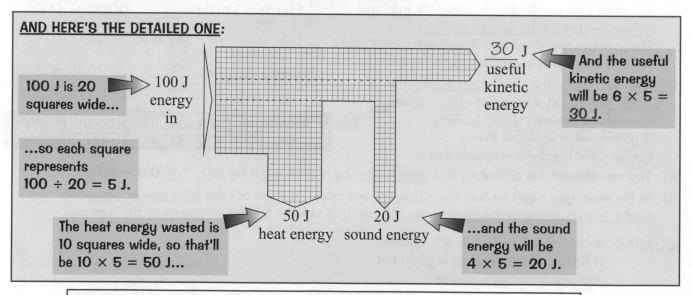

100 J is 20 squares wide...

100 J energy in

...so each square represents 100 ÷ 20 = 5 J.

The heat energy wasted is 10 squares wide, so that'll be 10 × 5 = 50 J...

50 J heat energy

20 J sound energy

...and the sound energy will be 4 × 5 = 20 J.

30 J useful kinetic energy

And the useful kinetic energy will be 6 × 5 = <u>30 J</u>.

EXAM QUESTIONS:

In an exam, the most likely question you'll get about detailed Sankey diagrams is filling in one of the numbers or calculating the efficiency. The efficiency is straightforward enough if you can work out the numbers (see p.103).

Skankey diagrams — to represent the smelliness of your socks...

If they ask you to <u>draw your own</u> Sankey diagram in the exam, and don't give you the figures, a sketch is all they'll expect. Just give a rough idea of where the energy goes. E.g. a filament lamp turns most of the input energy into heat, and only a tiny proportion goes to useful light energy.

Power Stations and Nuclear Energy

There are different types of energy resource. They fit into two broad types: renewable and non-renewable.

Non-Renewable Energy Resources Will Run Out One Day

The non-renewables are:

1) Fossil fuels: coal, oil and natural gas
2) Nuclear fuels: uranium and plutonium

a) They will all 'run out' one day.
b) They all do damage to the environment.
c) But they provide most of our energy.

Energy Resources can be Burned to Drive Turbines in Power Stations

Most of the electricity we use is generated from NON-RENEWABLE sources of energy in big thermal power stations, which are all pretty much the same apart from the boiler.

The basic features of a typical thermal power station are shown here:

1) The fuel is burned to convert its stored chemical energy into heat (thermal) energy.

2) The heat energy is used to heat water (or air in some power stations) to produce steam.

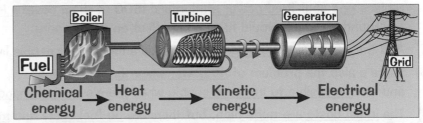

3) The steam turns a turbine, converting heat energy into kinetic energy.

4) The turbine is connected to a generator, which transfers kinetic energy into electrical energy (see p.112).

Nuclear Reactors are Just Fancy Boilers

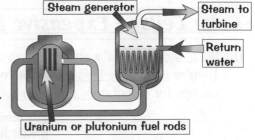

1) A nuclear power station is mostly the same as the one above, but with nuclear fission of uranium or plutonium producing the heat to make steam to drive turbines, etc. The difference is in the boiler, as shown here:

2) Nuclear power stations take the longest time of all the power stations to start up. But they produce loads more energy per gram of fuel than fossil fuels, and nuclear fission does not produce carbon dioxide.

Nuclear Power Produces Radioactive Waste

1) Nuclear power stations produce radioactive waste — this can be very dangerous and difficult to dispose of as it emits ionising radiation (see p.124) and stays radioactive for a long time.

2) Radioactive waste can put people at risk through:
   - IRRADIATION — being exposed to radiation without coming into contact with the source. The damage to your body stops as soon as you leave the area where the radioactive waste is. This means you're only exposed for a short period of time, so will receive a lower dose.
   - CONTAMINATION — picking up some radioactive waste, e.g. by breathing it in, drinking contaminated water or getting it on your skin. You'll still be exposed to the radiation once you've left the area. Contamination is worse because it leaves people exposed to ionising damage for a long time, leading to more damage.

3) Nuclear power needs extra safety precautions — waste needs disposing of carefully (e.g. it's buried deep underground), the surrounding area needs to be tested for contamination of the soil and water, and workers need to be tested regularly to check they've not been exposed to too much radiation.

4) Nuclear power is supported by some people, but people who live close are often more scared of the risks.

It all boils down to steam...

So we're still using steam engines to produce our electricity today, over 300 years after they were invented...

Wind and Solar Energy

Renewable energy sources, like wind, waves and solar energy, will not run out. What's more, they do a lot less damage to the environment. They don't generate as much electricity as non-renewables though — if they did we'd all be using solar-powered toasters by now.

Wind Power — Lots of Little Wind Turbines

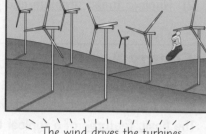

1) This involves putting lots of windmills (wind turbines) up in exposed places like on moors or round coasts.

2) Each wind turbine has its own generator inside it so the electricity is generated directly from the wind turning the blades, which turn the generator.

3) There's no pollution (except for a little bit when they're manufactured).

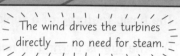
The wind drives the turbines directly — no need for steam.

4) But they do spoil the view. You need about 1500 wind turbines to replace one coal-fired power station and 1500 of them cover a lot of ground — which would have a big effect on the scenery.

5) And they can be very noisy, which can be annoying for people living nearby.

6) There's also the problem of no power when the wind stops, and it's impossible to increase supply when there's extra demand.

7) The initial costs are quite high, but there are no fuel costs and minimal running costs.

8) There's no permanent damage to the landscape — if you remove the turbines, you remove the noise and the view returns to normal.

Solar Cells — Expensive but No Environmental Damage

1) Solar cells generate electric currents directly from sunlight. *(well, there may be a bit caused by making the cells)* They're expensive initially. Solar cells are often the best source of energy for calculators and watches which don't use much electricity.

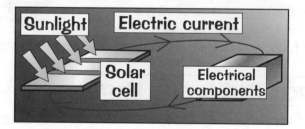

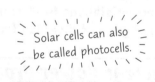
Solar cells can also be called photocells.

2) Solar power is often used in remote places where there's not much choice (e.g. the Australian outback) and to power electric road signs and satellites.

3) There's no pollution. (Although they do use quite a lot of energy to manufacture in the first place.)

4) In sunny countries solar power is a very reliable source of energy — but only in the daytime. Solar power can still be cost-effective even in cloudy countries like Britain.

5) Initial costs are high but after that the energy is free and running costs almost nil.

6) Solar cells are usually used to generate electricity on a relatively small scale, e.g. powering individual homes.

7) It's often not practical or too expensive to connect them to the National Grid (see p.113) — the cost of connecting them can be enormous compared with the value of the electricity generated.

People love the idea of wind power — just not in their backyard...

Did you know you can now get rucksacks with built-in solar cells to charge up your mobile phone, MP3 player and digital camera while you're wandering around. Pretty cool, huh.

Wave and Tidal Energy

More renewable energy sources — <u>wave power</u> and <u>tidal power</u>. It's easy to get confused between these two because they're both to do with the seaside — but don't. They're <u>completely different</u>.

Wave Energy — Lots of Little Wave-Powered Turbines

1) You need lots of small <u>wave-powered turbines</u> located <u>around the coast</u>.

2) As waves come in to the shore they provide an <u>up and down motion</u> that can be used to <u>directly</u> drive a <u>turbine</u>, which then drives a <u>generator</u>.

3) There's <u>no pollution</u>. The main problems are <u>spoiling the view</u> and being a <u>hazard to boats</u>.

4) They are <u>fairly unreliable</u>, since waves tend to die out when the <u>wind drops</u>.

5) <u>Initial costs are high</u>, but there are <u>no fuel costs</u> and <u>minimal running costs</u>. Wave power is never likely to provide energy on a <u>large scale</u>, but it can be <u>very useful</u> on <u>small islands</u>.

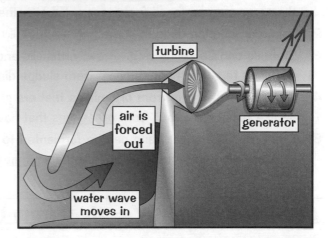

Tidal Barrages — Using the Sun and Moon's Gravity

1) <u>Tidal barrages</u> are <u>big dams</u> built across <u>river estuaries</u>, with <u>turbines</u> in them.

2) As the <u>tide comes in</u> it fills up the estuary to a height of <u>several metres</u> — it also drives the <u>turbines</u>. This water can then be allowed out <u>through the turbines</u> at a controlled speed.

3) The source of the energy is the <u>gravity</u> of the <u>Sun</u> and the <u>Moon</u>.

4) There's <u>no pollution</u>. The main problems are <u>preventing free access by boats</u>, <u>spoiling the view</u> and <u>altering the habitat</u> of the wildlife, e.g. wading birds, sea creatures and beasties who live in the sand.

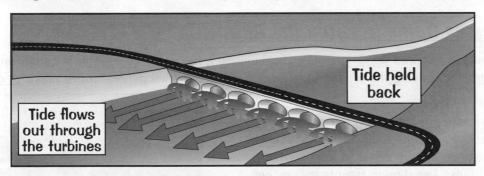

Tide flows out through the turbines

Tide held back

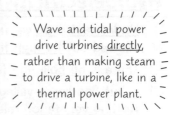

Wave and tidal power drive turbines <u>directly</u>, rather than making steam to drive a turbine, like in a thermal power plant.

5) Tides are <u>pretty reliable</u> in the sense that they happen <u>twice a day without fail</u>, and always near to the <u>predicted height</u>. The only drawback is that the <u>height</u> of the tide is <u>variable</u> so lower (neap) tides will provide <u>significantly less energy</u> than the bigger 'spring' tides. They also don't work when the water level is the <u>same</u> either side of the barrage — this happens four times a day because of the tides. But tidal barrages are <u>excellent</u> for <u>storing energy</u> ready for periods of <u>peak demand</u>.

6) <u>Initial costs are moderately high</u>, but there are <u>no fuel costs</u> and <u>minimal running costs</u>. Even though it can only be used in <u>some</u> of the <u>most suitable estuaries</u> tidal power has the potential for generating a <u>significant amount</u> of energy.

Learn about Wave Power — and bid your cares goodbye...

I do hope you appreciate the <u>big big differences</u> between <u>tidal power</u> and <u>wave power</u>. They both involve salty seawater, sure — but there the similarities end. Lots of jolly details then, just waiting to be absorbed into your cavernous intracranial void. Smile and enjoy. And <u>learn</u>.

Biofuels, Geothermal and Hydroelectricity

Well, whaddaya know — there's <u>more renewable energy</u> lurking about in piles of rubbish, rocks and rainwater.

Biofuels are Made from Plants and Waste

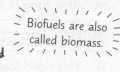
Biofuels are also called biomass.

1) Biofuels are <u>renewable energy resources</u>. They're used to generate electricity in <u>exactly</u> the same way as fossil fuels (see p.105) — they're <u>burnt</u> to heat up <u>water</u>.

2) They can be also used in some <u>cars</u> — just like fossil fuels (see p. 88).

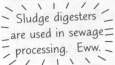
Sludge digesters are used in sewage processing. Eww.

3) Biofuels can be <u>solids</u> (e.g. straw, nutshells and woodchips), <u>liquids</u> (e.g. ethanol) or <u>gases</u> (e.g. methane 'biogas' from sludge digesters).

4) We can get <u>biofuels</u> from organisms that are <u>still alive</u> or from dead organic matter — like fossil fuels, but from <u>organisms</u> that have been living much more <u>recently</u>.

5) E.g. <u>crops</u> like sugar cane can be fermented to produce <u>ethanol</u>, or plant oils can be modified to produce <u>biodiesel</u>.

Geothermal Energy — Heat from Underground

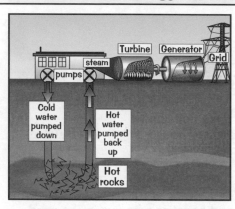

1) This is <u>only possible</u> where <u>hot rocks</u> lie quite near to the <u>surface</u>.

2) Geothermal energy is used to drive generators in <u>thermal power stations</u> (see p.105). E.g. <u>water is pumped</u> in pipes down to <u>hot rocks</u> and <u>returns as steam</u> to drive a <u>turbine</u>.

3) This is actually <u>brilliant free, renewable energy</u> with no real environmental problems.

4) The <u>main disadvantage</u> is the <u>cost of drilling</u> down <u>several km</u> to the hot rocks.

5) Unfortunately there are <u>very few places</u> where this seems to be an <u>economic option</u> (for now).

Hydroelectricity uses Dams to catch the Rain

1) <u>Hydroelectric power</u> usually requires <u>flooding</u> a <u>valley</u> by building a <u>big dam</u>. <u>Rainwater</u> is caught and allowed out <u>through turbines</u>, driving them directly. The turbines then drive generators to make <u>electricity</u>.

2) There is <u>no pollution</u> (as such)...

3) ...but flooding a valley has a <u>big impact</u> on the <u>environment</u>. <u>Rotting vegetation</u> releases methane and CO_2, some species <u>lose their habitat</u>, and the reservoirs can also look very <u>unsightly</u> when they <u>dry up</u>. Location in <u>remote valleys</u> can reduce the human impact.

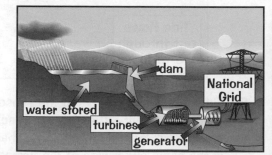

4) A <u>big advantage</u> is <u>immediate response</u> to increased demand, and it's fairly <u>reliable</u> except in times of <u>drought</u>.

5) <u>Initial costs are high</u>, but there's <u>no fuel</u> and <u>minimal running costs</u>.

6) The <u>block diagram</u> for the process looks like this:

1) Water stored in <u>reservoir</u> above the <u>turbines</u> using a <u>dam</u>.	2) <u>Gravity</u> causes the water to rush through the <u>turbines</u>.	3) A <u>generator</u> converts the movement of the turbines (<u>kinetic</u> energy) into <u>electricity</u>.

Hydroelectric power — pretty dam good...

There's <u>so much</u> to learn on this page — I'll not keep you a minute longer. <u>Get and learn it</u>...

Energy Sources and the Environment

They might fly you to Spain for your holidays and power your games consoles, but using <u>non-renewable energy sources</u> and <u>biofuels</u> to generate electricity can have <u>damaging effects</u> on the <u>environment</u>.

Non-Renewables are Linked to Environmental Problems

1) All three <u>fossil fuels</u> (coal, oil and gas) release CO_2 into the atmosphere when they're burned. For the same amount of energy produced, coal releases the most CO_2, followed by oil then gas. All this CO_2 adds to the <u>greenhouse effect</u>, and contributes to <u>global warming</u> (see p. 126-127).

2) Burning coal and oil releases <u>sulfur dioxide</u>, which causes <u>acid rain</u>. Acid rain can be harmful to trees and soils and can have far-reaching effects in ecosystems.

3) Acid rain can be reduced by taking the sulfur out <u>before</u> the fuel is burned, or cleaning up the <u>emissions</u>.

4) <u>Coal mining</u> makes a <u>mess</u> of the <u>landscape</u>, especially "<u>open-cast mining</u>".

5) <u>Oil spillages</u> cause <u>serious environmental problems</u>, affecting mammals and birds that live in and around the sea. We try to avoid them, but they'll always happen.

6) <u>Nuclear power</u> is <u>clean</u> but the <u>nuclear waste</u> is very <u>dangerous</u> and difficult to <u>dispose of</u> (see p.105).

7) Nuclear <u>fuel</u> (i.e. uranium) is <u>relatively cheap</u> but the <u>overall cost</u> of nuclear power is <u>high</u> due to the cost of the <u>power plant</u> and final <u>decommissioning</u>.

8) <u>Nuclear power</u> always carries the risk of a <u>major catastrophe</u> like the <u>Chernobyl disaster</u> in 1986.

Biofuels Have Their Disadvantages Too

1) Biofuels (p.108) are a relatively <u>quick</u> and 'natural' source of energy and are supposedly <u>carbon neutral</u>:

> The <u>plants</u> that grew to <u>produce the waste</u> (or to <u>feed the animals</u> that produced the dung) <u>absorbed carbon dioxide</u> from the atmosphere as they were growing. When the waste is burnt, this CO_2 is <u>re-released</u> into the <u>atmosphere</u>. So it has a <u>neutral effect</u> on <u>atmospheric CO_2 levels</u> (although this only really works if you keep growing plants at the same rate you're burning things).

Huge areas of land are needed to produce biofuels on a large scale.

2) Biofuel production also creates <u>methane</u> emissions — a lot of this comes from the <u>animals</u>. Nice.

3) There is still debate into the impact of biofuels on the environment, once the <u>full energy</u> that goes into the <u>production</u> is considered.

4) In some regions, large areas of <u>forest</u> have been <u>cleared</u> to make room to grow <u>biofuels</u>, resulting in lots of species losing their <u>natural habitats</u>. The <u>decay</u> and <u>burning</u> of this vegetation also increases CO_2 and <u>methane</u> emissions.

5) Biofuels have <u>potential</u>, but their use is limited by the amount of available <u>farmland</u> that can be dedicated to their production.

Carbon Capture can Reduce the Impact of Carbon Dioxide

1) <u>Carbon capture and storage</u> (CCS) is used to <u>reduce</u> the amount of CO_2 building up in the atmosphere and <u>reduce</u> the strength of the <u>greenhouse effect</u> (see page 126).

2) CCS works by <u>collecting</u> the CO_2 from power stations <u>before</u> it is released into the atmosphere.

3) The captured CO_2 can then be <u>pumped</u> into empty <u>gas fields</u> and <u>oil fields</u> like those under the North Sea. It can be safely <u>stored</u> without it adding to the greenhouse effect.

4) CCS is a <u>new technology</u> that's <u>developing quickly</u>. New ways of storing CO_2 are being explored, including <u>storing</u> CO_2 dissolved in <u>seawater</u> at the bottom of the ocean and <u>capturing</u> CO_2 with <u>algae</u>, which can then be used to <u>produce oil</u> that can be used as a <u>biofuel</u>.

Biofuels are great — but don't burn your biology notes just yet...

<u>Wowsers</u>. There certainly is a lot to bear in mind with all the different energy sources and all the good things and nasty things associated with each of them. The next page is <u>really handy</u> for making <u>comparisons</u> between different energy sources — it'll tell you everything you need to know. (Secret hint: you should definitely read it.)

Comparison of Energy Resources

Setting Up a Power Station

Because coal and oil are running out fast, many old <u>coal- and oil-fired power stations</u> are being <u>taken out of use</u>. Often they're being <u>replaced</u> by <u>gas-fired power stations</u> because they're <u>quick</u> to <u>set up</u>, there's still quite a lot of <u>gas left</u> and gas <u>doesn't pollute as badly</u> as coal and oil.

But gas is <u>not</u> the <u>only option</u>, as you really ought to know if you've been concentrating at all over the last few pages. When looking at the options for a <u>new power station</u>, there are <u>several factors</u> to consider: How much it <u>costs</u> to set up and run, <u>how long</u> it takes to <u>build</u>, <u>how much power</u> it can generate, etc. Then there are also the trickier factors like <u>damage to the environment</u> and <u>impact on local communities</u>. And because these are often <u>very contentious</u> issues, getting <u>permission</u> to build certain types of power station can be a <u>long-running</u> process, and hence <u>increase</u> the overall <u>set-up time</u>. The time and <u>cost</u> of <u>decommissioning</u> (shutting down) a power plant can also be a crucial factor.

Set-Up Costs

<u>Renewable</u> resources often need <u>bigger power stations</u> than non-renewables for the <u>same output</u>. And as you'd expect, the <u>bigger</u> the power station, the <u>more expensive</u>.

<u>Nuclear reactors</u> and <u>hydroelectric dams</u> also need <u>huge</u> amounts of <u>engineering</u> to make them <u>safe</u>, which bumps up the cost.

Set-Up/Decommissioning Time

These are both affected by the <u>size</u> of the power station, the <u>complexity</u> of the engineering and also the <u>planning issues</u> (e.g. <u>discussions</u> over whether a nuclear power station should be built on a stretch of <u>beautiful coastline</u> can last years). <u>Gas</u> is one of the <u>quickest</u> to set up. <u>Nuclear</u> power stations take by far the <u>longest</u> (and cost the most) to <u>decommission</u>.

Reliability Issues

All the <u>non-renewables</u> are <u>reliable energy providers</u> (until they run out).

Many of the <u>renewable</u> sources <u>depend on the weather</u>, which means they're pretty <u>unreliable</u> here in the UK. The <u>exceptions</u> are <u>tidal</u> power and <u>geothermal</u> (which <u>don't</u> depend on weather).

Running/Fuel Costs

<u>Renewables</u> usually have the <u>lowest running costs</u>, because there's <u>no</u> actual <u>fuel</u> involved.

Environmental Issues

If there's a <u>fuel</u> involved, there'll be <u>waste pollution</u> and you'll be <u>using up resources</u>.

If it <u>relies on the weather</u>, it's often got to be in an <u>exposed place</u> where it sticks out like a <u>sore thumb</u>.

Atmospheric Pollution
Coal, Oil, Gas,
(+ others, though less so)

Visual Pollution
Coal, Oil, Gas, Nuclear,
Tidal, Waves, Wind,
Hydroelectric,

Other Problems
Nuclear (dangerous waste, explosions, contamination),
Hydroelectric (dams bursting)

Using Up Resources
Coal, Oil, Gas, Nuclear

Noise Pollution
Coal, Oil, Gas, Nuclear,
Wind,

Disruption of Habitats
Hydroelectric, Tidal,
Biofuels.

Disruption of Leisure Activities (e.g. boats)
Waves, Tidal

Location Issues

This is fairly <u>common sense</u> — a <u>power station</u> has to be <u>near</u> to the <u>stuff it runs on</u>.

<u>Solar</u> — pretty much <u>anywhere</u>, though the sunnier the better

<u>Gas</u> — pretty much <u>anywhere</u> there's piped gas (most of the UK)

<u>Hydroelectric</u> — <u>hilly</u>, <u>rainy</u> places with <u>floodable valleys</u>, e.g. the Lake District, Scottish Highlands

<u>Wind</u> — <u>exposed</u>, <u>windy</u> places like moors and coasts or out at sea

<u>Oil</u> — near the <u>coast</u> (oil transported by sea)

<u>Waves</u> — on the <u>coast</u>

<u>Coal</u> — near <u>coal mines</u>, e.g. Yorkshire, Wales

<u>Nuclear</u> — <u>away from people</u> (in case of disaster), <u>near water</u> (for cooling)

<u>Tidal</u> — big <u>river estuaries</u> where a dam can be built

<u>Geothermal</u> — fairly limited, only in places where <u>hot rocks</u> are <u>near the Earth's surface</u>

Of course — the biggest problem is we need too much electricity...

It would be <u>lovely</u> if we could get rid of all the <u>nasty polluting power stations</u> and replace them with clean, green fuel, just like that... but it's not quite that simple. Renewable energy has its <u>own</u> problems too, and probably isn't enough to power the whole country without having a wind farm in everyone's back yard.

Revision Summary for Section 7

And that was the first bout of physics — but it's not quite over yet.
Try these questions, and if there's something you don't know, go back and learn it.

1) True or false? A hot object cools faster in a cool room than in a warm room.
2) Describe the arrangement and movement of the particles in a) solids   b) liquids   c) gases.
3) What is the name of the process where vibrating particles
pass on their extra kinetic energy to neighbouring particles?
4) Which type of heat transfer can't take place in solids — convection or conduction?
5) Explain why solar hot water panels have a matt black surface.
6) Draw a diagram of Leslie's cube and explain why the thermometer facing the black side gets hottest.
7) What happens to the particles of a gas as it turns to a liquid?
8) What is the name given to the process where a gas turns to a liquid?
9) Why does evaporation have a cooling effect on a liquid?
10) The two designs of car engine shown are made from the same material.
Which engine will transfer heat quicker? Explain why.   Engine A   Engine B
11) Describe two features of a vacuum flask that make it good at keeping hot liquids hot.
12) Do animals that live in hot climates tend to have large or small ears?
Give one reason why this might be an advantage in a hot climate.
13) Name five ways of improving energy efficiency in the home. Explain how each improvement
reduces the amount of energy lost from a house.
14)* If it costs £4000 to double glaze your house and the double glazing saves you
£100 on energy bills every year, calculate the payback time for the double glazing.
15) What can you tell from a material's U-value?
16) What property of a material tells you how much energy it can store?
17)* An ornament has a mass of 0.5 kg. The ornament is made from a material that has a specific heat capacity
of 1000 J/kg°C. How much energy does it take to heat the ornament from 20 °C to 200 °C?
18) Do heaters use materials that have a high or low specific heat capacity?
19) Name nine types of energy and give an example of each.
20) State the principle of the conservation of energy.
21) List the energy transformations that occur in a battery-powered toy car.
22)*What is the efficiency of a motor that converts 100 J of electrical energy into 70 J of useful kinetic energy?
23)*The following Sankey diagram shows how energy is converted in a catapult.

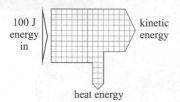

a) How much energy is converted into kinetic energy?
b) How much energy is wasted?
c) What is the efficiency of the catapult?

24) Why can't we carry on using fossil fuels forever?
25) Draw a diagram showing energy conversion in a thermal power station.
26) What process produces heat in nuclear power stations?
27) Give one advantage and one disadvantage for using the following types of power:
a) wind,   b) solar,   c) wave,   d) tidal,   e) biofuels,   f) geothermal.
28) Describe the process of generating hydroelectricity. Draw this as a block diagram.
29) Describe two disadvantages of using hydroelectricity.
30) Give three examples of environmental problems caused by fossil fuels.
31) Name two places that carbon dioxide can be stored after carbon capture.
32) Name six factors that should be considered when a new power station is being planned.
33) Which three energy sources are linked most strongly with habitat disruption?

Generating Electricity

Generators (e.g. in power stations) use something called electromagnetic induction to make electricity. It's a bit mysterious, but don't get bogged down — there's not that much to it.

Moving a Magnet in a Coil of Wire Induces a Voltage

1) You can induce (create) a voltage, and maybe a current, in a conductor by moving a magnet in or near a coil of wire. This is called electromagnetic induction or the dynamo effect.

2) As you move the magnet, the magnetic field through the coil changes — this change in the magnetic field induces a voltage, and a current flows in the wire (if it's part of a complete circuit).

3) The direction of the voltage and current depends on which way you move the magnet:

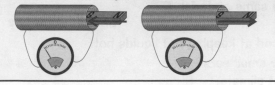

| If you move the magnet into the coil the voltage and current are induced in the opposite direction from when you move it out of the coil. | If you reverse the magnet's North-South polarity — so that the opposite pole points into the coil, the voltage and current are induced in the opposite direction. |

4) You can also create a voltage and current in a conductor by either rotating a magnet in or near a coil of wire, or by rotating a coil of wire in a magnetic field (see below).

Four Factors Affect the Size of the Induced Voltage and Current

1) If you want a bigger peak voltage (and current) you have to increase at least one of these four things:

> 1) The **STRENGTH** of the **MAGNET**   2) The **AREA** of the **COIL**
> 3) The **number of TURNS** on the **COIL**   4) The **SPEED** of movement

2) To reduce the voltage, you would reduce one of those factors, obviously.

3) If you move or turn the magnet faster, you'll get a higher peak voltage, but also get a higher frequency — because the magnetic field is reversing more frequently.

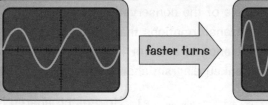

faster turns

This is How All Generators Work

1) Generators generate alternating current (a.c.) by electromagnetic induction, either by rotating a magnet or by rotating a coil of wire and keeping the magnet fixed.

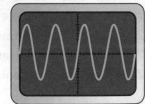

Applied Force

axis

Induced AC voltage

2) All generators just need something to do the turning. That could be anything from a steam-driven turbine (like in a power station — see p.105) to a water-wheel (like the one in the River Thames to generate electricity for the Queen's pad at Windsor).

3) A dynamo is a particular type of generator which is often used on bikes to power the lights. Here the magnet is rotated instead of the coil. The dynamo is attached to a wheel — so as you turn the wheels, you're turning the magnet inside the dynamo.

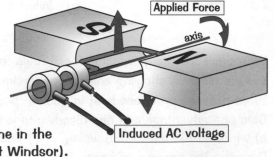

So THAT's how they make electricity — I always wondered...

The National Grid (see next page) is fed by hundreds of generators — mostly powered by burning things to make steam, which turns a turbine, which turns a coil in a magnetic field. Then, you get electricity. Great.

Electricity and the National Grid

The National Grid is the network of pylons and cables that covers the whole of Britain, getting electricity to homes everywhere. Whoever you pay for your electricity, it's the National Grid that gets it to you.

Electricity is Distributed via the National Grid...

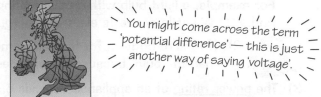

1) The National Grid takes electrical energy from power stations to where it's needed in homes and industry.

2) It enables power to be generated anywhere on the grid, and then be supplied anywhere else on the grid.

3) To transmit the huge amount of power needed, you need either a high voltage or a high current.

4) The problem with a high current is that you lose loads of energy through heat in the cables.

5) It's much cheaper to boost the voltage up really high (to 400 000 V) and keep the current very low.

You might come across the term 'potential difference' — this is just another way of saying 'voltage'.

...With a Little Help from Pylons and Transformers

1) To get the voltage to 400 000 V to transmit power requires transformers as well as big pylons with huge insulators — but it's still cheaper.

2) The transformers have to step the voltage up at one end, for efficient transmission, and then bring it back down to safe, usable levels at the other end.

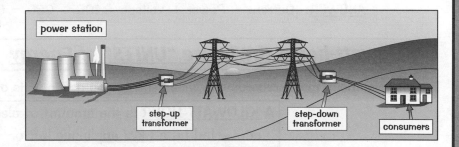

3) The voltage is increased ('stepped up') using a step-up transformer. (Yep, does what it says on the tin.)

4) It's then reduced again ('stepped down') at the consumer end using a step-down transformer.

5) Consumers receive the electricity at the mains supply voltage — 230 V.

There are Different Ways to Transmit Electricity

1) Electrical energy can be moved around by cables buried in the ground, as well as in overhead power lines.

2) Each of these different options has its pros and cons:

	Setup cost	Maintenance	Faults	How it looks	Affected by weather	Reliability	How easy to set up	Disturbance to land
Overhead Cables	lower	lots needed	easy to access	ugly	yes	less reliable	easy	minimal
Underground Cables	higher	minimal	hard to access	hidden	no	more reliable	hard	lots

Supply and Demand

1) The National Grid needs to generate and direct all the energy that the country needs — our energy demands keep on increasing too.

2) In order to meet these demands in the future, the energy supplied to the National Grid will need to increase, or the energy demands of consumers will need to decrease.

3) In the future, supply can be increased by opening more power plants or increasing their power output (or by doing both).

4) Demand can be reduced by consumers using more energy-efficient appliances, and being more careful not to waste energy in the home (e.g. turning off the lights or running washing machines at cooler temperatures).

Transformers — NOT robots in disguise...

Transformers are dead important for energy transport around the country. They increase and decrease the voltage to minimise power losses in the National Grid — this saves us loads of money, hooray.

Power and the Cost of Electricity

Electrical power is the <u>amount of energy converted per second</u>. It's a hoot.

Running Costs Depend on an Appliance's Power Rating

1) Power's measured in <u>watts</u> (W) or <u>kilowatts</u> (kW) — where <u>1 watt means 1 joule per second</u>.

   For example, a light bulb with a power rating of 100 W uses 100 J of electrical energy <u>every second</u>. And a 2 kW kettle converts electrical energy at the rate of 2000 J <u>per second</u>. Easy.

2) If they're both on for the same amount of <u>time</u>, the <u>kettle</u> is much more <u>expensive</u> to run than the bulb, because it consumes <u>more energy</u> (and it's energy you pay for — see below).

3) The <u>power rating</u> of an appliance depends on the <u>voltage</u> and the <u>current</u> it uses. Equation time...

> \ \ \ \ \ | \ | / / / /
> ~ So to transmit a lot of power, you ~
> ~ need either a high voltage or a ~
> ~ high current — see p. 113. ~
> / / / | / | \ \ \ \ \ \

> ## Power (in W) = Voltage (in V) × Current (in A) ←

Learn how to use <u>the equation</u>, and <u>how to rearrange it</u>.

> <u>EXAMPLE:</u> Find the current flowing through a 100 W light bulb if the voltage is **230 V**.
> <u>ANSWER:</u> Current = Power ÷ Voltage = 100 ÷ 230 = 0.43 amps

Kilowatt-hours (kWh) are "UNITS" of Energy

Your electricity meter records how much <u>energy</u> you use in units of <u>kilowatt-hours</u>, or <u>kWh</u>.

> A <u>KILOWATT-HOUR</u> is the amount of electrical energy
> converted by a <u>1 kW appliance</u> left on for <u>1 HOUR</u>.

The <u>higher</u> the <u>power rating</u> of an appliance, and the <u>longer</u> you leave it on, the <u>more energy</u> it consumes, and the <u>more it costs</u>. Learn how to use and rearrange this equation too...

> ## ENERGY SUPPLIED = POWER × TIME
> (in kWh)   (in kW)   (in hours)

And this one (but this one's easy):   ## COST = NUMBER OF UNITS × PRICE PER UNIT

> <u>EXAMPLE:</u> Find the cost of leaving a 60 W light bulb on for 30 minutes if one kWh costs 10p.
> <u>ANSWER:</u> Energy (in kWh) = Power (in kW) × Time (in hours) = 0.06 kW × ½ hr = <u>0.03 kWh</u>
> Cost = number of units × price per unit = 0.03 × 10p = <u>0.3p</u>

Off-Peak Electricity is Cheaper

Electricity supplied <u>during the night</u> (off-peak) is sometimes cheaper. <u>Storage heaters</u> take advantage of this — they heat up at night and then release the heat slowly throughout the day. If you can put <u>washing machines</u>, <u>dishwashers</u>, etc. on at night, so much the better.

<u>ADVANTAGES</u> of using off-peak electricity	<u>DISADVANTAGES</u> of using off-peak electricity
1) <u>Cost-effective</u> for the <u>electricity company</u> — power stations <u>can't</u> be <u>turned off</u> at night, so it's good if there's a demand for electricity at night. 2) <u>Cheaper</u> for <u>consumers</u> if they buy electricity during the <u>off-peak</u> hours.	1) There's a slightly increased <u>risk of fire</u> with more appliances going at night but no one watching. 2) You start fitting your <u>routine</u> around the <u>cheap rate</u> hours — i.e. you might stop enjoying the use of electricity during the day.

<u>Watt's the answer — well, part of it...</u>

Get a bit of <u>practice</u> with the equations in those lovely bright red boxes, and try these questions*:
1) A kettle draws a current of 12 A from the 230 V mains supply. Calculate its power rating.
2) With 0.5 kWh of energy, for how long could you run the kettle?

Choosing Electrical Appliances

Unfortunately, this isn't about what <u>colour</u> MP3 player to get. There's a bit more to it than that...

Sometimes You Have a Choice of Electrical Equipment

1) There are often a few <u>different appliances</u> that do the <u>same job</u>. In the exam, they might ask you to <u>weigh up</u> the <u>pros and cons</u> of different appliances and decide which one is <u>most suitable</u> for a particular <u>situation</u>.

2) You might need to work out whether one appliance uses <u>less energy</u> or is <u>more cost-effective</u> than another.

3) You might also need to think about the <u>practical</u> advantages and disadvantages of using different appliances. E.g. 'Can an appliance be used in areas with <u>limited electricity supplies</u>?'

4) You might get asked to compare two appliances that <u>you haven't seen before</u>. Just take your time and think about the <u>advantages</u> and <u>disadvantages</u> — you should be able to make a <u>sensible judgement</u>.

Here are some examples of the sorts of things you might have to compare:

E.G. CLOCKWORK RADIOS AND BATTERY RADIOS

1) <u>Battery radios</u> and <u>clockwork radios</u> are both handy in areas where there is <u>no mains electricity</u> supply.

2) Clockwork radios work by storing <u>elastic potential energy</u> in a spring when someone winds them up. The elastic potential energy is <u>slowly released</u> and used to power the radio.

3) <u>Batteries</u> can be <u>expensive</u>, but powering a clockwork radio is <u>free</u>.

4) Battery power is also only useful if you can get hold of some <u>new batteries</u> when the old ones <u>run out</u>. You don't get that problem with clockwork radios — but it can get annoying to have to <u>keep winding them up</u> every few hours to recharge them.

5) Clockwork radios are also better for the <u>environment</u> — a lot of <u>energy</u> and <u>harmful chemicals</u> go into making batteries, and they're often <u>tricky</u> to dispose of safely.

You Might Be Asked to Use Data to Compare Two Appliances

EXAMPLE

A company is deciding whether to install a <u>720 W low-power heater</u>, or a <u>high-power 9 kW</u> heater. The heater they choose will be on for <u>30 hours each week</u>. Their electricity provider charges <u>7p per kWh</u> of electricity. How much money per week would they save by choosing the low-power heater?

<u>ANSWER:</u> Weekly electricity used by the low-power heater = 0.720 kW × 30 h = 21.6 kWh
Weekly electricity used by the high-power heater = 9 kW × 30 h = 270 kWh
Total saving = (270 − 21.6) × 7 = <u>£17.39</u> (to the nearest penny)

Standard of Living is Affected by Access to Electricity

1) Most people in <u>developed countries</u> have access to <u>mains electricity</u>. However, many people living in the world's <u>poorest</u> countries <u>don't</u> — this has a big effect on their <u>standard of living</u>.

2) In the UK, our houses are full of devices that <u>transform electrical energy</u> into <u>other</u> useful types of energy. For example, not only is electric lighting <u>useful</u> and <u>convenient</u>, but it can also help <u>improve safety</u> at night.

3) <u>Refrigerators</u> keep <u>food fresh</u> for longer by <u>slowing</u> down the <u>growth</u> of <u>bacteria</u>. Refrigerators are also used to keep <u>vaccines</u> cold. Without refrigeration it's difficult to distribute important vaccines — this can have <u>devastating</u> effects on a country's population.

4) Electricity also plays an important role in <u>improving public health</u> in other ways. <u>Hospitals</u> in developed countries rely heavily on electricity, e.g. for <u>X-ray</u> machines. Without access to these modern machines, the <u>diagnosis</u> and <u>treatment</u> of patients would be <u>poorer</u> and could reduce <u>life expectancy</u>.

5) <u>Communications</u> are also affected by a <u>lack</u> of electricity. No electricity means no <u>internet</u> or <u>phones</u> — making it hard for people to keep <u>in touch</u>, or for people to send or receive <u>news</u> and <u>information</u>.

I'm definitely a fan of things running like clockwork...

Make sure you're happy with <u>comparing electrical devices</u>, and you know how important <u>access to electricity</u> can be.

Section 8 — Electricity and Waves

Wave Basics

Waves transfer <u>energy</u> from one place to another without transferring any <u>matter</u> (stuff).

Waves Have Amplitude, Wavelength and Frequency

1) The <u>amplitude</u> is the displacement from the <u>rest position</u> to the <u>crest</u> (NOT from a trough to a crest).

2) The <u>wavelength</u> is the length of a <u>full cycle</u> of the wave, e.g. from <u>crest to crest</u>.

3) <u>Frequency</u> is the <u>number of complete waves</u> passing a certain point <u>per second</u> OR the <u>number of waves</u> produced by a source <u>each second</u>. Frequency is measured in hertz (Hz). 1 Hz is <u>1 wave per second</u>.

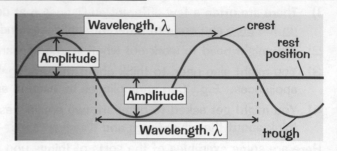

Transverse Waves Have Sideways Vibrations

<u>Most waves</u> are <u>transverse</u>:

1) <u>Light</u> and <u>all other electromagnetic (EM) waves</u>.
2) <u>Ripples</u> on water.
3) <u>Waves</u> on <u>strings</u>.
4) A <u>slinky spring</u> wiggled up and down.

In <u>TRANSVERSE</u> waves the vibrations are <u>PERPENDICULAR</u> (at <u>90°</u>) to the <u>DIRECTION OF ENERGY TRANSFER</u> of the wave.

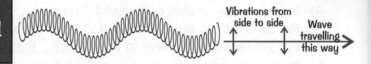

Vibrations from side to side | Wave travelling this way

Longitudinal Waves Have Vibrations Along the Same Line

Examples of <u>longitudinal</u> waves are:

1) <u>Sound waves</u> and <u>ultrasound</u>.
2) <u>Shock waves</u>, e.g. seismic waves.
3) A <u>slinky spring</u> when you <u>push</u> the end.

~ Water waves, shock waves and waves in springs and ropes are all examples of <u>mechanical waves</u>.

In <u>LONGITUDINAL</u> waves the vibrations are <u>PARALLEL</u> to the <u>DIRECTION OF ENERGY TRANSFER</u> of the wave.

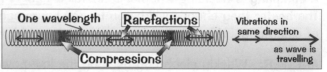

One wavelength | Rarefactions | Vibrations in same direction
Compressions | as wave is travelling

Wave Speed = Frequency × Wavelength

The equation below applies to <u>all waves</u>. You need to <u>practise using it</u>.

$$\text{Speed} = \text{Frequency} \times \text{Wavelength}$$
$$\text{(m/s)} \qquad \text{(Hz)} \qquad \text{(m)}$$

OR $v = f \times \lambda$

Speed (v is for <u>velocity</u>)   Frequency   Wavelength (that's the Greek letter 'lambda')

<u>EXAMPLE</u>: A radio wave has a frequency of 92.2×10^6 Hz. Find its wavelength. (The speed of all EM waves is 3×10^8 m/s.)

<u>ANSWER</u>: You're trying to find λ using f and v, so you've got to rearrange the equation. So $\lambda = v \div f = 3 \times 10^8 \div 9.22 \times 10^7 = \underline{3.25 \text{ m}}$.

$\dfrac{v}{f \times \lambda}$

The <u>speed</u> of a wave is <u>usually independent</u> of the <u>frequency</u> or <u>amplitude</u> of the wave.

Waves — dig the vibes, man...

The first thing to learn is that diagram at the top of the page. Then get that $v = f \times \lambda$ business <u>imprinted</u> on your brain. When you've done <u>that</u>, try this question: A sound wave travelling in a solid has a frequency of <u>1.9×10^4 Hz</u> and a wavelength of <u>12.5</u> cm. Find its speed.*

Wave Properties

If you're anything like me, you'll have spent hours gazing into a mirror in <u>wonder</u>. Here's why...

All Waves Can be Reflected, Refracted and Diffracted

1) When waves arrive at an obstacle (or meet a new material), their direction of travel can be changed.
2) This can happen by <u>reflection</u> (see below) or by <u>refraction</u> or <u>diffraction</u> (see p.118).

Reflection of Light Lets Us See Things

1) <u>Reflection of light</u> is what allows us to <u>see</u> objects. Light bounces off them into our eyes.
2) When light travelling in the <u>same direction</u> reflects from an <u>uneven surface</u> such as a <u>piece of paper</u>, the light reflects off <u>at different angles</u>.
3) When light travelling in the <u>same direction</u> reflects from an <u>even surface</u> (<u>smooth and shiny</u> like a <u>mirror</u>) then it's all reflected at the <u>same angle</u> and you get a <u>clear reflection</u>.

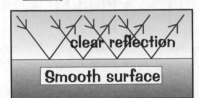

clear reflection
Smooth surface

\ \ \ \ \ \ \ \ \ / / / /
~The <u>normal</u> is an imaginary line that's
~ perpendicular (at right angles) to
— the surface at the point of incidence —
~ (where the light hits the surface).
/ / / / / / \ \ \ \ \ \ \

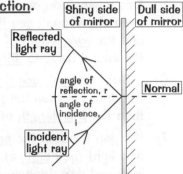

Shiny side of mirror | Dull side of mirror
Reflected light ray
angle of reflection, r | Normal
angle of incidence, i
Incident light ray

4) The <u>LAW OF REFLECTION</u> applies to <u>every</u> reflected ray:

> Angle of <u>INCIDENCE</u> = Angle of <u>REFLECTION</u>

Note that these two angles are <u>ALWAYS</u> defined between the ray itself and the <u>NORMAL</u>, dotted above. <u>Don't ever</u> label them as the angle between the ray and the <u>surface</u>. Definitely uncool.

Draw a Ray Diagram for an Image in a Plane Mirror

I said ANGLE

The diagrams below show <u>how an image is formed</u> in a <u>PLANE MIRROR</u>.
Learn these <u>important points</u>:

1) The <u>image</u> is the <u>same size</u> as the <u>object</u>.
2) It is <u>AS FAR BEHIND</u> the mirror as the object is <u>in front</u>.
3) The image is <u>virtual</u> and <u>upright</u>. The image is virtual because the object appears to be <u>behind</u> the mirror.
4) The image is <u>laterally inverted</u> — the left and right sides are <u>swapped</u>, i.e. the object's <u>left</u> side becomes its <u>right</u> side in the <u>image</u>.

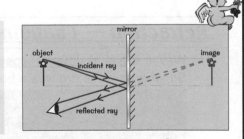

mirror
object | image
incident ray
reflected ray

1) First off, draw the <u>virtual image</u>. <u>Don't</u> try to draw the rays first. Follow the rules in the above box — the image is the <u>same size</u>, and it's <u>as far behind</u> the mirror as the object is in <u>front</u>.

2) Next, draw a <u>reflected ray</u> going from the top of the virtual image to the top of the eye. Draw a <u>bold line</u> for the part of the ray between the mirror and eye, and a <u>dotted line</u> for the part of the ray between the mirror and virtual image.

3) Now draw the <u>incident ray</u> going from the top of the object to the mirror. The incident and reflected rays follow the <u>law of reflection</u> — but you <u>don't</u> actually have to measure any angles. Just draw the ray from the <u>object</u> to the <u>point</u> where the reflected ray <u>meets the mirror</u>.

4) Now you have an <u>incident ray</u> and <u>reflected ray</u> for the <u>top</u> of the image. Do <u>steps 2 and 3</u> again for the <u>bottom</u> of the <u>eye</u> — a reflected ray going from the image to the bottom of the eye, then an incident ray from the object to the mirror.

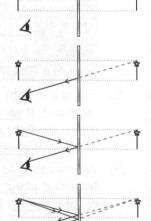

Plane mirrors — what pilots use to look behind them...

Make sure you can draw clear <u>ray diagrams</u> and you'll be well on your way to picking up lotsa marks in the exam.

Diffraction and Refraction

If you thought <u>reflection</u> was good, you'll just love <u>diffraction</u> and <u>refraction</u> — it's awesome. If you didn't find reflection interesting then I'm afraid it's tough luck — you'll have to read about them anyway. Sorry.

Diffraction — Waves Spreading Out

1) All waves <u>spread out</u> ('<u>diffract</u>') at the edges when they pass through a <u>gap</u> or <u>pass an object</u>.

2) The <u>amount</u> of diffraction depends on the <u>size</u> of the gap relative to the <u>wavelength</u> of the wave. The <u>narrower the gap</u>, or the <u>longer the wavelength</u>, the <u>more</u> the wave spreads out.

3) A <u>narrow gap</u> is one about the same size as the <u>wavelength</u> of the wave. So whether a gap counts as narrow or not depends on the wave.

4) <u>Light</u> has a very <u>small wavelength</u> (about 0.0005 mm), so it can be diffracted but it needs a <u>really small gap</u>.

5) This means you can <u>hear</u> someone through an open door even if you <u>can't see them</u>, because the <u>size of the gap</u> and the <u>wavelength of sound</u> are roughly <u>equal</u>, causing the sound wave to <u>diffract</u> and fill the room...

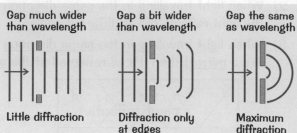

Gap much wider than wavelength — Little diffraction

Gap a bit wider than wavelength — Diffraction only at edges

Gap the same as wavelength — Maximum diffraction

6) ...But you <u>can't see them</u> unless you're <u>directly facing</u> the door because the gap is about a <u>million</u> times <u>bigger</u> than the <u>wavelength</u> of <u>light</u>, so it <u>won't</u> diffract enough.

7) If a gap is about the <u>same size</u> as the wavelength of a light, you <u>can</u> get a <u>diffraction pattern</u> of light and dark fringes, as shown here.

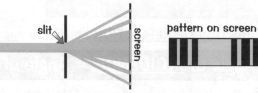

light — slit — screen — pattern on screen

8) You get diffraction around the edges of <u>obstacles</u> too. The <u>shadow</u> is where the wave is <u>blocked</u>. The <u>wider</u> the obstacle compared to the <u>wavelength</u>, the <u>less diffraction</u> it causes, so the <u>longer</u> the shadow.

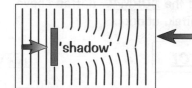

'shadow'

Refraction — Changing the Speed of a Wave Can Change its Direction

1) Waves travel at <u>different speeds</u> in substances which have <u>different densities</u>. So when a wave crosses a boundary between two substances (from glass to air, say) it <u>changes speed</u>:

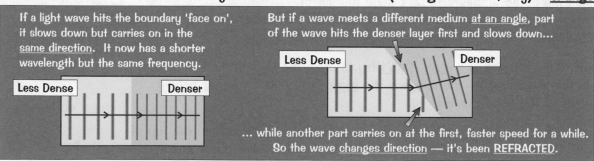

If a light wave hits the boundary 'face on', it slows down but carries on in the <u>same direction</u>. It now has a shorter wavelength but the same frequency.

Less Dense — Denser

But if a wave meets a different medium <u>at an angle</u>, part of the wave hits the denser layer first and slows down...

Less Dense — Denser

... while another part carries on at the first, faster speed for a while. So the wave <u>changes direction</u> — it's been <u>REFRACTED</u>.

2) E.g. when light passes from <u>air</u> into the <u>glass</u> of a window pane (a <u>denser</u> medium), it <u>slows down</u> — causing the light to refract <u>towards</u> the normal. When the light reaches the 'glass to air' boundary on the <u>other side</u> of the window, it <u>speeds up</u> and refracts <u>away</u> from the normal.

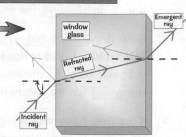

Emergent ray — window glass — Refracted ray — Incident ray

3) Waves are <u>only</u> refracted if they meet a new medium <u>at an angle</u>. If they're travelling <u>along the normal</u> (i.e. the angle of incidence is zero) they will <u>change speed</u>, but are <u>NOT refracted</u> — they don't change direction.

Lights, camera, refraction...

Remember that <u>all</u> waves can be <u>diffracted</u>. It doesn't matter what <u>type</u> of wave it is — sound, light, water... The key point to remember about <u>refraction</u> is that the wave has to meet a boundary <u>at an angle</u>.

Sound Waves

We hear sounds when <u>vibrations</u> reach our <u>eardrums</u>. Read on to find out how sound waves work.

Sound Travels as a Wave

1) <u>Sound waves</u> are caused by <u>vibrating objects</u>.
These mechanical vibrations are passed through the
surrounding medium as a series of compressions.
They're a type of <u>longitudinal wave</u> (see p.116).

2) Sometimes the sound will eventually travel through someone's <u>ear</u> and reach their
<u>eardrum</u>, at which point the person might <u>hear it</u>.

3) Sound generally travels <u>faster in solids</u> than in liquids, and faster in liquids than in
gases.

4) Sound can't travel in <u>space</u>, because it's mostly a <u>vacuum</u> (there are no particles).

Sound Waves Can Reflect and Refract

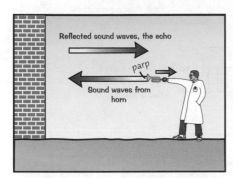

1) Sound waves will be <u>reflected</u> by <u>hard flat surfaces</u>.

2) This is very noticeable in an <u>empty room</u>. A big empty room
sounds <u>completely different</u> once you've put <u>carpet</u>, <u>curtains</u>
and a bit of <u>furniture</u> in it. That's because these things <u>absorb</u>
the sound quickly and stop it <u>echoing</u> around the room.
<u>Echoes</u> are just <u>reflected</u> sound waves.

3) You hear a <u>delay</u> between the <u>original</u> sound
and the <u>echo</u> because the echoed sound
waves have to <u>travel further</u>, and so take
<u>longer</u> to reach your ears.

4) <u>Sound waves</u> will also refract (see page 118) as they enter <u>different media</u>.
As they enter <u>denser</u> material, they <u>speed up</u>. (However, since sound waves are always
<u>spreading out so much</u>, the change in direction is <u>hard to spot</u> under normal circumstances.)

The Higher the Frequency, the Higher the Pitch

1) <u>High frequency</u> sound waves sound <u>high-pitched</u> like a <u>squeaking mouse</u>.

2) <u>Low frequency</u> sound waves sound <u>low-pitched</u> like a <u>mooing cow</u>.

1 kHz = 1000 Hz

3) <u>Frequency</u> is the number of <u>complete vibrations</u> each second — so a wave that has a
frequency of 100 Hz vibrates 100 times each second.

4) <u>High frequency</u> (or high pitch) also means <u>shorter wavelength</u> (see p. 116).

5) The <u>loudness</u> of a sound depends on the <u>amplitude</u> (p. 116) of the sound wave.
The <u>bigger</u> the amplitude, the <u>louder</u> the sound.

Electrical devices can be made which produce <u>electrical oscillations</u> of <u>any frequency</u>. These can easily
be converted into <u>mechanical vibrations</u> to produce <u>sound</u> waves <u>beyond the range of human hearing</u>:

1) Sound that has a frequency <u>above</u> the range of human hearing (about <u>20 kHz</u>) is called <u>ultrasound</u>.

2) It's used for <u>pre-natal scanning</u>, and <u>sonar</u>.

3) Sound that's too <u>low</u> for humans to hear (below <u>20 Hz</u>) is called <u>infrasound</u>.

The room always feels big and empty whenever I tell a joke... (It must be the carpets.)

The thing to do here is learn the facts. There's a simple equation that says <u>the more you learn now</u>, the <u>more
marks you'll get</u> in the exam. A lot of questions just test whether you've learnt the facts. Easy marks, really.

Analogue and Digital Signals

Sound and images can be sent as analogue or digital signals, but digital technology is gradually taking over.

Information is Converted into Signals

Information is being transmitted everywhere all the time.

1) Whatever kind of information you're sending (text, sound, pictures...) it's converted into electrical signals before it's transmitted.

2) It's then sent long distances down telephone lines or...

3) ...superimposed (mixed) onto 'carrier' EM waves (see next page).

4) It's then sent out as either analogue or digital signals.

Analogue Signals Vary but Digital's Either On or Off

1) The amplitude or frequency of an analogue signal varies continuously. An analogue signal can take any value in a particular range.

2) Digital signals can only take one of a small number of discrete values (usually two), e.g. 0 or 1, on or off, true or false.

3) The information is carried by switching the EM carrier wave on or off.

4) This creates pulses — short bursts of waves, e.g. where 0 = off (no pulse) and 1 = on (pulse).

5) A digital receiver will decode these pulses to get a copy of the original signal.

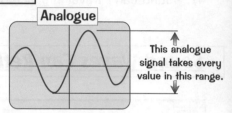

Analogue

This analogue signal takes every value in this range.

Digital

This digital signal only takes these two values.

Signals Have to be Amplified

Both digital and analogue signals weaken as they travel, so they may need to be amplified along their route. They also pick up interference or noise from electrical disturbances or other signals.

A nice smooth analogue signal

The same signal with noise

Digital Signals are Far Better Quality

1) Noise is less of a problem with digital signals than with analogue. If you receive a 'noisy' digital signal, it's pretty obvious what it's supposed to be. So it's easy to 'clean up' the signal — the noise doesn't get amplified.

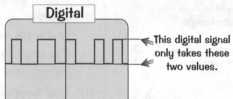

This noisy digital signal... ...is obviously supposed to be this.

2) But if you receive a noisy analogue signal, it's difficult to know what the original signal would have looked like. And if you amplify a noisy analogue signal, you amplify the noise as well.

But this noisy analogue signal... ...could have started like this... ...or this...

3) This is why digital signals are much higher quality — the information received is the same as the original.

4) Another advantage of digital technology is you can transmit several signals at once using just one cable or EM wave — so you can send more information (in a given time) than using analogue signals.

5) Also, digital signals are easy to process using computers, since computers are digital devices.

6) The amount of information used to store a digital image or sound is measured in bytes. Images and sounds will be of higher quality when the amount of information stored is higher.

I've got loads of digital stuff — watch, radio, fingers...

Digital signals are great — unless you live in a part of the country which currently has poor reception of digital broadcasts, in which case you get no benefit at all. This is because if you don't get spot-on reception of digital signals in your area, you won't get a grainy picture (as with analogue signals) — you'll get nothing at all.

EM Waves and Communication

Types of <u>electromagnetic</u> (EM) wave have a lot in common with one another, but their <u>differences</u> make them useful to us in different ways. These pages are packed with loads of dead important info, so pay attention...

There's a Continuous Spectrum of EM Waves

EM waves with <u>different wavelengths</u> (or frequencies) have different properties. We group them into <u>seven basic types</u>, but the different regions actually merge to form a <u>continuous spectrum</u>. They're shown below with <u>increasing frequency</u> and <u>energy</u> (decreasing wavelength) from left to right.

RADIO WAVES	MICRO WAVES	INFRA RED	VISIBLE LIGHT	ULTRA VIOLET	X-RAYS	GAMMA RAYS
wavelength → $1\ m - 10^4\ m$	$10^{-2}\ m$ (1 cm)	$10^{-5}\ m$ (0.01 mm)	$10^{-7}\ m$	$10^{-8}\ m$	$10^{-10}\ m$	$10^{-15}\ m$

1) EM waves vary in <u>wavelength</u> from around $10^{-15}\ m$ to more than $10^4\ m$.
2) All the different types of EM wave travel at the <u>same speed</u> (3×10^8 m/s) in a <u>vacuum</u> (e.g. space).
3) EM waves with <u>higher frequencies</u> have <u>shorter wavelengths</u>.
4) Because of their <u>different properties</u>, different EM waves are used for <u>different purposes</u>.

Radio Waves are Used Mainly for Communication

1) <u>Radio waves</u> are EM waves with wavelengths longer than about 10 cm.
2) <u>Long-wave radio</u> (wavelengths of <u>1 – 10 km</u>) can be transmitted from London, say, and received halfway round the world. That's because long wavelengths <u>diffract</u> (<u>bend</u>) (see p.118) around the curved surface of the Earth.

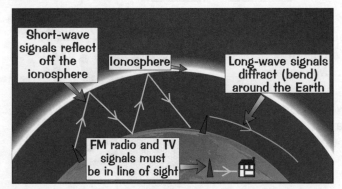

Short-wave signals reflect off the ionosphere

Ionosphere

Long-wave signals diffract (bend) around the Earth

FM radio and TV signals must be in line of sight

Other EM waves can be used for communications too, in different ways — such as microwaves (p. 122), infrared and visible light (p. 123).

3) <u>Long-wave radio</u> wavelengths can also <u>diffract</u> around <u>hills</u>, into <u>tunnels</u> and all sorts.
4) This <u>diffraction effect</u> makes it possible for radio signals to be <u>received</u> even if the receiver <u>isn't</u> in <u>line of the sight</u> of the <u>transmitter</u>.
5) The radio waves used for <u>TV and FM radio</u> transmissions have very short wavelengths (10 cm – 10 m). To get reception, you must be in <u>direct sight of the transmitter</u> — the signal doesn't bend around hills or travel far <u>through</u> buildings.
6) <u>Short-wave radio</u> signals (wavelengths of about <u>10 m – 100 m</u>) can, like long-wave, be received at <u>long distances</u> from the transmitter. That's because they are <u>reflected</u> (p.117) off the <u>ionosphere</u> — an <u>electrically charged layer</u> in the Earth's upper atmosphere.
7) <u>Medium-wave</u> signals (well, the shorter ones) can also reflect from the ionosphere, depending on atmospheric conditions and the time of day.

Size matters — and my wave's longer than yours...

You might have to <u>name</u> and <u>order</u> of the different types of EM waves in terms of their <u>energy</u>, <u>frequency</u> and <u>wavelength</u>. To remember the order of <u>increasing frequency</u> and <u>energy</u>, I use the mnemonic <u>R</u>ock <u>M</u>usic <u>I</u>s <u>V</u>ery <u>U</u>seful for e<u>X</u>periments with <u>G</u>oats. It sounds stupid but it <u>does</u> work — why not make up your own...

Microwaves

No phones, no dinner — what would we do without <u>microwaves</u>?

Microwaves are Used for Satellite Communication and Mobile Phones

microwaves

clouds and water vapour

1) Communication to and from <u>satellites</u> (including satellite TV signals and satellite phones) uses microwaves. But you need to use microwaves which can <u>pass easily</u> through the Earth's <u>watery atmosphere</u>.

2) For satellite TV, the signal from a <u>transmitter</u> is transmitted into space...

3) ... where it's picked up by the satellite receiver dish <u>orbiting</u> thousands of kilometres above the Earth. The satellite <u>transmits</u> the signal back to Earth in a different direction...

4) ... where it's received by a <u>satellite dish</u> on the ground. There is a slight <u>time delay</u> between the signal being sent and <u>received</u>, e.g. from the UK to Australia, because of the <u>long distance</u> the signal has to travel.

5) Mobile phone signals also travel from your phone to the nearest <u>transmitter</u> as <u>microwaves</u>.

Microwave Ovens Use a Different Microwave Wavelength from Satellites

1) In <u>communications</u>, the microwaves used need to <u>pass through</u> the Earth's watery atmosphere.

2) In <u>microwave ovens</u>, the microwaves need to be <u>absorbed</u> by <u>water molecules</u> in food to be able to heat it up — so they use a <u>different</u> wavelength to those used in satellite communications.

3) The microwaves penetrate up to a few centimetres into the food before being <u>absorbed</u> by water molecules. The energy from the absorbed microwaves causes the food to heat up. The heat energy is then <u>conducted</u> or <u>convected</u> to other parts of the food.

Microwave radiation would heat up the water in your body's <u>cells</u> if you were exposed to it. Microwave ovens have <u>metal cases</u> and <u>screens</u> over their glass doors which <u>reflect</u> and <u>absorb</u> the microwaves, stopping them getting out.

Some People Say There are Health Risks with Using Microwaves

1) Microwaves are used to <u>send signals</u> between <u>mobile phones</u> and mobile phone <u>masts</u>.

2) When you make a call on your mobile, the phone <u>emits</u> microwave radiation. Some of this radiation is <u>absorbed</u> by your body, and causes <u>heating</u> of your body tissues (which all contain <u>water</u>).

3) It's the absorption that's <u>harmful</u> — if microwaves are absorbed by water molecules in living tissue, <u>cells</u> may be <u>burned</u> or killed.

4) Some people <u>think</u> that the microwaves emitted into your body from <u>using</u> a <u>mobile phone</u> or <u>living near</u> a mobile phone <u>mast</u> could damage your <u>health</u>.

5) There's <u>no conclusive proof</u> either way yet though. Lots of studies have been published, which has allowed the results to be checked, but so far they have given <u>conflicting evidence</u>.

Microwaves — for when you're only slightly sad to say goodbye...

In a microwave, the whole idea is for <u>water molecules</u> to <u>absorb</u> the microwave energy. But that's <u>not</u> ideal for communication — if all the energy was absorbed by water molecules, the signals would never get through clouds.

Infrared and Visible Light

Infrared radiation (or IR) may sound space-age but it's actually as common as beans on toast.

Infrared Waves are Used for Remote Controls and Optical Fibres

1) Infrared waves are used in lots of wireless remote controllers.

2) Remote controls work by emitting different patterns of infrared waves to send different commands to an appliance, e.g. a TV.

3) Optical fibres (e.g. those used in phone lines) can carry data over long distances very quickly.

4) They use both infrared waves and visible light.

5) The signal is carried as pulses of light or infrared radiation and is reflected off the sides of a very narrow core from one end of the fibre to the other.

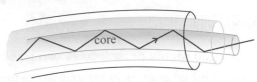

IR Can be Used to Monitor Temperature

1) Infrared radiation is also known as heat radiation. It's given out by hot objects — and the hotter the object, the more IR it gives out.

2) This means infrared can be used to monitor temperatures. For example, heat loss through a house's uninsulated roof can be detected using infrared sensors, and security systems detect body heat.

3) Infrared is also detected by night-vision equipment. The equipment turns it into an electrical signal, which is displayed on a screen as a picture. The hotter an object is, the brighter it appears. Police and the military use this to spot baddies running away, like you've seen on TV.

IR Has Many Other Uses Around the Home

1) As well as remote controls, optical fibres and night vision, infrared radiation is also used for cooking, e.g. in grills and toasters.

2) It can also be used to transmit information between mobile phones or computers — but only over short distances.

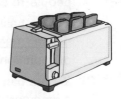

Visible Light is Useful for Photography

It sounds pretty obvious, but photography would be kinda tricky without visible light.

1) Cameras use a lens to focus visible light onto a light-sensitive film or electronic sensor.

2) The lens aperture controls how much light enters the camera (like the pupil in an eye).

3) The shutter speed determines how long the film or sensor is exposed to the light.

4) By varying the aperture and shutter speed (and also the sensitivity of the film or the sensor), a photographer can capture as much or as little light as they want in their photograph.

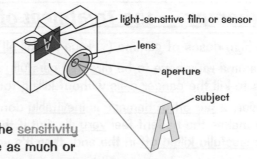

light-sensitive film or sensor
lens
aperture
subject

Don't lose control of your sensors — this page isn't remotely hard...

Because infrared technology is relatively cheap and cheerful we can afford to use it to make our lives a bit easier (and safer) around the home. Bad news for criminals. Remember — crime doesn't pay, revision does. Fact.

X-Rays and Gamma Rays

Generally, high-energy EM radiation (like X-rays and gamma rays) is more harmful than low-energy radiation.

Some EM Radiation Causes Ionisation

1) All substances are made of atoms and molecules.

2) When radiation hits an atom or molecule, it sometimes has enough energy to remove an electron and change the atom or molecule. This process is called ionisation:

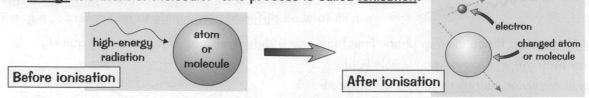

3) The changed atoms or molecules can go on to initiate (start) other chemical reactions.

4) It takes a lot of energy to remove an electron from an atom or molecule. So only the types of radiation with high enough energy can cause ionisation — ultraviolet, X-rays and gamma rays. These types of electromagnetic radiation are called ionising radiation.

5) Some substances (radioactive materials) emit ionising gamma radiation all the time.

Ionisation is Dangerous if it Happens in Your Cells

1) In the cells in your body, there are many important molecules, including DNA molecules.

2) If your cells are exposed to ionising radiation, the damage to DNA molecules can cause mutations, and the cells might start dividing over and over again, without stopping — this is cancer.

3) Very high doses of radiation can kill your cells altogether — this is what happens in 'radiation sickness'.

4) The longer you're exposed to the radiation the more damage it causes.

X-Rays are Used to Look Inside Objects

1) Radiographers in hospitals take X-ray 'photographs' of people to see if they have any broken bones.

2) X-rays pass easily through flesh but not so easily through denser material like bones or metal. So it's the amount of radiation that's absorbed (or not absorbed) that gives you an X-ray image.

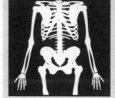

The brighter bits are where fewer X-rays get through. This is a negative image. The plate starts off all white.

3) X-rays can cause cancer, so radiographers wear lead aprons and stand behind a lead screen or leave the room to keep their exposure to X-rays to a minimum.

4) Airport security use X-rays to scan luggage to check for suspicious-looking objects.

5) Some airports now use X-ray scanners on passengers to look for concealed weapons or explosives — low-level X-rays are used so they aren't as harmful as the X-rays used in hospitals.

Radiotherapy — the Treatment of Cancer Using Gamma Rays

1) Since high doses of gamma (γ) rays will kill all living cells, they can be used to treat cancers.

2) The gamma rays have to be directed carefully and at just the right dosage so as to kill the cancer cells without killing too many normal cells.

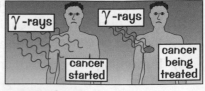

3) However, a fair bit of damage is inevitably done to normal cells, which makes the patient feel very ill. But if the cancer is successfully killed off in the end, then it's worth it.

4) Gamma rays can also be used to diagnose cancer. A radioactive isotope is injected into the patient — a gamma camera is then used to detect where the radioactive isotope travels in the body. This creates an image which can then be used to detect where there might be cancer.

Don't lie to an X-ray — they can see right through you...

X-rays and gamma rays can be harmful, but really useful too — as long as you're not exposed to them too much.

UV Radiation and Ozone

UV radiation also causes ionisation. The Sun emits loads of UV, but the ozone layer can absorb it.

Ultraviolet Radiation Causes Skin Cancer

1) If you spend a lot of time in the sun, you can expect to get a tan and maybe sunburn.

2) But the more time you spend in the sun, the more chance you also have of getting skin cancer. This is because the Sun's rays include ultraviolet radiation (UV) which damages the DNA in your cells.

3) UV radiation can also cause you eye problems, such as cataracts, as well as premature skin aging (eek!).

4) Darker skin gives some protection against UV rays — it absorbs more UV radiation. This prevents some of the damaging radiation from reaching the more vulnerable tissues deeper in the body.

5) Everyone should protect themselves from the Sun, but if you're pale skinned, you need to take extra care, and use a sunscreen with a higher Sun Protection Factor (SPF).

6) An SPF of 15 means you can spend 15 times as long as you otherwise could in the sun without burning.

7) We're kept informed of the risks of exposure to UV — research into its effects is made public through the media and advertising, and the government tells people how to keep safe to improve public health.

8) It's not just exposure to the Sun that's a problem — we are now being warned of the risks of prolonged use of sunbeds too. Tanning salons have time limits to make sure people are not over-exposed.

The Ozone Layer Protects Us from UV Radiation

1) There's a layer of ozone high up in the Earth's atmosphere which absorbs some of the UV rays from the Sun — so it reduces the amount of UV radiation reaching the Earth's surface.

2) Ozone is a form of oxygen. An ozone molecule is just three oxygen atoms joined together — O_3. It's formed like this:

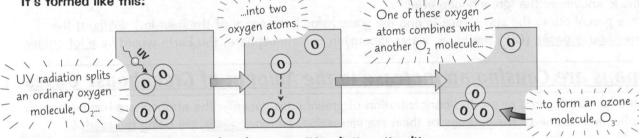

UV radiation splits an ordinary oxygen molecule, O_2...

...into two oxygen atoms.

One of these oxygen atoms combines with another O_2 molecule....

...to form an ozone molecule, O_3.

3) When an ozone molecule, O_3, absorbs more UV radiation, it splits into O_2 and O again. So the reaction is reversible (can go forwards and backwards) — causing a chemical change each time.

4) Recently, the ozone layer has got thinner because of pollution from CFCs — these are gases which react with ozone molecules and break them up. This depletion of the ozone layer allows more UV rays to reach us at the surface of the Earth (which, as you know, can be a danger to our health).

There's a Hole in the Ozone Layer over Antarctica

1) In winter, special weather effects cause the concentration of ozone over Antarctica to drop dramatically. It increases again in spring, but the winter concentration has been dropping. The low concentration looks like a 'hole' on satellite images.

2) Scientists now monitor the ozone concentration very closely to get a better understanding of why it's decreasing, and how to prevent further depletion.

3) Many different studies have been carried out internationally, using different equipment, to get accurate results — this helps scientists to be confident that their hypotheses and predictions are correct.

4) Studies led scientists to confirm that CFCs were causing the depletion of the ozone layer, so the international community banned them. We used to use CFCs all the time but now international bans and restrictions on CFC use have been put in place because of their environmental impact.

Use protection — wear a hat...

Things are slowly getting better for the ozone layer since lots of countries agreed to reduce their use of CFCs.

The Greenhouse Effect

The atmosphere <u>keeps us warm</u> by <u>trapping heat</u>.

Some Radiation from the Sun Passes Through the Atmosphere

1) The Earth is surrounded by an <u>atmosphere</u> made up of various gases — the <u>air</u>.

2) The gases in the atmosphere <u>filter out</u> certain types of radiation from the Sun — they <u>absorb</u> or <u>reflect</u> radiation of <u>certain wavelengths</u> (<u>infrared</u>).

3) However, some wavelengths of radiation — mainly <u>visible light</u> and some <u>radio waves</u> — pass through the atmosphere quite easily.

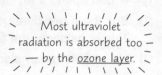
Most ultraviolet radiation is absorbed too — by the <u>ozone layer</u>.

The Greenhouse Effect Helps Regulate Earth's Temperature

1) The Earth <u>absorbs</u> <u>short wavelength</u> <u>EM radiation</u> from the Sun. This warms the Earth's surface up. The Earth then <u>emits</u> some of this EM radiation back out into space — this tends to cool us down.

2) Most of the radiation <u>emitted</u> from Earth is <u>longer wavelength</u> infrared radiation — <u>heat</u>.

3) A lot of this infrared radiation is <u>absorbed</u> by atmospheric gases, including <u>carbon dioxide</u>, <u>methane</u> and <u>water vapour</u>.

4) These gases then re-radiate heat in all directions, including <u>back towards the Earth</u>.

5) So the atmosphere acts as an insulating layer, stopping the Earth losing all its heat at night.

6) This is known as the 'greenhouse effect'. (In a greenhouse, the sun shines in and the glass helps keep some of the heat in.) <u>Without</u> the <u>greenhouse gases</u> (CO_2, methane, water vapour) in our atmosphere, the Earth would be <u>a lot colder</u>.

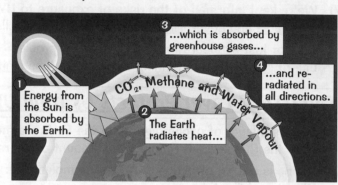

③ ...which is absorbed by greenhouse gases...

④ ...and re-radiated in all directions.

CO_2, Methane and Water Vapour

① Energy from the Sun is absorbed by the Earth.

② The Earth radiates heat...

Humans are Causing an Increase in the Amount of Greenhouse Gases

Over the last 200 years or so, the concentration of greenhouse gases in the atmosphere has been <u>increasing</u>. This is because some of the <u>sources</u> of them are increasing, so <u>more gases</u> are being <u>released</u>:

Carbon Dioxide

People use more energy (e.g. travel more in <u>cars</u>) — which we get mainly from <u>burning fossil fuels</u>, which releases <u>more carbon dioxide</u>.

More <u>land</u> is needed for <u>houses</u> and <u>food</u> and the space is often made by <u>chopping down</u> and <u>burning trees</u> — fewer trees mean less CO_2 is absorbed, and burning releases more CO_2.

CO_2 also comes from <u>natural</u> sources — e.g. <u>respiration</u> in animals and plants, and volcanic eruptions can release it.

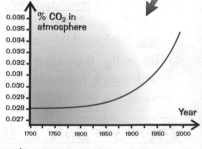
% CO_2 in atmosphere

Year

You might have to interpret data on greenhouse gases — there's more on interpreting data on pages 6-7.

Methane

<u>Cattle</u> farming has increased to feed the growing <u>population</u> — cattle <u>digestion</u> produces <u>methane</u>, so the amount of methane is increasing.

<u>Decaying</u> waste in <u>landfill</u> sites produces methane — the <u>amount</u> of waste is increasing, causing, you guessed it, an increase in methane.

Methane is released naturally by <u>volcanoes</u>, <u>wetlands</u> and wild <u>animals</u>.

Water Vapour

Most water vapour comes from <u>natural</u> sources — mainly <u>oceans</u>, seas, rivers and lakes. As global temperature increases (see next page), so <u>could</u> the amount of water vapour. <u>Power stations</u> also produce water vapour, which can affect the amount in the local area.

A biologist, a chemist and a physicist walk into a greenhouse...

...it works out badly. <u>Without</u> the greenhouse effect the Earth would be pretty nippy. Brrrrr.

Global Warming and Climate Change

Without any 'greenhouse gases' in the atmosphere, the Earth would be about 30 °C colder than it is now. So we <u>need</u> the greenhouse effect — just <u>not too much</u> of it...

Upsetting the Greenhouse Effect Has Led to Global Warming

1) Since we started burning fossil fuels in a big way, the level of <u>carbon dioxide</u> in the atmosphere has increased (see previous page).

2) The <u>global temperature</u> has also risen during this time (<u>global warming</u>). There's a <u>link</u> between concentration of CO_2 and global temperature.

3) A lot of evidence shows that the <u>rise in CO$_2$</u> level is <u>causing</u> global warming by <u>increasing</u> the greenhouse effect (see previous page).

4) So there's now a <u>scientific consensus</u> (general agreement) that <u>humans</u> are causing global warming.

5) Global warming is a type of <u>climate change</u>, and it also causes other types, e.g. changing <u>weather</u> patterns.

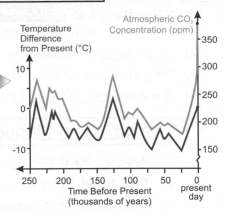

Scientists Use Computer Models to Understand Climate Change

The climate is very complicated — conditions in the <u>atmosphere</u>, <u>oceans</u> and <u>land</u> all affect one another.

1) A <u>climate model</u> is a great big load of <u>equations</u> linking these various parts of the climate system. The idea is to mimic what goes on in the real climate by doing <u>calculations</u>.

2) Once you've programmed a big <u>computer</u> with your equations, you need some <u>data</u> to start the calculations off. E.g. you might put in some data about <u>temperature</u> at the surface of the ocean in various places. The computer uses this data to work out, say, the speed and direction of ocean <u>currents</u>... then uses those results to work out <u>air temperatures</u> around the world. (It's a lot more complicated than this, but you don't have to know any details.)

3) Climate models can also be used to explain why the climate is changing <u>now</u>. We know that the Earth's climate <u>varies naturally</u> — changes in our orbit around the Sun cause ice ages, for instance. Climate modelling over the last few years has shown that <u>natural changes</u> <u>don't explain</u> the current 'global warming' — and that the increase in greenhouse gases due to human activity is the cause.

The Consequences of Global Warming Could be Pretty Serious

1) As the sea gets warmer, it <u>expands</u>, causing sea level to <u>rise</u>. Sea level <u>has risen</u> a little bit over the last 100 years. If it keeps rising it'll be <u>bad news</u> for people living in <u>low-lying</u> places like the Netherlands, East Anglia and the Maldives — they'd be <u>flooded</u>.

2) Higher temperatures also make <u>ice melt</u>. Water that's currently 'trapped' on land as ice runs into the sea, causing sea level to rise even more.

3) Global warming has <u>changed weather patterns</u> in many parts of the world. It's thought that many regions will suffer <u>more extreme weather</u> because of this, e.g. longer, hotter droughts. <u>Hurricanes</u> form over water that's warmer than 27 °C — so with more warm water, you'd expect <u>more hurricanes</u>.

4) The <u>extra heat</u> in the atmosphere will also <u>increase convection</u> (<u>stronger winds</u>) and result in <u>more water vapour</u> (<u>more rain</u>), causing more storms and <u>floods</u>.

5) <u>Changing weather patterns</u> also affect <u>food production</u> — some regions are now <u>too dry</u> to grow food, some <u>too wet</u>. This will <u>get worse</u> as <u>temperature increases</u> and weather patterns change more.

Be a climate model — go on a diet and solve lots of equations...

'Global warming' could mean that some parts of the world cool down. For instance, as ice melts, lots of cold fresh water will enter the sea and this could disrupt the <u>ocean currents</u>. This could be bad news for us in Britain — if the nice <u>warm</u> currents we get at the moment weaken, we'll be a lot colder.

Seismic Waves

Earthquakes produce <u>seismic waves</u> that travel through the Earth.
Scientists can detect these waves and use them to investigate the Earth's <u>inner structure</u>.

Earthquakes Cause Different Types of Seismic Waves

1) When there's an <u>earthquake</u>, it produces <u>wave motions</u> (<u>shock waves</u>) which travel on the <u>surface</u> and <u>inside</u> the Earth. We <u>record</u> these <u>seismic waves</u> all over the surface of the planet using <u>seismographs</u>.

2) <u>Seismologists</u> measure the <u>time</u> it takes for the shock waves to reach each seismograph.

3) They also note which parts of the Earth <u>don't receive the shock waves</u> at all.

4) There are <u>two different types</u> of seismic waves that travel through the Earth — <u>P-waves</u> and <u>S-waves</u>.

P-Waves Travel Through Solids and Liquids

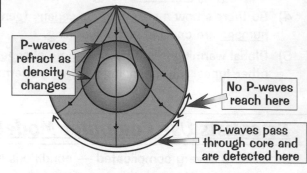

P-waves refract as density changes

No P-waves reach here

P-waves pass through core and are detected here

1) P-waves travel through <u>solids</u> and <u>liquids</u>.

2) They travel <u>faster</u> than <u>S-waves</u>.

3) P-waves are <u>longitudinal</u> (see p. 116).

S-Waves Only Travel Through Solids

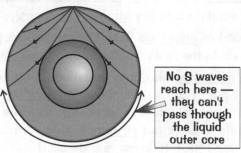

No S waves reach here — they can't pass through the liquid outer core

1) <u>S-waves</u> only travel through <u>Solids</u>.

2) They are <u>Slower</u> than <u>P-waves</u>.

3) S-waves are <u>transverse</u> (see p. 116).

Earthquakes can also produce waves called surface waves.

The Waves Curve with Increasing Depth

1) When seismic <u>waves</u> reach a <u>boundary</u> between different layers of the Earth, some waves will be <u>reflected</u>.

2) The waves also <u>change speed</u> as the <u>properties</u> (e.g. density) of the mantle and core change. This change in speed causes the waves to <u>change direction</u> — which is <u>refraction</u>.

3) Most of the time the waves change speed <u>gradually</u>, resulting in a <u>curved path</u>. But when the properties change <u>suddenly</u>, the wave speed changes abruptly, and the path has a <u>kink</u>.

The Seismograph Results Tell Us What's Down There

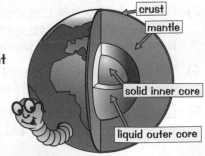

crust

mantle

solid inner core

liquid outer core

1) About <u>halfway through</u> the Earth, P-waves <u>change direction</u> abruptly. This indicates that there's a <u>sudden change</u> in <u>properties</u> — as you go from the <u>mantle</u> to the <u>core</u>.

2) The fact that <u>S-waves</u> are <u>not detected</u> in the core's <u>shadow</u> tells us that the <u>outer core</u> is <u>liquid</u> — <u>S</u> waves only pass through <u>Solids</u>.

3) <u>P-waves</u> seem to travel <u>slightly faster</u> through the <u>middle</u> of the core, which strongly suggests that there's a <u>solid inner core</u>.

4) Note that <u>S-waves</u> do travel through the <u>mantle</u>, which shows that it's <u>solid</u>. It only melts to form magma in small 'hot spots'.

What's that coming straight through the core? Is it a P-wave, is it a P-wave?

Try and remember that <u>P-waves</u> are <u>longitudinal</u> and <u>S-waves</u> are <u>transverse</u>. You might find it helpful to think of them as <u>Push-waves</u> and <u>Shake-waves</u>. Gosh — what a useful little trick. You can thank me later...

Revision Summary for Section 8

It's all very well reading the pages and looking at the diagrams — but you won't have a hope of remembering it for your exam if you don't understand it. Have a go at these questions to see how much has gone in so far. If you struggle with any of them, have another read through the section and give the questions another go.

1) Explain how generators magically generate electricity.

2) What is the National Grid?

3) Explain why a very high electrical voltage is used to transmit electricity in the National Grid.

4)* a) Calculate how many kWh of electrical energy are used by a 0.5 kW heater used for 15 minutes.
   b) Calculate the cost of the electrical energy used in a) if energy costs 10p per kWh.

5) Describe three ways in which access to electricity can affect peoples standard of living.

6) Draw a diagram to illustrate the frequency, wavelength and amplitude of a wave.

7)* Find the speed of a wave with frequency 50 kHz and wavelength 0.3 cm.

8) a) Sketch a diagram of a ray of light being reflected in a plane mirror.
   b) Label the normal and the angles of incidence and reflection.

9) Draw a diagram showing a wave diffracting through a gap.

10) What size should the gap be in order to maximise diffraction?
    a) much larger than the wavelength b) the same size as the wavelength c) a bit bigger than the wavelength.

11) Why does light bend if it hits a boundary between air and water at an angle?

12) Why can't sound waves travel in space?

13) Are high frequency sound waves high-pitched or low-pitched?

14) Draw diagrams of an analogue and a digital signal and briefly explain the differences between them.

15) Why are digital signals better quality than analogue signals?

16) Sketch the EM spectrum with all its details. Put the lowest frequency waves on the left.

17) Explain why radio waves can be transmitted across long distances.

18) Describe how satellites are used for communication.

19) Briefly explain how microwaves cook food.

20) What type of wave do remote controls usually use?

21) Which two types of EM wave are commonly used to send signals along optical fibres?

22) Why is ionisation dangerous if it occurs in your cells?

23) Explain how both X-rays and gamma rays can be useful in hospitals.

24) Give three health problems that can be caused by exposure to UV radiation.

25) How is ozone made in the atmosphere?

26) Briefly describe what is meant by the 'greenhouse effect'.

27) What two effects does chopping down and burning trees have on the atmospheric carbon dioxide level?

28) What is global warming?

29) What's causing global warming? How do we know this?

30) Give two possible consequences of global warming.

31) Name the two types of seismic waves caused by earthquakes, and state whether each type is a transverse or longitudinal wave.

32) What type of seismic wave cannot pass through liquids?

Galileo and Copernicus

Back in the day, people thought the Earth was at the centre of the Universe. It turns out they were wrong.

Ancient Greeks Thought the Earth was the Centre of the Universe

1) Most ancient Greek astronomers believed that the Sun, Moon, planets and stars all orbited the Earth in perfect circles — this is known as the geocentric model or Ptolemaic model.

2) The Ptolemaic model was the accepted model of the Universe from the time of the ancient Greeks until the 1500s. It was only in the 1600s that it began to be replaced by the Copernican model...

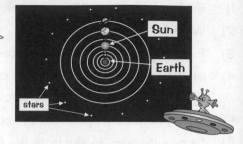

Copernican Model — Sun at the Centre

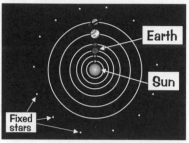

The Copernican model.

1) The Copernican model states that the Earth and planets all orbit the Sun, which is at the centre of the Universe, in perfect circles.

2) The idea had already been around for 2000 years, but the model was first introduced in a book by Copernicus in 1543. This book showed astronomical observations could be explained without having the Earth at the centre of the Universe.

3) The Copernican model is also a heliocentric model (Sun at the centre).

4) Galileo found one of the best pieces of evidence for this theory:

Around 1610, Galileo was observing Jupiter using a telescope (a new invention at the time) when he saw some stars in a line near the planet. When he looked again, he saw these stars never moved away from Jupiter and seemed to be carried along with the planet — which suggested they weren't stars, but moons orbiting Jupiter.
This showed not everything was in orbit around the Earth — evidence that the Ptolemaic model was wrong.

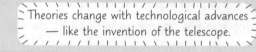
Theories change with technological advances — like the invention of the telescope.

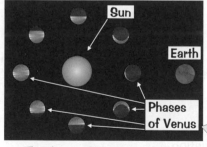

The phases of Venus as it orbits the Sun, as seen from Earth.

5) In the autumn of 1610, Galileo noticed that Venus has phases — where the amount of the planet that's lit by the Sun seems to change over time.

6) If the Ptolemaic model was right then these changes would be very small because Venus would always be in front of the Sun.

7) But if the Copernican model was right, Venus could move in front of and behind the Sun and so the changes in the amount Venus was lit would be really big — just like Galileo saw.

8) Copernicus' ideas weren't very popular at that time because the current models had been around for a long time.

9) The model was also condemned by the church. They claimed that the model went against the Bible, which said the Earth was at the centre of the Universe.

10) Gradually, evidence for the Copernican model increased thanks to more technological advances.

11) The current model still says that the planets in our Solar System orbit the Sun — but that these orbits are actually elliptical rather than circular and the Sun isn't really at the centre of the Universe.

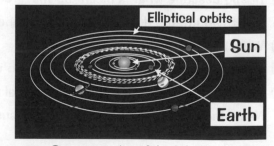

Our current view of the Solar System.

Copernicus — not a brand of metal underwear...

It's taken thousands of years for us to reach our current model of the Solar System. Although these models turned out to be wrong, they played a really important part in helping us reach the model we have today. And unsurprisingly, there's loads and loads that scientists still don't know about our Solar System.

The Solar System

When I were a lad I was taught that there were <u>nine planets</u> in our Solar System. But in 2006 some pesky astrobods decided that Pluto wasn't really a proper planet, so now there's only <u>eight</u> — for now...

Planets Reflect Sunlight and Orbit the Sun in Ellipses

Our Solar System consists of a <u>star</u> (<u>the Sun</u>) and lots of stuff <u>orbiting</u> it in <u>slightly elongated</u> circles (called ellipses).

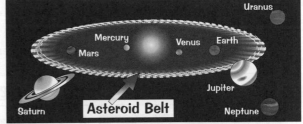

Closest to the Sun are the <u>inner planets</u> — Mercury, Venus, Earth and Mars.

Then the <u>asteroid belt</u>.

Then the <u>outer planets</u>, much further away — Jupiter, Saturn, Uranus, Neptune.

The <u>order</u> of the planets is made easier by using the little jollyism below:

Mercury,	Venus,	Earth,	Mars,	(Asteroids),	Jupiter,	Saturn,	Uranus,	Neptune
(Mad	Vampires	Eat	Mangoes	And	Jump	Straight	Up	Noses)

1) You can <u>see</u> some planets with the <u>naked eye</u>. They look like <u>stars</u>, but they're <u>totally different</u>.

2) Stars are <u>huge</u>, very <u>hot</u> and very <u>far away</u>. They <u>give out</u> lots of <u>light</u> — which is why you can see them, even though they're very far away.

3) The planets are <u>smaller</u> and <u>nearer</u> and they just <u>reflect sunlight</u> falling on them.

4) Planets often have <u>moons</u> orbiting around them. Jupiter has at least 63 of 'em. We've just got one.

There's a Belt of Asteroids Orbiting Between Mars and Jupiter

1) When the Solar System was forming, the rocks between Mars and Jupiter <u>didn't form a planet</u> — the large <u>gravitational attraction</u> of Jupiter kept interfering.

2) This left millions of <u>asteroids</u> — <u>piles of rubble and rock</u> measuring up to about 1000 km in diameter. They orbit the Sun between the orbits of <u>Jupiter</u> and <u>Mars</u> (see diagram above).

3) Asteroids usually <u>stay in their orbits</u> but sometimes they're <u>pushed</u> or <u>pulled</u> into different ones and can even <u>crash into planets</u>.

Comets Orbit the Sun in Very Elliptical Orbits

1) <u>Comets</u> are balls of <u>rock</u>, <u>dust</u> and <u>ice</u> which orbit the Sun in very <u>elongated</u> ellipses, often in different planes from the planets.

2) They <u>come</u> from objects orbiting the Sun <u>way beyond</u> the planets.

3) As a comet approaches the Sun, its ice <u>melts</u>, leaving a bright <u>tail</u> of gas and debris which can be millions of kilometres long. This is what we see from the Earth.

4) Comets <u>speed up</u> as they approach the Sun, because the Sun's gravitational pull <u>increases</u> as you get <u>closer</u>.

Comet in an elliptical orbit (red line).

The Solar System is Held Together by Gravitational Attraction

1) <u>Gravity</u> pulls <u>everything</u> in the Universe towards <u>everything else</u>. The effect is tiny between 'small' things (e.g. between you and a car, or between a house and a hat) — so tiny you don't notice it.

2) But when you're talking about things as big as <u>stars</u> and <u>planets</u>, the pull of gravity can be <u>huge</u> (the bigger the 'thing', the bigger its pull). So it's <u>gravity</u> that makes planets orbit stars, and moons orbit planets. <u>Gravity</u> keeps satellites, comets and asteroids in their orbits, and so on.

Asteroids... my dad had those — very nasty...

So, the <u>planets</u>, asteroids and comets all orbit the <u>Sun</u>. The whole lot's called the <u>Solar System</u>. Simple as that.

Beyond the Solar System

The <u>Universe</u> is big — huge in fact...

We're in the Milky Way Galaxy

1) Our <u>Sun</u> is one of <u>thousands of millions</u> of <u>stars</u> which form the <u>Milky Way</u> <u>galaxy</u> — about 1 in 100 000 000 000 (or 10¹¹) if you had to write it out.

2) The Sun is about halfway along one of the <u>spiral arms</u> of the Milky Way.

3) The <u>distance</u> between neighbouring stars in a galaxy is usually <u>millions</u> <u>of times greater</u> than the distance between <u>planets</u> in the Solar System.

The Whole Universe Has More Than a Thousand Million Galaxies

1) Every galaxy is made up of thousands of millions of stars, and the Universe is made up of <u>thousands of millions</u> of <u>galaxies</u> — that's a lot of stars.

2) Galaxies themselves are often <u>millions of times further apart</u> than the stars are within a galaxy.

3) So even the slowest among you will have worked out that the Universe is <u>mostly empty space</u> and is <u>really really BIG</u>.

Distances in Space Can Be Measured Using Light Years

1) Once you get outside our Solar System, the distances between stars and between galaxies are <u>so enormous</u> that kilometres seem too <u>pathetically small</u> for measuring them.

2) For example, the <u>closest</u> star to us (after the Sun) is about 40 000 000 000 000 kilometres away (give or take a few hundred billion kilometres). Numbers like that soon get out of hand.

3) So we use <u>light years</u> instead. A <u>light year</u> is the <u>distance</u> that <u>light travels</u> through a vacuum (like space) in one <u>year</u>. Simple as that.

4) Light travels <u>really fast</u> — <u>300 000 km/s</u>. So 1 light year is equal to about 9 460 000 000 000 km.

5) Just remember — a light year is a measure of <u>DISTANCE</u> (<u>not</u> time).

Astronomers can Work Out the Distances to Stars and Galaxies

1) To work out <u>how far away</u> a star is, you can use various methods.

2) For 'nearby' stars, you can use <u>parallax</u>. Astronomers take <u>pictures</u> of the sky six months apart (when Earth is at <u>opposite sides</u> of its orbit).

> <u>Parallax</u> is when something <u>appears to move</u> when you look at it from <u>different places</u> (e.g. hold your finger at arm's length and look at it first through your left eye, then your right — it seems to move against the background).

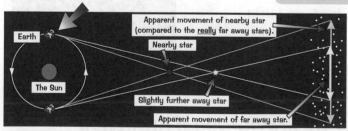

3) The <u>apparent movement</u> of a star between the two photos lets you work out <u>how far away</u> it is. Stars <u>further away</u> appear to move less (the <u>really</u> distant stars don't appear to move at all — the movement is too small to detect).

4) Another way to get an idea of the distance to a star is to measure its <u>brightness</u>.

5) Unfortunately, a star that <u>looks</u> very bright to us here on Earth could be either:
a) quite <u>close</u> to Earth but <u>not</u> actually that <u>bright</u>, or b) a <u>long way away</u> and <u>very bright indeed</u>.

6) However, astronomers know <u>how much radiation</u> certain types of star <u>actually</u> emit, and so by examining how bright they look <u>from Earth</u>, they can tell <u>how far away</u> those stars must be.

You may think it's a long way down the street to the chip shop...

...but that's <u>nothing</u> compared to <u>distances in space</u>. Space is also <u>less tasty</u> (and even worse for your health).

Looking Into Space

We can't travel to stars to study them — it'd take 'a while' (thousands of years, at the very least). All we can realistically do is measure the radiation (e.g. light, microwaves...) coming from them.

The Atmosphere and Light Pollution Cause Some Problems

1) If you're trying to detect light, Earth's atmosphere can be a bit of a pain — it absorbs quite a bit of the light coming from space before it can reach us.

2) And light pollution (light thrown upwards from streetlamps, etc.) makes it hard to see dim objects.

3) That's why scientists put the Hubble Space Telescope in space — where you don't get these problems.

We See Stars and Galaxies as They Were In The Past

1) Electromagnetic (EM) radiation (including light) travels pretty fast in space — 300 000 km/s (p.121).

2) Since the Sun is about 150 million km away from Earth, the radiation from the Sun that reaches us must have left about 8 minutes before we actually see it.

3) That means that when we look at the Sun, we see it as it was about 8 minutes ago. So if it suddenly exploded (but, fingers crossed, it won't for a while), we wouldn't know anything about it for about 8 minutes.

4) Since the nearest star to us after the Sun is about 4.2 light years away, light from it takes 4.2 years to reach us. This means we see it as it was 4.2 years ago.

5) When we look at other stars, this effect is even more extreme. For example, we see the North Star as it was during the time of William Shakespeare (it's about 430 light years away).

Different Telescopes Detect Different Types of EM Wave

To get a full picture of the Universe, you need telescopes that detect different kinds of EM wave.

1) The earliest telescopes were all optical telescopes which detect visible light. They're used to look at objects close by and in other galaxies.

2) From the 1940s onwards, telescopes were developed for all parts of the EM spectrum. These modern telescopes mean we can now 'see' parts of the Universe that we couldn't see before.

3) Cygnus A is a nearby galaxy. When you look at it through an optical telescope, you see the galaxy as a small blob, surrounded by stars. When observed using a radio telescope instead, you see two 'radio jets' moving away from the centre of the galaxy in opposite directions — these create two massive 'lobes' of hot radiation. Impressive stuff.

An image of Cygnus A using an optical telescope.

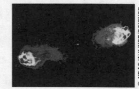
An image of Cygnus A using a radio telescope.

© NRAO/AUI/NSF/SCIENCE PHOTO LIBRARY

4) X-ray telescopes are a good way to 'see' violent, high-temperature events in space, like exploding stars.

5) Telescopes are improving all the time — bigger telescopes give us better resolution (i.e. a lot of detail) and can gather more light, so we can see things we couldn't before as they were too faint. Improved magnification means we can now look further into space, so more and more galaxies are being discovered.

6) Discovering more galaxies is important to help scientists learn more about their life cycle. Some pictures taken by the Hubble Space Telescope show galaxies at all different stages of their life. These images are used to help scientists learn more about how galaxies are formed and how they evolve.

7) Modern telescopes often work alongside computers. Computers help create clearer and sharper images and make it easy to capture these pictures so they can be analysed later.

Constant stars, in them I read such art...   (From a Shakespeare Sonnet)

A bit of culture there. Now then... most telescopes contain a lot of delicate, easily damaged parts. This makes it really expensive to put them in space — they've got to be strong enough to withstand all the shaking on board the vehicle which takes them into orbit, but they need to be lightweight too. It's hard work being a boffin.

The Life Cycle of Stars

Stars go through many traumatic stages in their lives — just like teenagers.

Nebula

1) Stars initially form from clouds of dust and gas called NEBULAS.

2) The force of gravity makes the gas and dust spiral in together. Gravitational energy is converted into heat energy, so the temperature rises.

Main Sequence Star

3) When the temperature gets high enough, hydrogen nuclei undergo thermonuclear fusion to form helium nuclei and give out massive amounts of energy. A star is born. It immediately enters a long stable period where the heat created by the nuclear fusion provides an outward pressure to balance the force of gravity pulling everything inwards. In this stable period it's called a MAIN SEQUENCE STAR and it can last for several billion years. (The Sun is in the middle of this stable period — or to put it another way, the Earth has already had half its innings before the Sun engulfs it.)

4) Eventually the hydrogen in the core begins to run out and the star then swells into a RED GIANT (it becomes red because the surface cools).

Red Giant

Small stars

Big stars

5) A small-to-medium-sized star like the Sun then becomes unstable and ejects its outer layer of dust and gas as a planetary nebula.

planetary nebula.... and a White Dwarf

6) This leaves behind a hot, dense solid core — a WHITE DWARF, which just cools down and eventually disappears. (That's going to be really sad.)

Supernova

Neutron Star...

...or Black Hole

7) Big stars, however, start to glow brightly again as they undergo more fusion and expand and contract several times, forming heavier elements in various nuclear reactions. Eventually they'll explode in a SUPERNOVA.

8) The exploding supernova throws the outer layers of dust and gas into space, leaving a very dense core called a NEUTRON STAR. If the star is big enough this will become a BLACK HOLE.

Red Giants, White Dwarfs, Black Holes, Green Ghosts...

Erm. Now how do they know that exactly... Anyway, now you know what the future holds — our Sun is going to fizzle out, and it'll just get very very cold and very very dark. Great. On a brighter note, the Sun's got a good few years in it yet, so it's still worth passing those exams.

The Life of the Universe

Physicists have got some <u>ideas</u> about how the <u>Universe started</u> based on their <u>observations of the stars</u>.

The Universe Seems to be Expanding

As big as the Universe already is, it looks like it's getting <u>even bigger</u>.
All its <u>galaxies</u> seem to be <u>moving away</u> from each other. There's good evidence for this...

1) Light from Other Galaxies is Red-shifted

1) Different chemical elements <u>absorb</u> different <u>frequencies</u> of light.

2) Each element produces a <u>specific pattern</u> of <u>dark lines</u> at the frequencies that it <u>absorbs</u> in the visible spectrum.

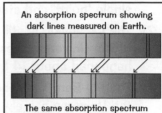

An absorption spectrum showing dark lines measured on Earth.

3) When we look at <u>light from distant galaxies</u> we can see the <u>same patterns</u> but at <u>slightly lower frequencies</u> than they should be — they're shifted towards the <u>red end</u> of the spectrum. This is called <u>red-shift</u>.

4) It's the same effect as the vrrroomm from a racing car — the engine sounds <u>lower-pitched</u> when the car's gone past you and is <u>moving away</u> from you. This is called the Doppler effect:

The same absorption spectrum measured from light from a distant galaxy. The dark lines in this spectrum are red-shifted.

THE DOPPLER EFFECT

1) The <u>frequency</u> of a source moving <u>towards</u> you will seem <u>higher</u> and its <u>wavelength</u> will seem <u>shorter</u>.

2) The <u>frequency</u> of a source moving <u>away</u> from you will seem <u>lower</u> and its <u>wavelength</u> will seem <u>longer</u>.

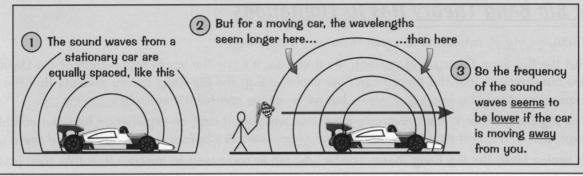

① The sound waves from a stationary car are equally spaced, like this

② But for a moving car, the wavelengths seem longer here... ...than here

③ So the frequency of the sound waves <u>seems</u> to be <u>lower</u> if the car is moving <u>away</u> from you.

2) The Further Away a Galaxy is, the Greater the Red-shift

1) <u>Measurements</u> of the red-shift suggest that <u>all the galaxies</u> are <u>moving away from us</u> very quickly — and it's the <u>same result</u> whichever direction you look in.

2) <u>More distant</u> galaxies have <u>greater</u> red-shifts than nearer ones.

3) This means that more distant galaxies are <u>moving away</u> from us <u>faster</u> than nearer ones.

4) This provides evidence that the whole Universe is <u>expanding</u>.

There's a Uniform Microwave Radiation from All Directions

1) Scientists have detected <u>low-frequency electromagnetic radiation</u> coming from <u>all parts</u> of the Universe.

2) This radiation is largely in the <u>microwave</u> part of the EM spectrum (p.121). It's known as the <u>cosmic microwave background radiation</u> (CMBR).

3) The <u>Big Bang theory</u> (see next page) is the <u>only</u> theory that explains the CMBR.

4) Just after the Big Bang while the Universe was still <u>extremely hot</u>, everything in the Universe emitted very <u>high-frequency radiation</u>. As the Universe <u>expanded</u> it has <u>cooled</u>, and this radiation has dropped in frequency and is now seen as <u>microwave radiation</u>.

If a tree falls down in the forest and you're driving away from it...

Listen out for the Doppler effect next time you hear a fast <u>motorbike</u> or a police <u>siren</u> — physics in <u>action</u>.

The Life of the Universe

Once upon a time there was a really Big Bang — that's the most convincing theory we've got.

It All Started Off with a Very Big Bang (Probably)

Right now, distant galaxies are moving away from us — the further away a galaxy is from us, the faster it's moving away (see previous page). But something must have got them going. That 'something' was probably a big explosion — so they called it the Big Bang...

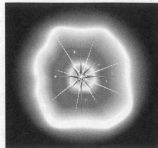

1) According to this theory, all the matter and energy in the Universe must have been compressed into a very small space. Then it exploded from that single 'point' and started expanding.

2) The expansion is still going on. We can use the current rate of expansion of the Universe to estimate its age. Our best guess is that the Big Bang happened about 14 billion years ago.

3) The Big Bang isn't the only game in town. The 'Steady State' theory says that the Universe has always existed as it is now, and it always will do. It's based on the idea that the Universe appears pretty much the same everywhere. This theory explains the apparent expansion by suggesting that matter is being created in the spaces as the Universe expands. But there are some big problems with this theory.

4) The discovery of the cosmic microwave background radiation (CMBR) was strong evidence that the Big Bang was the more likely explanation of the two.

The Big Bang Theory Has Its Limitations

1) Today nearly all astronomers agree there was a Big Bang.

2) But the Big Bang theory isn't perfect. As it stands, it's not the whole explanation of the Universe — there are observations that the theory can't yet explain. E.g. the Big Bang theory predicts that the Universe's expansion should be slowing down — but as far as we can tell it's actually speeding up.

3) The Big Bang explains the Universe's expansion well, but it isn't an explanation for what actually caused the explosion in the first place, or what the conditions were like before the explosion (or if there was a 'before').

4) It seems likely the Big Bang theory will be adapted in some way to improve it, rather than just being dumped — it explains so much so well that scientists will need a lot of persuading to drop it altogether.

We Don't Know How (or If) the Universe Will End...

1) The Universe's ultimate fate depends on how fast it's expanding and the total mass there is in it.
(The mass affects the gravitational pull that stops the Universe expanding so quickly.)

2) But these things are hard to measure, so determining the fate of the Universe is difficult.

3) To calculate how fast it's moving, you need to measure large distances, but the Universe is huge, so it's hard to accurately measure the distances involved.

4) You also need to accurately observe the motion of objects (e.g. galaxies). This is difficult because they're far away, you have to make lots of assumptions about their motion, and pollution gets in the way (p.133).

5) It's also tricky to measure how much mass there is because most of it appears to be invisible. Astronomers can only detect this dark matter by the way it affects the movement of the things we can see.

- If there's enough mass compared to how fast the galaxies are currently moving, the Universe will eventually stop expanding — and then begin contracting. This would end in a Big Crunch.

- If there's not enough mass in the Universe to stop the expansion, it could expand forever, with the Universe becoming more and more spread out into eternity.

Time and space — it's funny old stuff isn't it...

Proving a scientific theory is impossible. If enough evidence points a certain way, then a theory can look pretty convincing. But that doesn't prove it's a fact — new evidence may change people's minds.

Revision Summary for Section 9

It's business time — another chance for you to see which bits went in and which bits you need to flick back and have another read over. You know the drill by now. Do as many of the questions as you can and then try the tricky ones after you've had another chance to read the pages you struggled on. You know it makes sense.

1) Describe Copernicus's model of the Universe.

2) Explain the evidence that Galileo produced that supported Copernicus' theory.

3) Briefly explain why we can see planets, even though they don't give out any light.

4) What are asteroids and where are they found?

5) What are comets made of?

6) Roughly how many stars make up the Milky Way galaxy?

7) What is a light year?

8) Briefly describe parallax and how it's used to measure the distance to nearby stars.

9) Explain why we see stars and galaxies as they were in the past.

10) Explain why we need telescopes for other parts of the EM spectrum, as well as visible light.

11) Describe the first stages of a star's formation.

12) Where does the initial energy come from to form a star?

13) What is a 'main sequence' star?

14) How long does the stable period of a star last?

15) What are the final two stages of a small star's life?

16) What are the two final stages of a big star's life?

17) If a wave source is moving towards you, will the observed frequency of its waves be higher or lower than their actual frequency?

18) What do red-shift observations tell us about the Universe?

19) Describe the 'Big Bang' theory for the origin of the Universe.

20) What evidence is there for the 'Big Bang' theory?

Index

Index

Index and Answers

Answers

Revision Summary for Section 1 (page 19)

7) a) Response A   b) Response B

Revision Summary for Section 2 (page 33)

2) Professional runner, mechanic, secretary

11) a) Dave because he has a more stressful job than Tricia / he smokes / he does less exercise than Tricia / he has a diet higher in saturated fats and salt than Tricia.

   b) Improve your diet, e.g. eat less fatty foods and salt / be less stressed / stop smoking / don't use drugs like ecstasy and cannabis / reduce the amount of alcohol you consume / do regular moderate exercise.

Revision Summary for Section 3 (page 51)

5)

All the offspring love Aston Villa, but half of them carry the allele for being normal.

6)

Offspring:
Two Aa genotypes so half the offspring will love Aston Villa. Two aa genotypes, so the other half of the offspring will be normal.

Revision Summary for Section 4 (page 66)

3) Calcium

7) a) Could be hydrogen/oxygen/nitrogen (or any other diatomic gaseous element).

   b) Could be carbon dioxide (water molecules are bent).

8) a) $CaCO_3 + 2HCl \rightarrow CaCl_2 + H_2O + CO_2$

   b) $Ca + 2H_2O \rightarrow Ca(OH)_2 + H_2$

Revision Summary for Section 5 (page 79)

2) b) 2 cm   c) 3.5 years

20) phosphoric acid + potassium hydroxide → potassium phosphate + water

21) $H_2SO_4 + Na_2CO_3 \rightarrow Na_2SO_4 + H_2O + CO_2$

Revision Summary for Section 6 (page 94)

13) Propane — the fuel needs to be a gas at −10 °C to work in a camping stove.

Revision Summary for Section 7 (page 111)

14) Payback time = initial cost ÷ annual saving.
   Payback time = 4000 ÷ 100 = 40 years.

17) $E = m \times c \times \theta = 0.5 \times 1000 \times (200 - 20)$
   $E = 500 \times 180 = 90\,000$ J

22) Efficiency =
   useful energy output ÷ total energy input
   = 70 ÷ 100 = 0.7 (or 70%)

23) a) 80 J
   b) 20 J
   c) Efficiency = 80 ÷ 100 = 0.8 (or 80%)

Power and the Cost of Electricity (page 114)

1) Power = voltage × current
   Power = 230 × 12 = 2760 W = 2.76 kW

2) Energy supplied = power × time
   So, time = energy supplied ÷ power
   Time = 0.5 ÷ 2.76 = 0.181 h

Wave Basics (page 116)

Speed = frequency × wavelength
Frequency = 1.9×10^4 Hz = 19 000 Hz
Wavelength = 12.5 cm = 0.125 m
Speed = 19 000 × 0.125 = 2375 m/s

Revision Summary for Section 8 (page 129)

4) a) Energy supplied = power × time
   Time = 0.25 h
   Energy supplied = 0.5 × 0.25 = 0.125 kWh

   b) Cost = number of units × price per unit
   Cost = 0.125 × 10 = 1.25p

7) Speed = frequency × wavelength
   Frequency = 50 kHz = 50 000 Hz
   Wavelength = 0.3 cm = 0.003 m
   Speed = 50 000 Hz × 0.003 m = 150 m/s